Absolute Beginner's Guide

to

Computer Basics

Fifth Edition

Michael Miller

800 East 96th Street,
Indianapolis, Indiana 46240

Absolute Beginner's Guide to Computer Basics, Fifth Edition

ISBN-13: 978-0-789-74253-7
ISBN-10: 0-7897-4253-5

Library of Congress Cataloging-in-Publication Data:

Miller, Michael, 1958-
  Absolute beginner's guide to computer basics / Michael Miller. — 5th ed.
    p. cm.
  Includes index.
  ISBN 978-0-7897-4253-7
  1. Computers. I. Title.
  QA76.5.M531412 2009
  004—dc22

                                    2009026988

Printed in the United States of America

First Printing: September 2009

Trademarks

Warning and Disclaimer

Bulk Sales

Que Publishing offers excellent discounts on this book when ordered in quantity for bulk purchases or special sales. For more information, please contact

U.S. Corporate and Government Sales
1-800-382-3419
corpsales@pearsontechgroup.com

For sales outside of the U.S., please contact

International Sales
international@pearson.com

Associate Publisher
Greg Wiegand

Acquisitions Editor
Michelle Newcomb

Development Editor
The Wordsmithery LLC

Managing Editor
Patrick Kanouse

Project Editor
Bethany Wall

Copy Editor
Karen A. Gill

Indexer
Publishing Works Inc.

Proofreader
Language Logistics LLC

Technical Editor
Vince Averello

Publishing Coordinator
Cindy Teeters

Cover Designer
Anne Jones

Compositor
Bronkella Publishing LLC

Contents at a Glance

Table of Contents

About the Author

Michael Miller is a successful and prolific author with a reputation for practical advice, technical accuracy, and an unerring empathy for the needs of his readers.

Mr. Miller has written more than 90 best-selling books over the past two decades. His books for Que include *Absolute Beginner's Guide to eBay*, *How Microsoft Windows Vista Works*, *Speed It Up! A Non-Technical Guide for Speeding Up Slow Computers*, and *Googlepedia: The Ultimate Google Resource*. He is known for his casual, easy-to-read writing style and his practical, real-world advice—as well as his ability to explain a wide variety of complex topics to an everyday audience.

You can email Mr. Miller directly at abg@molehillgroup.com. His website is located at www.molehillgroup.com.

Dedication

To Sherry—finally and forever.

Acknowledgments

Thanks to the usual suspects at Que Publishing, including but not limited to Greg Wiegand, Michelle Newcomb, Charlotte Kughen, Bethany Wall, Karen Gill, and technical editor Vince Averello.

We Want to Hear from You!

As the reader of this book, *you* are our most important critic and commentator. We value your opinion and want to know what we're doing right, what we could do better, what areas you'd like to see us publish in, and any other words of wisdom you're willing to pass our way.

As an associate publisher for Que Publishing, I welcome your comments. You can email or write me directly to let me know what you did or didn't like about this book—as well as what we can do to make our books better.

Please note that I cannot help you with technical problems related to the topic of this book. We do have a User Services group, however, where I will forward specific technical questions related to the book.

When you write, please be sure to include this book's title and author as well as your name, email address, and phone number. I will carefully review your comments and share them with the author and editors who worked on the book.

Email: feedback@quepublishing.com

Mail: Greg Wiegand
         Associate Publisher
         Que Publishing
         800 East 96th Street
         Indianapolis, IN 46240 USA

Reader Services

Visit our website and register this book at www.informit.com/title/9780789742537 for convenient access to any updates, downloads, or errata that might be available for this book.

INTRODUCTION

Because this is the *Absolute Beginner's Guide to Computer Basics*, let's start at the absolute beginning, which is this: Computers aren't supposed to be scary. Intimidating? Sometimes. Difficult to use? Perhaps. Inherently unreliable? Most definitely. (Although they're better than they used to be.)

But scary? Definitely not.

Computers aren't scary because there's nothing they can do to hurt you (unless you drop your notebook PC on your foot, that is). And there's not much you can do to hurt them, either. It's kind of a wary coexistence between man and machine, but the relationship has the potential to be beneficial—to you, anyway.

Many people think that they're scared of computers because they're unfamiliar with them. But that isn't really true.

You see, even if you've never actually used a computer before, you've been exposed to computers and all they can do for the past three decades or so. Whenever you make a deposit at your bank, you're working with computers. Whenever you make a purchase at a retail store, you're working with computers. Whenever you watch a television show or read a newspaper article or look at a picture in a magazine, you're working with computers.

That's because computers are used in all those applications. Somebody, somewhere, is working behind the scenes with a computer to manage your bank account and monitor your credit card purchases.

In fact, it's difficult to imagine, here in the twenty-first century, how we ever got by without all those keyboards, mice, and monitors. (Or, for that matter, the Internet.)

However, just because computers have been around for awhile doesn't mean that everyone knows how to use them. It's not unusual to feel a little trepidation the first time you sit down in front of that intimidating display and keyboard. Which keys should you press? What do people mean by double-clicking the mouse? And what are all those little pictures onscreen?

As foreign as all this might seem at first, computers really aren't that hard to understand—or use. You have to learn a few basic concepts, of course (all the pressing and clicking and whatnot), and it helps to understand exactly what part of the system does what. But once you get the hang of things, computers really are easy to use.

Which, of course, is where this book comes in.

Absolute Beginner's Guide to Computer Basics, Fifth Edition, will help you figure out how to use your new computer system. You'll learn how computers work, how to connect all the pieces and parts, and how to start using them. You'll learn about computer hardware and software, about the Microsoft Windows 7 operating system, and about the Internet. And after you're comfortable with the basic concepts (which won't take too long, trust me), you'll learn how to actually do stuff.

You'll learn how to do useful stuff, such as writing letters, balancing your check-book, and creating presentations; fun stuff, such as listening to music, watching movies, and editing your digital photos; online stuff, such as searching for informa-tion, sending email, and keeping up with friends and family via Facebook and MySpace; and essential stuff, such as copying files, troubleshooting problems, and protecting against thieves and hackers.

All you have to do is sit yourself down in front of your computer, try not to be scared (there's nothing to be scared of, really), and work your way through the chapters and activities in this book. And remember that computers aren't difficult to use, they don't break easily, and they let you do all sorts of fun and useful things once you get the hang of them. Really!

How This Book Is Organized

This book is organized into six main parts, as follows:

- **Part I, "Getting Started,"** describes all the pieces and parts of both desk-top and notebook PCs and how to connect everything to get your new system up and running.

- **Part II, "Using Windows,"** introduces the backbone of your entire system, the Microsoft Windows operating system. You'll learn how Windows works and how to use it to perform basic tasks, such as copying and deleting files and folders. (You'll also learn fun stuff, such as how to change the picture on your computer desktop.)

- **Part III, "Upgrading and Maintaining Your System,"** contains all the boring (but necessary) information you need to know to keep your new PC in tip-top shape. You'll learn how to add new pieces of hardware to your sys-tem, how to set up a wireless home network, how to perform routine mainte-nance, how to track down and fix common PC problems, and how to protect your system against viruses, spyware, and other forms of computer attack.

- **Part IV, "Using Computer Software,"** tells you everything you need to know about running the most popular computer programs. You'll learn how to use Microsoft Works, Microsoft Office, Microsoft Word, Microsoft Excel, and Microsoft PowerPoint. That's a lot.

- **Part V, "Using the Internet,"** is all about going online. You'll discover how to connect to the Internet and surf the Web with Internet Explorer. You'll also learn how to shop online, buy and sell in eBay auctions and craigslist classifieds, search the Web with Google and research topics with Wikipedia, watch and upload YouTube videos, and create your own personal web page. This is the fun part of the book.

- **Part VI, "Communicating via the Internet,"** is all about keeping in touch. You'll find out how to send and receive email, chat online via instant messaging, navigate the blogosphere, and network socially with Facebook, MySpace, and Twitter.

- **Part VII, "Exploring the Digital Lifestyle,"** is even more fun. You'll see how to use your PC with your digital camera to edit and manage your digital photos, how to listen to CDs and download music to your iPod or iPhone, how to watch DVDs on your computer screen, and how to create your own digital home movies on DVD. It's amazing all the things you can do with your PC!

Taken together, the 38 chapters in this book will help you progress from absolute beginner to experienced computer user. Just read what you need, and before long you'll be using your computer like a pro!

Which Version of Windows?

This Fifth Edition of the *Absolute Beginner's Guide to Computer Basics* is written for computers running the latest version of Microsoft's operating system, Windows 7. If you're running the previous version, Windows Vista, most of the advice and information will still work. But if you're running the even older Windows XP, you should read the earlier Third Edition of this book instead; it covers XP exclusively.

Conventions Used in This Book

I hope that this book is easy enough to figure out on its own, without requiring its own instruction manual. As you read through the pages, however, it helps to know precisely how I've presented specific types of information.

Menu Commands

Most computer programs operate via a series of pull-down menus. You use your mouse to pull down a menu and then select an option from that menu. This sort of operation is indicated like this throughout the book:

Select File, Save

or

Click the Start button and select All Programs, Accessories, Notepad.

All you have to do is follow the instructions in order, using your mouse to click each item in turn. When submenus are tacked onto the main menu (as in the All Programs, Accessories, Notepad example), just keep clicking the selections until you come to the last one—which should open the program or activate the command you want!

Shortcut Key Combinations

When you're using your computer keyboard, sometimes you have to press two keys at the same time. These two-key combinations are called *shortcut keys* and are shown as the key names joined with a plus sign (+).

For example, Ctrl+W indicates that you should press the W key while holding down the Ctrl key. It's no more complex than that.

Web Page Addresses

This book contains a lot of web page addresses. (That's because you'll probably be spending a lot of time on the Internet.)

Technically, a web page address is supposed to start with http:// (as in http://www.molehillgroup.com). Because Internet Explorer and other web browsers automatically insert this piece of the address, however, you don't have to type it—and I haven't included it in any of the addresses in this book.

Special Elements

This book also includes a few special elements that provide additional information not included in the basic text. These elements are designed to supplement the text to make your learning faster, easier, and more efficient.

tip

A *tip* is a piece of advice—a little trick, actually—that helps you use your computer more effectively or maneuver around problems or limitations.

note

A *note* is designed to provide information that is generally useful but not specifically necessary for what you're doing at the moment. Some are like extended tips—interesting, but not essential.

caution

A *caution* tells you to beware of a potentially dangerous act or situation. In some cases, ignoring a caution could cause you significant problems—so pay attention to them!

Let Me Know What You Think

I always love to hear from readers. If you want to contact me, feel free to email me at abg@molehillgroup.com. I can't promise that I'll *answer* every message, but I do promise that I'll *read* each one!

If you want to learn more about me and any new books I have cooking, check out my Molehill Group website at www.molehillgroup.com. Who knows, you might find some other books there that you would like to read.

PART

i

GETTING STARTED

1

HOW PERSONAL COMPUTERS WORK

Chances are you're reading this book because you just bought a new computer, are thinking about buying a new computer, or maybe even had someone give you his old computer. (Nothing wrong with high-tech hand-me-downs!) At this point you might not be totally sure what it is you've gotten yourself into. Just what is this mess of boxes and cables, and what can you—or *should* you—do with it?

This chapter serves as an introduction to the entire concept of personal computers in general—what they do, how they work, that sort of thing—and computer hardware in particular. It's a good place to start if you're not that familiar with computers or want a brief refresher course in what all those pieces and parts are and what they do.

Of course, if you want to skip the background and get right to using your computer, that's okay, too. For step-by-step instructions on how to connect and configure your new PC, go directly to Chapter 2, "Setting Up Your New Computer System"—everything you need is there.

What Your Computer Can—and *Can't*—Do

What good is a personal computer, anyway?

Everybody has one, you know. (Including you, now!) In fact, it's possible you bought your new computer just so that you wouldn't feel left out. But now that you have your very own personal computer, what do you do with it?

Good for Work

A lot of people use their home PCs for work-related purposes. You can bring your work (reports, spreadsheets, you name it) home from the office and finish it on your home PC at night or on weekends. Or if you work at home, you can use your computer to pretty much run your small business—you can use it to do everything from typing memos and reports to generating invoices and setting budgets.

In short, anything you can do with a normal office PC, you can probably do on your home PC.

Good for Play

All work and no play make Jack a dull boy, so there's no reason not to have a little fun with your new PC. Not only can you use your PC to play some really cool games, you can also use it to listen to music you download from the Internet, view and edit photos you take with your digital camera, and even edit home movies you make with your video camcorder. Then there are all the movies, TV shows, and videos you can watch online at sites like YouTube. There's a lot of fun to be had with your new PC!

Good for Getting Online

A lot of the work and play you do with your PC happens online over the Internet. The Internet's a great tool; in addition to music and movies, you can buy and sell just about anything online, read the latest news from popular blogs, and browse the World Wide Web—which is chock-full of interesting and informative content and services. Now you won't feel left out when people start talking about "double-you double-you double-you" this and "dot-com" that—because you'll be online, too.

Good for Keeping in Touch

Want to send a letter to a friend? With your new PC (and a word processing program, such as Microsoft Word), it's a cinch. Even better, save a stamp and send that friend an email or instant message over the Internet. Or keep in touch with any number of friends and colleagues via a social network site such as Facebook, MySpace, or Twitter.

That's far from all you can do with your new PC, of course. Many people use their computers to do online banking; others use them to keep up with their favorite hobbies and pastimes. Chances are there's a software program or website devoted to what you want to do. The biggest challenge is finding time to do everything you want!

Getting to Know Your Personal Computer System

Now that you know *why* you have that brand-new personal computer sitting on your desk, you might be interested in just *what* it is that you have. It's important to know what each part of your system is, what it does, and how to hook it all together.

note

This book is written for users of relatively new personal computers—in particular, PCs running the Microsoft Windows 7 operating system. If you have an older PC running an older version of Windows, most of the advice here is still good, although not all the step-by-step instructions will apply.

Pieces and Parts—Computer Hardware

We'll start by looking at the physical components of your system—the stuff we call computer *hardware*.

When it comes to computers, there are two basics types: desktops and notebooks. A desktop PC is assembled from various pieces and parts, while a notebook PC has everything built into a single compact and portable unit. These days, the majority of new PCs sold are notebooks, probably because they're more flexible in how and where they can be used. They're certainly easier to set up and find space for.

Figure 1.1 shows a typical notebook PC. Everything you need is contained within the case—the screen, the keyboard, the touchpad (to control the onscreen cursor), even a pair of stereo speakers. That's a lot more compact than the desktop computer system shown in Figure 1.2, which contains all the same components but as separate pieces, called *peripherals*; as you can imagine, all this hardware requires a bit of desk space.

FIGURE 1.1
A typical note-
book computer.

FIGURE 1.2
A typical desktop
computer sys-
tem.

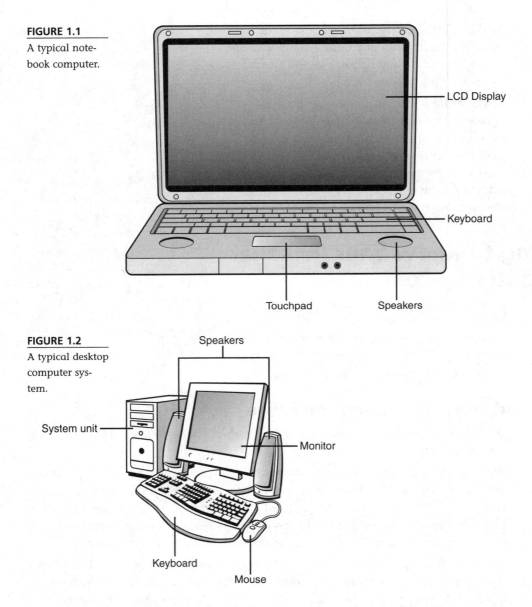

LCD Display

Keyboard

Touchpad

Speakers

Speakers

System unit

Monitor

Keyboard

Mouse

You should note, however, that whether you're talking about notebook or desktop
units, no two computer systems are identical. You can always add new components
to your system—or, in the case of a desktop system, disconnect other pieces you
don't have a use for.

The PC itself is just a part of your entire computer system. You can add lots of other
items to your system, including *printers* (to make printouts of documents and pictures), *scanners* (to convert a printed document or picture to electronic format),

webcams (to send live video of yourself to friends and family), *joysticks* (to play the most challenging games), and external *hard disks* (to back up your precious data). You can also hook up all manner of portable devices to your PC, including *digital cameras, camcorders,* and *portable music players* (such as the ubiquitous Apple iPod). You can even add the appropriate devices to connect multiple PCs in a *network,* which is useful if you have more than one computer in your house. Fortunately, connecting a new device is as easy as plugging in a single cable; anyone can do it!

The Right Tools for the Right Tasks— Computer Software

By themselves, the beige and black boxes that comprise a typical computer system aren't that useful. You can connect them and set them in place, but they won't do anything until you have some software to make things work.

> **note**
>
> Learn more about these pieces and parts in "Inside a Personal Computer," later in this chapter. If you need help connecting all the pieces and parts, turn to Chapter 2. And if you want to add a new piece of hardware to your basic system, check out Chapter 6, "Adding New Hardware and Devices to Your System."

Computer *hardware* are those things you can touch—the keyboard, monitor, system unit, and the like. Computer *software,* on the other hand, is something you *can't* touch because it's nothing more than a bunch of electronic bits and bytes. These bits and bytes, however, combine into computer programs—sometimes called *applications*—that provide specific functionality to your system.

For example, if you want to crunch some numbers, you need a piece of software called a *spreadsheet* program. If you want to write a letter, you need a *word processing* program. If you want to make changes to some pictures you took with your digital camera, you need *graphics editing* software. And if you want to surf the Internet, you need a *web browser.*

In other words, you need separate software for each task you want to do with your computer. Fortunately, most new computer systems come with a lot of this software already installed. You may have to buy a few specific programs, but it shouldn't set you back a lot of money.

> **note**
>
> If you want or need any additional software, you'll have to find and install it yourself—as described in Chapter 11, "Installing New Software."

Making Everything Work—with Windows

Whatever program you're using at any given point in time, you interface with your computer via a special piece of software called an *operating system*. As the name implies, this program makes your system operate; it's your gateway to the hardware part of your system.

The operating system is also how your application software interfaces with your computer hardware. When you want to print a document from your word processor, that software works with the operating system to send the document to your printer.

Most computers today ship with an operating system called *Microsoft Windows*. This operating system has been around in one form or another for almost 25 years and is published by Microsoft Corporation.

Windows isn't the only operating system around, however. Computers manufactured by Apple Computing use a different operating system, called the *Mac OS*. Therefore, computers running Windows and computers by Apple aren't totally compatible with each other. Then there's *Linux*, which is compatible with most PCs sold today, but used primarily by uber-techie types; it's not an operating system I would recommend for general users.

But let's get back to Windows, of which there have been several different versions over the years. The newest version is called *Microsoft Windows 7* because it's the seventh major version of the operating system, more or less. If you've just purchased a brand-new PC, this is probably the version you're using. If your PC is a little older, you might be running *Windows Vista*, the immediate predecessor to Windows 7, or *Windows XP*, which came just before that. If you have a much older PC, or one used in a corporate environment, you could be running yet another version of Windows—*Windows 2000*, perhaps, or even *Windows 98* on a very old machine.

To some degree, Windows is Windows is Windows; all the different versions do pretty much the same things, although newer versions look prettier, are a bit more stable, and have a few more bells and whistles. Whichever version of Windows you have installed on your PC, you use it to launch specific programs and to perform various system maintenance functions, such as copying files and turning off your computer.

note

You can learn more about Windows 7 in Chapter 3, "Getting to Know Windows 7."

Don't Worry, You Can't Screw It Up—Much

The balance of this chapter goes into a bit more detail about the hardware components of your PC system. Before you proceed, however, there's one other important thing you need to know about computers.

A lot of people are afraid of their computers. They think if they press the wrong key or click the wrong button, they'll break something or will have to call in an expensive repairperson to put things right.

This really isn't true.

The important thing to know is that it's really difficult to break your computer system. Yes, it's possible to break something if you drop it, but in terms of breaking your system through normal use, it just doesn't happen that often.

It *is* possible to make mistakes, of course. You can click the wrong button and accidentally delete a file you didn't want to delete or turn off your system and lose a document you forgot to save. You can even take inadequate security precautions and find your system infected by a computer virus. But in terms of doing serious harm just by clicking your mouse, it's unlikely.

So don't be afraid of the thing. Your computer is a tool, just like a hammer or a blender or a camera. After you learn how to use it, it can be a very useful tool. But it's *your* tool, which means *you* tell *it* what to do—not vice versa. Remember that you're in control and that you're not going to break anything, and you'll have a lot of fun—and maybe even get some real work done!

Inside a Personal Computer

As you just read, computer hardware are those parts of your system you can actually see and touch. This includes those pieces inside the computer's case, which you really can't see unless you open it up. In fact, it's the stuff inside the case that's most important, as you'll see on our brief tour of what makes a personal computer.

The Motherboard: Home to Almost Everything

Inside every PC are all manner of computer chips and circuit boards. Most of these parts are connected to a big board called a *motherboard*, because it's the "mother" for the computer's microprocessor and memory chips, as well as for all other internal components that enable your system to function. On a desktop PC, the motherboard is located near the base of the computer, as shown in Figure 1.3; on a notebook PC, it's just under the keyboard.

FIGURE 1.3

What your PC looks like on the inside—a big motherboard with lots of add-on boards attached.

On a desktop PC, the motherboard contains several slots, into which you can plug additional *boards* (also called *cards*) that perform specific functions. Notebook PC motherboards can't accept additional boards and thus aren't expandable like desktop PCs are.

Most desktop PC motherboards contain six or more slots for add-on cards. For example, a video card enables your motherboard to transmit video signals to your monitor. Other available cards enable you to add sound and modem/fax capabilities to your system. (On a notebook PC, these video and audio functions are built into the motherboard, rather than being on separate cards.)

Microprocessors: The Main Engine

We're not done looking at the motherboard just yet. That's because buried somewhere on that big motherboard is a specific chip that controls your entire computer system. This chip is called a *microprocessor* or a *central processing unit (CPU)*.

The microprocessor is the brains inside your system. It processes all the instructions necessary for your computer to perform its duties. The more powerful the microprocessor chip, the faster and more efficiently your system runs.

Microprocessors carry out the various instructions that let your computer compute. Every input and output device connected to a computer—the keyboard, printer, monitor, and so on—either issues or receives instructions that the microprocessor

then processes. Your software programs also issue instructions that must be imple-
mented by the microprocessor. This chip truly is the workhorse of your system; it
affects just about everything your computer does.

Different computers have different types of microprocessor chips. Many IBM-compatible computers use chips manufactured by Intel. Some use Intel-compatible chips
manufactured by AMD and other firms. But all IBM-compatible computers that run
the Windows operating system use Intel-compatible chips.

In addition to having different chip manufacturers (and different chip families from
the same manufacturer), you'll run into microprocessor chips that run at different
speeds. CPU speed today is measured in *gigahertz (GHz)*. A CPU with a speed of 1GHz
can run at one *billion* clock ticks per second! The bigger the gigahertz number, the
faster the chip runs.

It gets better. Many chips today incorporate so-called *dual-core* or *quad-core* chips.
What this means is that a single chip includes the equivalent of two (dual-core) or
four (quad-core) CPUs. That's like doubling or quadrupling your processing power!
The more cores, the better—especially for processor-intensive tasks, such as editing
digital video files.

If you're still shopping for a new PC, look for one with the combination of a powerful microprocessor and a high clock speed for best performance. And don't forget to
count all the cores; a dual-core chip with two 1.8GHz CPUs is more powerful than a
single-core chip with a 2.0GHz CPU.

Computer Memory: Temporary Storage

Before a CPU can process instructions you give it, your instructions must be stored
somewhere in preparation for access by the microprocessor. These instructions—
along with other data processed by your system—are temporarily held in the computer's *random access memory (RAM)*. All computers have some amount of memory,
which is created by a number of memory chips. The more memory that's available
in a machine, the more instructions and data that can be stored at one time.

Memory is measured in terms of *bytes*. One byte is equal to approximately one character in a word processing document. A unit equaling approximately one thousand
bytes (1,024, to be exact) is called a *kilobyte (KB)*, and a unit of approximately one
thousand (1,024) kilobytes is called a *megabyte (MB)*. A thousand megabytes is a
gigabyte (GB).

Most computers today come with at least 1GB of memory, and it's not uncommon to
find machines with 4GB or more of RAM. To enable your computer to run as many
programs as quickly as possible, you need as much memory installed in your system
as it can accept—or that you can afford. (I'd say that 2GB is the bare minimum necessary to run a Windows 7-based system, and more is always better.) Extra memory

can be added to a computer by installing new memory modules, which is as easy as plugging a "stick" directly into a slot on your system's motherboard.

If your computer doesn't possess enough memory, its CPU must constantly retrieve data from permanent storage on its hard disk. This method of data retrieval is slower than retrieving instructions and data from electronic memory. In fact, if your machine doesn't have enough memory, some programs will run very slowly (or you might experience random system crashes), and other programs won't run at all!

Hard Disk Drives: Long-Term Storage

Another important physical component inside your system unit is the *hard disk drive*. The hard disk permanently stores all your important data. Some hard disks today can store up to 2 *terabytes* of data—that's 2,000 gigabytes—and even bigger hard disks are on the way. (Contrast this to your system's RAM, which stores only a few gigabytes of data, temporarily.)

A hard disk consists of numerous metallic platters. These platters store data *magnetically*. Special read/write *heads* realign magnetic particles on the platters, much like a recording head records data onto magnetic recording tape.

However, before data can be stored on a disk, including your system's hard disk, that disk must be *formatted*. A disk that has not been formatted cannot accept data. When you format a hard disk, your computer prepares each track and sector of the disk to accept and store data magnetically. Fortunately, hard disks in new PCs are preformatted, so you don't have to worry about this. (And in most cases, your operating system and key programs are preinstalled.)

caution

If you try to reformat your hard disk, you'll erase all the programs and data that have been installed—so don't do it!

CD/DVD Drives: Storage on a Disc

Not all the storage on your PC is inside the system unit. As you can see in Figure 1.4, most PCs feature a combination *CD/DVD drive* that lets you play audio CDs and movie DVDs, install CD- or DVD-based software programs, and burn music, movies, or data to blank CD or DVD discs.

note

The *ROM* part of CD-ROM means that you can only read data from the disk; unlike normal hard disks and diskettes, you can't write new data to a standard CD-ROM. However, most PCs include recordable (CD-R) and rewritable (CD-RW) drives that *do* let you write data to CDs—so you can use your CD drive just like a regular disk drive.

FIGURE 1.4

Store tons of
data on a shiny
CD or DVD data
disc.

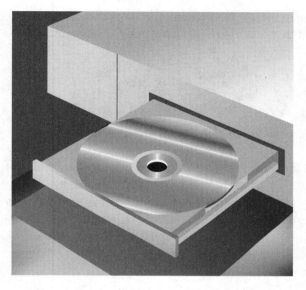

Computer CD discs, called CD-ROM discs (the ROM stands for "read-only memory), look just like the compact discs you play on your audio system. They're also similar in the way they store data (audio data in the case of regular CDs; computer data in the case of CD-ROMs).

If you need even more storage, consider writing to blank DVD discs. A DVD can contain up to 4.7GB of data (for a single-layer disc) or 8.5GB of data (for a double-layer disc). Compared to 650–700MB of storage for a typical CD-ROM, this makes DVDs ideally suited for large applications or games that otherwise would require multiple CDs. Similar to standard CD-ROMs, most DVDs are read-only—although all DVD drives can also read CD-ROMs.

Some high-end PCs do the standard DVD one step better and can read and write high-definition DVDs in the new *Blu-ray* format. The Blu-ray format lets you store 25GB or more of data on a single disc. While that storage for PC data may be overkill, it may be nice to play high-definition Blu-ray movies on your PC.

Keyboards: Fingertip Input

Computers receive data by reading it from disk, accepting it electronically over a modem, or receiving input directly from you, the user. You provide your input by way of what's called, in general, an *input device*; the most common input device you use to talk to your computer is the keyboard.

A computer keyboard, similar to the one in Figure 1.5, looks and functions just like a typewriter keyboard, except that computer keyboards have a few more keys. Some of these keys (such as the arrow, PgUp, PgDn, Home, and End keys) enable you to move around within a program or file. Other keys provide access to special program features. When you press a key on your keyboard, it sends an electronic signal to your system unit that tells your machine what you want it to do.

Most keyboards that come with desktop PCs hook up via a cable to the back of your system unit, although some manufacturers make *wireless* keyboards that connect to your system unit via radio signals—thus eliminating one cable from the back of your system. Keyboards on notebook PCs are built into the main unit, of course, and are typically a little smaller than desktop PC keyboards; most notebook keyboards, for example, lack a separate numeric keypad for entering numbers.

Mice and Touchpads: Point-and-Click Input Devices

It's a funny name but a necessary device. A computer *mouse*, like the one shown in Figure 1.6, is a small handheld device. Most mice consist of an oblong case with a roller underneath and two or three buttons on top. When you move the mouse along a desktop, an onscreen pointer (called a *cursor*) moves in response. When you click (press and release) a mouse button, this motion initiates an action in your program.

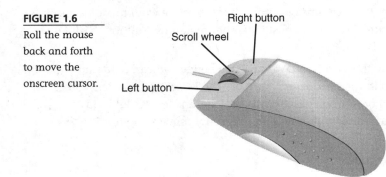

Right button

Scroll wheel

Left button

Mice come in all shapes and sizes. Some have wires, and some are wireless. Some are relatively oval in shape, and others are all curvy to better fit in the palm of your hand. Some have the typical roller ball underneath, and others use an optical sensor to determine where and how much you're rolling. Some even have extra buttons that can be programmed for specific functions or a scroll wheel you can use to scroll through long documents or web pages.

Of course, a mouse is just one type of input device you can hook up to your PC. Trackballs, joysticks, game controllers, and pen pads all count as input devices, whether they work in conjunction with a mouse or replace it. You can use one of these alternative devices to replace your original mouse or (in some cases) to supplement it.

If you have a notebook PC, you don't have a separate mouse. Instead, most notebooks feature a *touchpad* pointing device that functions like a mouse. You move your fingers around the touchpad to move the onscreen cursor and then click one of the buttons underneath the touchpad the same way you'd click a mouse button.

tip

If you have a portable PC, you don't have to use the built-in touchpad. Most portables let you attach an external mouse, which then can be used in addition to the internal device.

Modems: Going Online

Some PC systems today still include a dial-up *modem*, which enables your computer to connect to telephone lines and transmit data to and from the Internet and commercial online services (such as America Online). The word "modem" stands for "modulator-demodulator," which is how digital data is sent over traditional analog phone lines. The data is "modulated" for transmittal, and it's "demodulated" upon receipt.

That said, the traditional dial-up modem (and slow dial-up Internet connection) is a dying beast. That's because more and more users are opting for higher-speed broadband Internet connections (either via cable or DSL). If you sign up for cable or DSL Internet service, your Internet service provider (ISP) will provide you with an external *broadband modem* for their service. Most broadband modems connect to your PC either via USB or via an Ethernet connection.

note

Learn more about broadband Internet connections in Chapter 16, "Connecting to the Internet—at Home and on the Road."

Network Connections: Getting Connected

If you have more than one computer in your home, you may want to connect them in a home network. A network lets you share files between multiple computers, as well as connect multiple PCs to a single printer or scanner. In addition, you can use a home network to share a broadband Internet connection so that all your computers are connected to the Internet.

You can connect computers via either wired or wireless networks. Most home users prefer a wireless network, as there are no cables to run from one room of your house to another. Fortunately, connecting a wireless network is as easy as buying a wireless router, which functions as the hub of the network, and then connecting wireless adapters to each computer on the network. (And if you have a notebook PC, the wireless adapter is probably built-in.)

note

Learn more about wireless networks in Chapter 7, "Setting Up a Home Network."

Sound Cards and Speakers: Making Noise

Every PC comes with some sort of speaker system. Most desktop systems today let you set up separate right and left speakers, sometimes accompanied by a subwoofer for better bass. (Figure 1.7 shows a typical right-left-subwoofer speaker system.) Notebook PCs typically come with right and left speakers built in, but with the option of connecting external speakers if you want. You can even get so-called 5.1 surround sound speaker systems, with five satellite speakers (front and rear) and the ".1" subwoofer—great for listening to movie soundtracks or playing explosive-laden video games.

FIGURE 1.7

A typical set of right and left external speakers, complete with subwoofer.

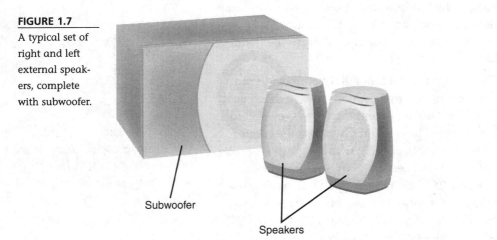

Subwoofer

Speakers

All speaker systems are driven by a sound card or chip that is installed inside your system unit. If you upgrade your speaker system, you also might need to upgrade your sound card accordingly. (You can easily switch sound cards on a desktop PC; that's really not an option on a notebook.)

Video Cards and Monitors: Getting the Picture

Operating a computer would be difficult if you didn't constantly receive visual feedback showing you what your machine is doing. This vital function is provided by your computer's monitor.

Most computer monitors today are built around an LCD display. On a notebook PC, this display is built into the unit; on a desktop PC, you connect a separate external monitor. You measure the size of a monitor from corner to corner, diagonally. Today's LCD monitors start at 15" or so and run up to 21" or larger.

A flat-screen LCD display doesn't take up a lot of desk space or use a lot of energy, both of which are good things. Many LCD monitors today come with a widescreen display that has the same 16:9 (or 16:10) aspect ratio used to display widescreen movies—which makes them ideal for viewing or editing movies on your PC.

Older computer monitors were built around a cathode ray tube, or CRT, similar to the picture tube found in normal television sets.

Know, however, that your computer monitor doesn't generate the images it displays. Instead, screen images are electronically crafted by a *video card* or chip installed inside your system unit. To work correctly, both the video card and monitor must be matched to display images of the same resolution.

Resolution refers to the size of the images that can be displayed onscreen and is measured in pixels. A *pixel* is a single dot on your screen; a full picture is composed of thousands of pixels. The higher the resolution, the sharper the resolution—which lets you display more (smaller) elements onscreen.

Resolution is expressed in numbers of pixels, in both the horizontal and vertical directions. Older video cards and monitors could display only 640×480 or 800×600 pixel resolution; you want a card/monitor combination that can display at least 1024×768 resolution—or, in the case of a widescreen monitor, 1280×800.

For most users, the video card or chip installed in their new PC works just fine. However, if you do a lot of heavy-duty gaming—especially with some of the newer graphics-intensive games—you may want to consider upgrading the video card in a desktop PC to one with more on-board memory, to better reproduce those cutting-edge graphics. And to display all of Windows 7's cutting-edge graphics, you'll need a card with a separate *graphics processing unit (GPU)*, which takes the graphics processing load off your PC's main CPU. The more graphics processing power, the better your system will look.

Desktop and Notebook PCs

As previously noted, personal computers today come in two different form factors—desktop and notebook. Both types contain the same basic internal pieces and parts, just configured differently.

Desktop PC Basics

On a desktop PC, the most important piece of hardware is the *system unit*. This is the big, ugly box that houses your disk drives and many other components. Most system units, like the one in Figure 1.8, stand straight up like a kind of tower—and are, in fact, called either *tower* or *mini-tower* PCs, depending on the size.

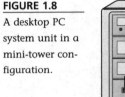

FIGURE 1.8

A desktop PC system unit in a mini-tower configuration.

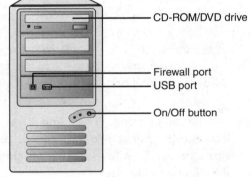

CD-ROM/DVD drive

Firewall port
USB port

On/Off button

Know, however, that some desktop systems combine the system unit and the monitor into a single unit. These all-in-one desktops take up less space and, in some instances, provide touch-screen functionalities that let you use your fingers (instead of a mouse) to navigate the screen. The only drawbacks I can see to these all-in-one units are the price (they're typically a bit more costly than traditional desktop PCs) and the fact that if one component goes bad, the whole system is out of commission. It's a lot easier to replace a single component than an entire system!

The system unit is where everything connects; it truly is the central hub for your entire system. For this reason, the back of the system unit typically is covered with all types of connectors. Because each component has its own unique type of connector, you end up with the assortment of jacks (called *ports* in the computer world) that you see in Figure 1.9.

As you've probably noticed, some PCs put some of these connectors on the front of the case—in addition to the back. This makes it easier to connect portable devices, such as an iPod music player or a digital video camcorder, without having to muck about behind your PC.

FIGURE 1.9

The back of a typical desktop PC system unit— just look at all those different connectors!

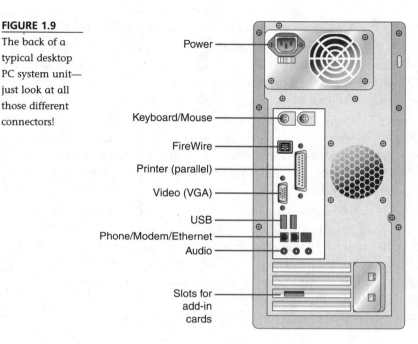

Power

Keyboard/Mouse

FireWire

Printer (parallel)

Video (VGA)

USB

Phone/Modem/Ethernet

Audio

Slots for add-in cards

While the connections are on the outside, all the good stuff in your system unit is inside the case. With most system units, you can remove the case to peek and poke around inside.

To remove your system unit's case, make sure the unit is unplugged and then look for some big screws or thumbscrews on either the side or back of the case. (Even better—read your PC's instruction manual for instructions specific to your unit.) With the screws loosened or removed, you should then be able to either slide off the entire case or pop open the top or back.

caution

Always turn off and unplug your computer before attempting to remove the system unit's case—and be careful about touching anything inside. If you have any built-up static electricity, you can seriously damage the sensitive chips and electronic components with an innocent touch.

Notebook PC Basics

While desktop systems used to dominate the market, the most popular type of computer today is the notebook PC. A notebook PC does everything a larger desktop PC does, but in a more compact package. A typical notebook PC combines all the various elements found in a desktop PC system into a single case and then adds a battery so that you can use it on the go. Many users find that portability convenient, even if it's just for using the computer in different rooms of the house.

A notebook PC looks like a smallish keyboard with a flip-up LCD screen attached. That's what you see, anyway; beneath the keyboard is a full-featured computer, complete with motherboard, CPU, memory chips, video and audio processing circuits, hard drive, and battery.

When the screen is folded down, the PC is portable; when the screen is flipped up, the keyboard is exposed. On the keyboard is some sort of built-in pointing device, like a touchpad, which is used in place of a standalone mouse.

If you look closely, you'll also see two built-in speakers, typically just above the top edge of the keyboard. Most notebooks also have an earphone jack, which you can use to connect a set of headphones or earbuds, the better to listen to music in a public place. (When you connect a set of headphones or earbuds, the built-in speakers are automatically muted.)

Somewhere on the notebook—either on the side or along the back edge—should be a row of connecting ports, like that shown in Figure 1.10. Most notebooks have two or more USB connectors, an Ethernet connector (for connecting to a wired network), a VGA video connector (for connecting to an external display monitor), and perhaps a FireWire connector (for connecting a digital camcorder). Some notebooks also have dedicated ports you can use to connect an external mouse and keyboard in case you don't like using the built-in keyboard and pointing device.

FIGURE 1.10

Connecting ports on a notebook PC.

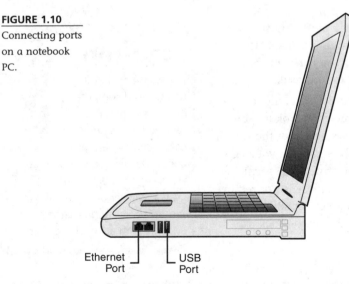

Ethernet Port   USB Port

In addition, your notebook probably has a built-in CD or CD/DVD drive, typically on the side of the case. Press the little button to open the drive and insert a disc; push the drive back in to begin playing the CD or DVD.

Inside the notebook case are the guts of the computer—everything you have in a desktop PC's system unit but more compact. In fact, most notebooks have *more* inside than does a typical desktop; in particular, most notebook PCs have a built-in

WiFi adapter so that the notebook can connect to a wireless home network or public WiFi hotspot.

In addition, virtually all notebook PCs come with some sort of built-in battery. That's because a portable PC is truly portable; in addition to running on normal AC power, a notebook PC can operate unplugged, using battery power. Depending on the PC (and the battery), you might be able to operate a laptop for three or four hours or more before switching batteries or plugging the unit into a wall outlet. That makes a notebook PC great for use on airplanes, in coffee shops, or anywhere plugging in a power cord is inconvenient.

Interestingly, although all notebook PCs have similar components, they're not all created alike. As you can see in Figure 1.11, some notebooks are smaller and lighter than others, whereas some models are more suited for multimedia use—for watching movies and listening to music while you're on the go.

FIGURE 1.11

Different types of notebooks.

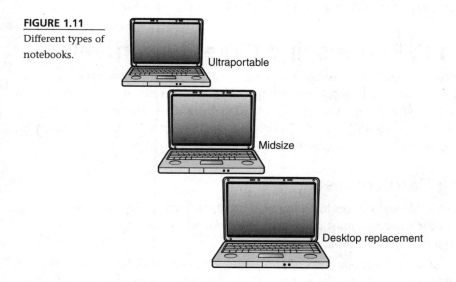

Ultraportable

Midsize

Desktop replacement

The smallest and most portable type of notebook PC is called an *ultraportable* or *netbook*. These models typically have a smallish screen (12" or so) with a traditional aspect ratio and weigh less than four pounds. Ultraportables are small and light enough to fit in a business briefcase and are perfect when all you need to do is check your email and do a little work when you're on the road. Because the screen is small and the PC horsepower is low, they get great battery life. On the downside, the screen is small and the horsepower is low, which means you can't do high-performance work; in addition, some users find the keyboards a trifle too compact.

In the middle of the pack is the appropriately named *midsize* or traditional notebook. These notebooks are a little bigger and a little heavier than ultraportables but also offer bigger screens and more comfortable keyboards. These notebooks have enough horsepower to do most traditional home or office computing tasks and typically have battery life in the 2–3 hour range.

If, on the other hand, you want a notebook that will do everything a desktop PC does and you won't be using it on batteries much, consider a *desktop replacement* model. These notebooks are big and heavy and have relatively poor battery life, so you won't be carrying them around much. They have big screens and lots of computing horsepower, so they can perform the most demanding tasks—including high-octane game playing and video editing. As the name implies, you can totally replace your desktop PC with one of these notebooks.

Which type of notebook is best for you? If you travel a lot but don't use your PC much, consider a lightweight notebook. If you use your notebook a lot and need to take your work with you, a midsize model is a good compromise. And if you want to totally replace your desktop with a notebook and know you won't be using it on battery power much, go with a more expensive desktop replacement model.

Beyond the PC: Printers and Other Peripherals

Whether you have a desktop or notebook PC, at some point or another you'll probably want to enhance your system by adding one or more peripherals. This may be a printer, a scanner, or perhaps an external hard disk (for more storage). Most likely, you'll connect your peripherals using a USB connection; that's the most common type of connection for outboard devices like these.

Printers: Making Hard Copies

Your monitor displays images in real time, but they're fleeting. For permanent records of your work, you must add a printer to your system. Printers create hard copy output from your software programs.

You can choose from various types of printers for your system, depending on your exact printing needs. The two main types of printers today are laser and inkjet printers.

Laser printers work much like copying machines, applying toner (powdered ink) to paper by using a small laser. *Inkjet* printers, on the other hand, shoot jets of ink to the paper's surface to create the printed image. Inkjet printers are typically a little lower priced than laser printers, although the price difference is shrinking.

You also can choose from either black-and-white or color printers. Black-and-white printers are faster than color printers and better if you're printing memos, letters, and other single-color documents. Color printers, however, are great if you have kids, and they're essential if you want to print pictures taken with a digital camera.

By the way, there's a type of "combination" printer available that combines a printer with a scanner, a fax machine, and a copier. If you need all these devices (sometimes called a *multifunction unit*, or *MFU*) and are short on space, these are pretty good deals.

Scanners: Making Digital Copies

Just a printer makes a hard copy of a digital file; a scanner makes a digital copy of a printed document or picture. You can use scanners to scan legal and other documents or to scan your favorite digital photographs. The process is similar, no matter the source.

A scanner works by running an image sensor across the face of the document, which is placed face-down on the scanner's glass bed. This image sensor digitizes the elements of the document, which are then converted into the appropriate file format. In most instances, it's as easy as pressing a button and letting the scanner do its thing; the resulting digital file is then stored somewhere on your computer's hard disk.

Most scanners cost in the $100 range and connect to your computer via USB. This is an affordable way to create digital copies of old photo prints, letters, and the like—which can then be stored along with your more-recent digital photo files.

THE ABSOLUTE MINIMUM

Here are the key points to remember from this chapter:

- There are two main types of computer systems today: desktop systems and notebook PCs.

- All personal computers are composed of various hardware components; in a desktop PC, they're separate devices, while a notebook PC combines them all into a single portable unit.

- You interface with your computer hardware via a piece of software called an operating system. The operating system on your new computer is probably some version of Microsoft Windows—Windows 7, Windows Vista, or Windows XP, depending on when it was purchased.

- You use specific software programs to perform specific tasks, such as writing letters and editing digital photos.

- The brains and engine of your system is the system unit, which contains the microprocessor, memory, disk drives, and all the connections for your other system components.

- To make your system run faster, get a faster microprocessor or more memory.

- Data is temporarily stored in your system's memory; you store data permanently on some type of disk drive—typically a hard disk or CD/DVD drive.

2

SETTING UP YOUR NEW COMPUTER SYSTEM

Chapter 1, "How Personal Computers Work," gave you the essential background information you need to understand how your computer system works. With that information in hand, it's now time to connect all the various pieces and parts of your computer system—and get your PC up and running!

Before You Get Started

It's important to prepare the space where you'll be putting your new PC. Obviously, the space has to be big enough to hold all the components—though you don't have to keep all the components together. You can, for example, spread out your left and right speakers, place your subwoofer on the floor, and separate the printer from the main unit. Just don't put anything so far away that the cables don't reach. (And make sure you have a spare power outlet—or even better, a multi-outlet power strip—nearby.)

You also should consider the ergonomics of your setup. You want your keyboard at or slightly below normal desktop height (if you have a separate keyboard, that is), and you want your monitor at or slightly below eye level. Make sure your chair is adjusted for a straight and firm sitting position with your feet flat on the floor, and then place all the pieces of your system in relation to that.

Wherever you put your computer, you should make sure that it's in a well-ventilated location free of excess dust and smoke. (The moving parts in your computer don't like dust and dirt or any other such contaminants that can muck up the way they work.) Because your computer generates heat when it operates, you must leave enough room around the system unit for the heat to dissipate. *Never* place your computer (especially a desktop PC's system unit) in a confined, poorly ventilated space; your PC can overheat and shut down if it isn't sufficiently ventilated.

For extra protection to your computer, connect the PC's power cable to a surge suppressor rather than directly into an electrical outlet. A *surge suppressor*—which looks like a power strip, but with an on/off switch and a circuit breaker button—protects your PC from power-line surges that could damage its delicate internal parts. When a power surge temporarily spikes your line voltage (causes the voltage to momentarily increase above normal levels), a surge suppressor helps to keep the level of the electric current as steady as possible. Most surge suppressors also include circuit breakers to shut down power to your system in the event of a severe power spike.

tip

When you unpack your PC, be sure you keep all the manuals, CD-ROMs, and cables. Put the ones you don't use in a safe place, in case you need to reinstall any software or equipment at a later date.

caution

Before you connect *any-thing* to your computer, make sure that the peripheral is turned off.

Connecting a Desktop PC

Now it's time to get connected—which can be a bit of a chore for a desktop computer system. (It's a lot easier for a notebook PC, as you'll see in a moment.)

Connect in Order

Start by positioning your system unit so that you easily can access all the connections on the back. Then you need to carefully run the cables from each of the other components so that they're hanging loose at the rear of the system unit. Now you're ready to get connected.

It's important that you connect the cables in a particular order. To make sure that the most critical devices are connected first, follow the instructions in Table 2.1.

caution

Make sure that every cable is *firmly* connected—both to the system unit and the specific piece of hardware. Loose cables can cause all sorts of weird problems, so be sure they're plugged in really well.

TABLE 2.1 Connecting Your System Components

Order	Connection	Looks Like
1.	Connect your mouse to the mouse connector—or, if you have a USB mouse, connect to an open USB port.	
2.	Connect your keyboard to the keyboard connector—or, if you have a USB keyboard, connect to an open USB port.	
3.	Connect your video monitor to the video connector. Most monitors connect via a standard VGA connector; some LCD monitors have the option of a higher-quality digital connection via a DVI connector—if your computer offers DVI output.	
4.	Most printers today connect via USB, so connect to an open USB port on your PC. If your printer uses an older parallel cable connection, connect to your PC's parallel connector (sometimes labeled "printer" or "LPT1").	

TABLE 2.1 (continued)

Order	Connection	Looks Like
5.	If you're using a dial-up Internet connection, connect a cable from your telephone line to the "line in" connector on your modem or modem board; then connect another cable from the "line out" connector on your modem to your telephone. If you're using a cable or DSL modem, connect a cable from your cable or telephone line to the modem; then connect the modem to your computer via either USB or Ethernet, as directed by your Internet service provider (ISP).	
6.	Connect the phono jack from your speaker system to the "audio out" or "sound out" connector. Run the necessary cables between your right and left speakers and your subwoofer, as directed by the manufacturer.	
7.	If you have a wired home network, connect an Ethernet cable between the network router and your computer. If you have a wireless home network, connect the WiFi adapter to a USB port on your computer.	
8.	Connect any external devices, such as your printer, to the appropriate USB or FireWire connector on your PC.	
9.	Plug the power cable of your video monitor into a power outlet.	
10.	If your system includes powered speakers, plug them into a power outlet.	
11.	Plug any other powered external component into a power outlet.	
12.	Plug the power cable of your system unit into a power outlet.	

Connect by Color

Most PC manufacturers color-code the cables and connectors to make the connection even easier—just plug the blue cable into the blue connector, and so on. If you're not sure which color cable goes to which device, take a look at the standard cable color coding in Table 2.2.

TABLE 2.2   Connector Color Codes

Connector	Color
VGA (analog) monitor	Blue
Digital monitor (DVI)	White
Video out	Yellow
Mouse	Green
Keyboard	Purple
Serial	Teal or turquoise
Parallel (printer)	Burgundy
USB	Black
FireWire (IEEE 1394)	Gray
Audio line out (right)	Red
Audio line out (left)	White
Audio line out (headphones)	Lime
Speaker out/subwoofer	Orange
Right-to-left speaker	Brown
Audio line in	Light blue
Microphone	Pink
Gameport/MIDI	Gold

Connecting a Notebook PC

One nice thing about notebook PCs is that you don't have nearly as many pieces to connect. Because the monitor, speakers, keyboard, mouse, and WiFi adapter are all built into the notebook unit, the only things you have to connect are a printer and a power cable. Connect your printer to a USB port on your notebook; then connect your notebook's power cable to a power strip or surge suppressor. Pretty easy, eh?

Turning It On and Setting It Up

Now that you have everything connected, sit back and rest for a minute. Next up is the big step—turning it all on.

It's important that you turn on things in the proper order. For a desktop PC, follow these steps:

1. Turn on your video monitor.

2. Turn on your speaker system—but make sure the speaker volume knob is turned down (toward the left).

3. Turn on any other system components that are connected to your system unit—such as your printer, scanner, external modem, and so on. (If your PC is connected to an Ethernet network, make sure that the network router is turned on.)

4. Turn on your system unit.

Note that your system unit is the *last* thing you turn on. That's because when it powers on, it has to sense the other components of your system—which it can do only if the other components are plugged in and turned on.

For a notebook PC, there's less to worry about. Just turn on any peripheral connected to the PC, such as your printer; then press your notebook's power button.

Powering On for the First Time

The first time you turn on your PC is a unique experience. A brand-new, out-of-the-box system will have to perform some basic configuration operations, which include asking you to input some key information.

This first-time startup operation differs from manufacturer to manufacturer, but it typically includes some or all of the following steps:

> **note**
>
> For full installation, activation, and registration, your PC will need to be connected to the Internet—typically via a cable or DSL modem connected either to your PC or to a network hub or router.

- **Windows Product Activation**—You may be asked to input the long and nonsensical product code found on the label attached to the rear of a desktop PC system unit or to the bottom of a notebook PC. Your system then connects to the Microsoft mother ship (via the Internet), registers your system information, and unlocks Windows for you to use. (Note that some manufacturers "pre-activate" Windows at the factory, so you might not have to go through this process.)

- **Windows Configuration**—During this process Windows asks a series of questions about your location, the current time and date, and other essential information. You also might be asked to create a username and password.

■ ***System Configuration***—This is where Windows tries to figure out all the different components that are part of your system, such as your printer, scanner, and so on. Enter the appropriate information when prompted; if asked to insert a component's installation CD, do so.

Many computer manufacturers supplement these configuration operations with setup procedures of their own. It's impossible to describe all the different options that might be presented by all the different manufacturers, so watch the screen carefully and follow all the onscreen instructions.

After you have everything configured, Windows finally starts, and then *you* can start using your system.

Powering On Normally

After everything is installed and configured, starting your computer is a much simpler affair. When you turn on your computer, you'll notice a series of text messages flash across your screen. These messages are there to let you know what's going on as your computer *boots up*.

After a few seconds (during which your system unit beeps and whirrs a little bit), the Windows Welcome screen appears, as shown in Figure 2.1. All registered users are listed on this screen. Click your username or picture, enter your password (if necessary), and then press the Enter key or click the right-arrow button. After you're past the Welcome screen, you're taken directly to the Windows desktop, and your system is ready to run.

note

Some installation procedures require your computer to be restarted. In most cases, this happens automatically; then the installation process resumes where it left off.

Technical types call the procedure of starting up a computer *booting* or *booting up* the system. Restarting a system (turning it off and then back on) is called *rebooting*.

note

If you have only a single user on your PC and that user doesn't have a password assigned, Windows moves past the Welcome screen with no action necessary on your part.

FIGURE 2.1

The first thing you see in Windows 7—the Welcome screen. (Looks slightly different in different versions of Windows.)

THE ABSOLUTE MINIMUM

Here are the key points to remember when connecting and configuring your new computer:

- Most cables plug into only a specific connector—and on most new systems, they're color-coded for easier hookup.
- Make sure your cables are firmly connected; loose cables are the cause of many computer problems.
- Connect all the cables to your system unit before you turn on the power.
- Remember to turn on your printer and monitor before you turn on the system unit.
- For full registration and activation, your computer needs to be connected to the Internet.

PART

Using Windows

3

GETTING TO KNOW WINDOWS 7

As you learned in Chapter 1, "How Personal Computers Work," the software and operating system make your hardware work. The operating system for most personal computers is Microsoft Windows, and you need to know how to use Windows to use your PC. Windows pretty much runs your computer for you; if you don't know your way around Windows, you won't be able to do much of anything on your new PC.

Introducing Microsoft Windows

Microsoft Windows is a type of software called an *operating system*. An operating system does what its name implies—*operates* your computer *system*, working in the background every time you turn on your PC.

Equally important, Windows is what you see when you first turn on your computer, after everything turns on and boots up. The "desktop" that fills your screen is part of Windows, as are the taskbar at the bottom of the screen and the big menu that pops up when you click the Start button.

Welcome to Windows 7

If you've recently purchased a new PC, the version of Windows on your PC is probably Windows 7. Microsoft has released different versions of Windows over the years, and Windows 7 is the latest—which is why it comes preinstalled on most new PCs.

If you've used a previous version of Windows—such as Windows Vista, Windows XP, Windows 2000, or Windows 98—on another PC, Windows 7 no doubt looks and acts somewhat differently from what you're used to. Don't worry; everything that was in the old Windows is still in the new Windows—it's just in a slightly different place.

Different Versions of Windows 7

There are actually several versions of Windows 7, each with a slightly different feature set. Which version you have depends on which was installed by your PC's manufacturer. Table 3.1 details the different versions available in the U.S. market.

note

If your PC is a little older, it's probably running Windows 7's predecessor, Windows Vista. Vista looks and works pretty much like Windows 7, with only a few minor exceptions. Older versions of Windows, such as Windows XP, look and act much different from Windows 7, however.

note

If you're currently using Windows Vista, you'll find that Windows 7 looks pretty much the same—except for the new taskbar. Beyond that, Windows 7 is more like an updated version of Vista than it is a totally new upgrade, as Vista was to Windows XP.

TABLE 3.1 Windows 7 Versions

	Starter	Home Premium	Ultimate	Professional	Enterprise
Target Market					
Home	Yes	Yes	Yes		
Small business			Yes	Yes	
Corporate				Yes	Yes
Sold at retail?	Yes	Yes	Yes	Yes	
Interface Features					
Basic user interface	Yes	Yes	Yes	Yes	Yes
Aero user interface		Yes	Yes	Yes	Yes
Aero Peek and Flip 3D		Yes	Yes	Yes	Yes
Live taskbar previews		Yes	Yes	Yes	Yes
Taskbar Jump Lists	Yes	Yes	Yes	Yes	Yes
Included Applications					
Internet Explorer 8	Yes	Yes	Yes	Yes	Yes
Windows Gadgets	Yes	Yes	Yes	Yes	Yes
Calculator	Yes	Yes	Yes	Yes	Yes
Paint	Yes	Yes	Yes	Yes	Yes
WordPad	Yes	Yes	Yes	Yes	Yes
Windows Fax and Scan	Yes	Yes	Yes	Yes	Yes
Premium games		Yes	Yes	Yes	Yes
Windows Photo Viewer	Yes	Yes	Yes	Yes	Yes
Windows Media Player 12	Yes	Yes	Yes	Yes	Yes
DVD playback		Yes	Yes	Yes	Yes
Windows DVD Maker		Yes	Yes	Yes	Yes
Windows Media Center		Yes	Yes	Yes	Yes
Performance Features					
Number of running applications supported	3	Unlimited	Unlimited	Unlimited	Unlimited
Maximum RAM (32-bit)	4GB	4GB	4GB	4GB	4GB
Maximum RAM (64-bit)	NA	16GB	192GB	192GB	192GB
Windows Backup	Yes	Yes	Yes	Yes	Yes
System image-based backup and recovery	Yes	Yes	Yes	Yes	Yes
BitLocker			Yes		Yes
HomeGroup sharing	Join only	Yes	Yes	Yes	Yes
Internet Connection Sharing		Yes	Yes	Yes	Yes
Windows Mobility Center		Yes	Yes	Yes	Yes
Multi-Touch support		Yes	Yes	Yes	Yes
XP Mode			Yes	Yes	Yes

Most new PCs should come with the Home Premium edition installed; this edition is also best for home users upgrading from a previous version of Windows. Some low-end PCs might come with the Starter edition, although it's pretty limited—and not available in an edition for 64-bit processors. The Professional and Enterprise editions are targeted at small and large businesses, respectively. And the Ultimate edition is for those users who want it all—and are prepared to pay for it.

Whichever version of Windows 7 you have installed on your PC, you can easily upgrade to another version by using the built-in Windows Anytime Upgrade feature, available from the Windows Control Panel. All you have to do is select the version you want, make sure you're connected to the Internet, and then give Microsoft your credit card number. The upgrade process is automatic, using files already installed on your PC's hard drive.

> **note**
>
> Microsoft is also distributing a stripped-down version of Windows 7 for emerging markets, called the Home Basic edition. This version is not available in the United States. It is similar to the Home Premium edition but without the Aero interface.

Working Your Way Around the Desktop

If you're already familiar with Windows, you can start using Windows 7 without much training. However, if this is your first PC, or if Windows 7 looks a little too different to you, take a few minutes to find your way around the Win7 desktop.

As you can see in Figure 3.1, the Windows 7 desktop includes a number of key elements. Get to know this desktop; you're going to be seeing a lot of it from now on.

The major parts of the Windows desktop include

- **Start button**—Opens the Start menu, which is what you can use to open all your programs and documents.

- **Taskbar**—Displays icons for your favorite applications and documents, as well as for any open window. Right-click an icon to see a Jump List of recent open documents and other operations for that application. (This is the most-changed feature from Windows Vista to Windows 7—which is why we'll discuss it in more depth later in this chapter.)

- **Notification area**—Sometimes known as the system tray, this part of the taskbar displays icons for a handful of key system functions, including the Action Center, power (on notebook PCs), networking/Internet, and audio (volume).

- **Aero Peek button**—Hover over this little rectangle, and all open windows go transparent so you can see what's on the desktop below. Click the Aero Peek button to immediately minimize all open windows.

- **Gadgets**—These are mini-applications that sit on the desktop and perform specific operations.

- **Shortcut icons**—These are links to software programs you can place on your desktop; a "clean" desktop includes just one icon, for the Windows Recycle Bin.

- **Recycle Bin**—This is where you dump any files you want to delete.

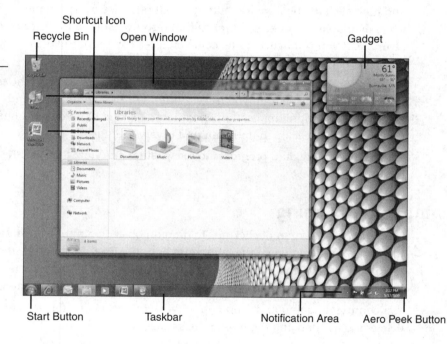

FIGURE 3.1

The Windows 7 desktop—click the Start button to get going.

Important Windows Operations

To use Windows efficiently, you must master a few simple operations, such as pointing and clicking, dragging and dropping, and right-clicking. You perform all these operations with your mouse.

Pointing and Clicking

The most common mouse operation is *pointing and clicking*. Simply move your computer's mouse or touchpad so that the cursor is pointing to the object you want to select, and then click the left mouse button once. Pointing and clicking is an effective way to select menu items, directories, and files.

Double-Clicking

To launch a program or open a file folder, single-clicking isn't enough. Instead, you need to *double-click* an item to activate an operation. This involves pointing at something onscreen with the cursor and then clicking the left mouse button twice in rapid succession. For example, to open program groups or launch individual programs, simply double-click a specific icon.

Right-Clicking

Here's one of the secret keys to efficient Windows operation. When you select an item and then click the *right* mouse button, you'll often see a pop-up menu. This menu, when available, contains commands that directly relate to the selected object. So for example, if you right-click a file icon, you'll see commands related to that file—copy, move, delete, and so forth.

Right-clicking is also key to Windows 7's new Jump List feature on the taskbar. Right-click any taskbar icon, and you'll see a Jump List that contains recently opened documents and essential application operations. It's kind of an extension of the traditional right-click pop-up menu and is very useful.

Refer to your individual programs to see whether and how they use the right mouse button.

Dragging and Dropping

Dragging is a variation of clicking. To drag an object, point at it with the cursor and then press and hold down the left mouse button. Move the mouse without releasing the mouse button and drag the object to a new location. When you're finished moving the object, release the mouse button to drop it onto the new location.

You can use dragging and dropping to move files from one folder to another or to delete files by dragging them onto the Recycle Bin icon.

Hovering

When you position the cursor over an item without clicking your mouse, you're *hovering* over that item. Many operations require you to hover your cursor and then perform some other action.

Moving and Resizing Windows

Every software program you launch is displayed in a separate onscreen window. When you open more than one program, you get more than one window—and your desktop can quickly become cluttered.

There are many ways to deal with desktop clutter. One way is to move a window to a new position. You do this by positioning your cursor over a blank area at the top of the window frame and then clicking and holding down the left button on your mouse. As long as this button is depressed, you can use your mouse to drag the window around the screen. When you release the mouse button, the window stays where you put it.

With Windows 7, you can quickly move a window to the left or right side of the desktop by using a new featured dubbed *Aero Snap*. Just drag the window to the left side of the screen to dock it there and resize it to the left half of the desktop; drag the window to the right side of the screen to dock it on that side.

You also can change the size of most windows. You do this by positioning the cursor over the edge of the window—any edge. If you position the cursor on either side of the window, you can resize the width. If you position the cursor on the top or bottom edge, you can resize the height. Finally, if you position the cursor on a corner, you can resize the width and height at the same time.

After the cursor is positioned over the window's edge, press and hold down the left mouse button; then drag the window border to its new size. Release the mouse button to lock in the newly sized window.

Peeking at the Desktop

Want to quickly see what's beneath all the open windows on the desktop? Have a gadget you want to look at?

Then you'll appreciate Windows 7's new *Aero Peek* feature. With Aero Peek you can, well, peek at the desktop beneath all that window clutter.

You activate Aero Peek from the little transparent rectangular button at the far right of the Windows taskbar. Hover the cursor over the Aero Peek button and every open window becomes transparent, as shown in Figure 3.2. This lets you see everything that's on the desktop below.

FIGURE 3.2

FIGURE 3.2

Aero Peek in action—a great way to view gadgets, shortcut icons, and your Windows desktop wallpaper.

Maximizing, Minimizing, and Closing Windows

Another way to manage a window in Windows is to make it display full-screen. You do this by maximizing the window. All you have to do is click the Maximize button at the upper-right corner of the window, as shown in Figure 3.3.

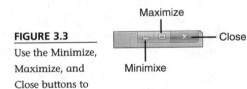

Maximize

Close

Minimixe

FIGURE 3.3

Use the Minimize, Maximize, and Close buttons to manage your desktop windows.

If the window is already maximized, the Maximize button changes to a Restore Down button. When you click the Restore Down button, the window resumes its previous (premaximized) dimensions.

If you would rather hide the window so that it doesn't clutter your desktop, click the Minimize button. This shoves the window off the desktop, onto the taskbar. The program in the window is still running, however—it's just not on the desktop. To restore a minimized window, all you have to do is click the window's icon on the Windows taskbar (at the bottom of the screen).

tip

Aero Snap provides another way to maximize a window. Use your mouse to drag the window to the top of the desktop, and it will automatically maximize.

If what you really want to do is close the window (and close any program running within the window), just click the window's Close button.

Scrolling Through a Window

Many windows contain more information than can be displayed at once. When you have a long document or web page, only the first part of the document or page is displayed in the window. To view the rest of the document or page, you have to scroll down through the window, using the various parts of the scrollbar (shown in Figure 3.4).

> **caution**
>
> If you try to close a window that contains a document you haven't saved, you'll be prompted to save the changes to the document. Because you probably don't want to lose any of your work, click Yes to save the document and then close the program.

FIGURE 3.4
Use the scrollbar to scroll through long pages.

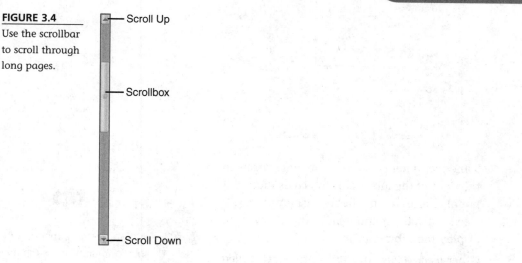

Scroll Up

Scrollbox

Scroll Down

There are several ways to scroll through a window. To scroll up or down a line at a time, click the up or down arrow on the window's scrollbar. To move to a specific place in a long document, use your mouse to grab the scroll box (between the up and down arrows) and drag it to a new position. You can also click the scrollbar between the scroll box and the end arrow, which scrolls you one screen at a time.

If your mouse has a scroll wheel, you can use it to scroll through a long document. Just roll the wheel back or forward to scroll down or up through a window. Likewise, some notebook touchpads let you drag your finger up or down to scroll through a window.

Using Menus

Many windows in Windows use a set of pull-down *menus* to store all the commands and operations you can perform. The menus are aligned across the top of the window, just below the title bar, in what is called a *menu bar*.

You open (or pull down) a menu by clicking the menu's name. The full menu then appears just below the menu bar, as shown in Figure 3.5. You activate a command or select a menu item by clicking it with your mouse.

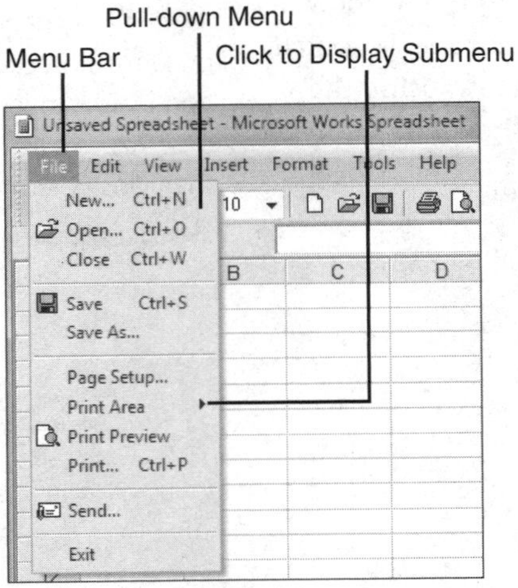

FIGURE 3.5
Navigating Windows' menu system.

Some menu items have a little black arrow to the right of the label. This indicates that additional choices are available, displayed on a *submenu*. Click the menu item or the arrow to display the submenu.

Other *menu items* have three little dots (called an ellipsis) to the right of the label. This indicates that additional choices are available, displayed in a dialog box. Click the menu item to display the dialog box.

tip

If an item in a menu, toolbar, or dialog box is dimmed (or grayed), that means it isn't available for the current task.

The nice thing is, after you get the hang of this menu thing in one program, the menus should be similar in all the other programs you use. For example, most of the Microsoft Office 2007 programs have an Office button that, when clicked, displays a pull-down menu of common file-oriented operations; older programs have a File menu that contains similar operations. Although each program has menus and menu items specific to its own needs, these common menus make it easy to get up and running when you install new software programs on your system.

Using Toolbars and Ribbons

Some Windows programs put the most frequently used operations on one or more *toolbars*, typically located just below the menu bar. (Figure 3.6 shows a typical Windows toolbar.) A toolbar looks like a row of buttons, each with a small picture (called an *icon*) and maybe a bit of text. You activate the associated command or operation by clicking the button with your mouse.

tip

If the toolbar is too long to display fully on your screen, you'll see a right arrow at the far-right side of the toolbar. Click this arrow to display the buttons that aren't currently visible.

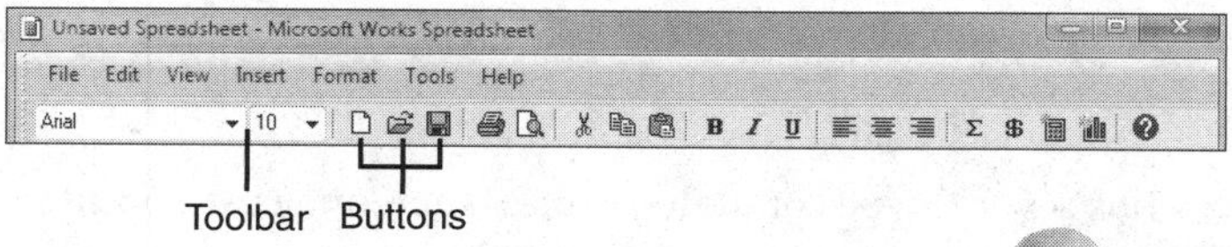

FIGURE 3.6
A typical
Windows toolbar.

Toolbar Buttons

Other programs substitute a *ribbon* for the toolbar. For example, most of the Microsoft Office 2007 programs have a ribbon that contains buttons for the most-used operations. As you can see in Figure 3.7, each ribbon has different tabs, each containing a unique collection of buttons. Click the tab to see the ribbon buttons for that particular type of operation.

tip

If you're not sure which button does what on a toolbar or ribbon, you can hover the cursor over the button to display a ToolTip. A *ToolTip* is a small text box that displays the button's label or other useful information.

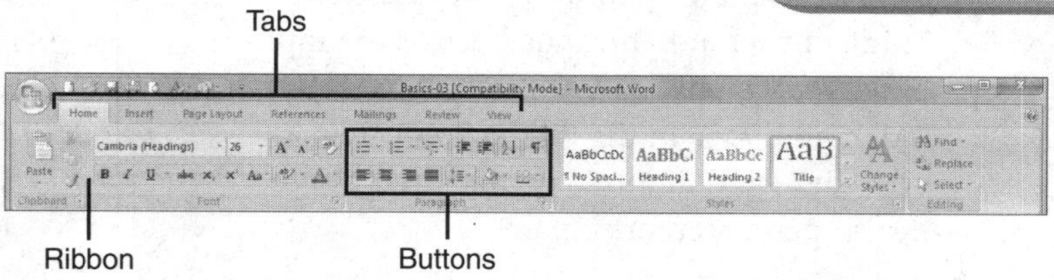

Tabs

FIGURE 3.7
A new-style ribbon, with tabs for different types of operations.

Ribbon Buttons

Using Dialog Boxes, Tabs, and Buttons

When Windows or an application requires a complex set of inputs, you are often presented with a *dialog box*. A dialog box is similar to a form in which you can input various parameters and make various choices—and then register those inputs and choices when you click OK. (Figure 3.8 shows the Save As dialog box, found in most Windows applications.)

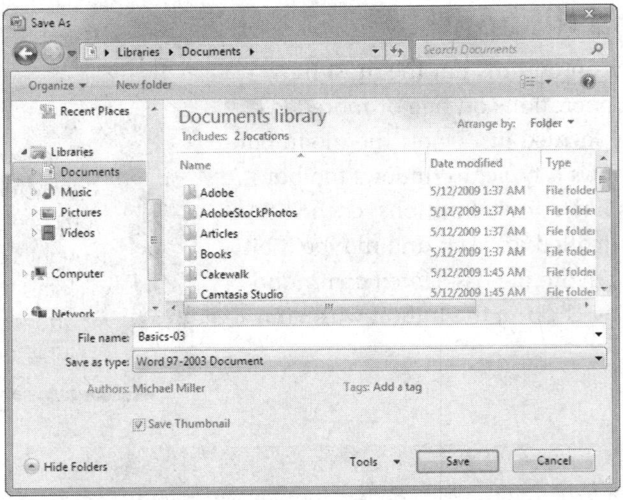

FIGURE 3.8

Use dialog boxes
to control vari-
ous aspects of
your Windows
applications.

Windows has several types of dialog boxes, each one customized to the task at
hand. However, most dialog boxes share a set of common features, which include
the following:

■ **Buttons**—Most buttons either register your
inputs or open an auxiliary dialog box. The
most common buttons are OK (to register
your inputs and close the dialog box),
Cancel (to close the dialog box without registering your inputs), and Apply (to register
your inputs without closing the dialog box).
Click a button once to activate it.

■ **Tabs**—These allow a single dialog box to
display multiple "pages" of information.
Think of each tab, arranged across the top
of the dialog box, as a "thumbtab" to the
individual page in the dialog box below it.
Click the top of a tab to change to that particular page of information.

■ **Text boxes**—These are empty boxes where
you type in a response. Position your cursor
over the empty input box, click your left
mouse button, and begin typing.

■ **Lists**—These are lists of available choices;
lists can either scroll or drop down from
what looks like an input box. Select an
item from the list with your mouse; you can

note

The operations pre-
sented in this chapter are
described as how they look and
act by default in a typical
Windows 7 installation. If you're
using someone else's PC, things
might not look or act exactly like
this. It's normal for two different
PCs to look and act a little differently because you can customize
so many options for your own personal tastes—as you'll learn in
Chapter 4, "Personalizing
Windows."

select multiple items in some lists by holding down the Ctrl key while clicking with your mouse.

- **Check boxes**—These are boxes that let you select (or deselect) various stand-alone options.
- **Sliders**—These are sliding bars that let you select increments between two extremes, similar to a sliding volume control on an audio system.

Using the Start Menu

All the software programs and utilities on your computer are accessed via Windows' Start menu. You display the Start menu by using your mouse to click the Start button, located in the lower-left corner of your screen.

As you can see in Figure 3.9, the Windows 7 Start menu consists of two columns of icons. Your most frequently and recently used programs are listed in the left column; basic Windows utilities and folders are listed in the right column. To open a specific program or folder, just click the name of the item.

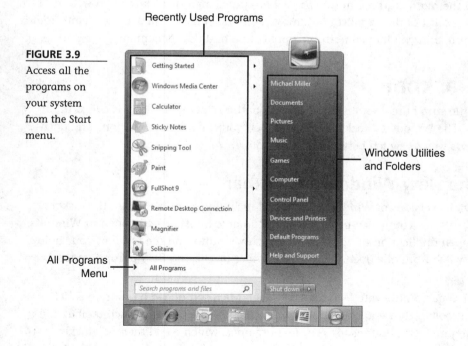

Recently Used Programs

FIGURE 3.9
Access all the programs on your system from the Start menu.

Windows Utilities and Folders

All Programs Menu

To view the rest of your programs, click the All Programs arrow. This displays a sub-menu called the Programs menu. From here you can access various programs, sorted by type or manufacturer. (When more programs are contained within a master folder, you'll see an arrow to the right of the title; click this arrow to expand the menu and display additional choices.)

Launching a Program

Now that you know how to work the Start menu, it's easy to start any particular software program. All you have to do is follow these steps:

1. Click the Start button to display the Start menu.
2. If the program is displayed on the Start menu, click the program's icon.
3. If the program isn't visible on the main Start menu, click the All Programs button, find the program's icon, and then click it.

Another way to find a program to launch is to use the Instant Search box on the Start menu. Just start entering the program's name into the search box, and a list of matching programs appears on the Start menu. When the program you want appears, click it to launch it.

Reopening Recent Documents

In Windows 7, you can quickly access the most recent documents opened with an application directly from the Start menu. Look for a right arrow next to an application on the main Start menu (not the All Programs menu); click this arrow, and you'll see a list of that application's most recent documents. Click a document from this menu, and you'll open both the application and that document.

Using the Taskbar

That little strip of real estate at the bottom of the Windows desktop is called the *taskbar*. The Windows 7 taskbar lets you open your favorite applications and documents, as well as switch between open windows.

Introducing the New Windows 7 Taskbar

In previous versions of Windows, up to and including Windows Vista, the taskbar existed to show you which programs or documents were currently open in Windows. Every open application or document had its own button on the taskbar; you could easily switch from one open window to another by clicking the appropriate taskbar button.

That changed a little with Windows XP, when Microsoft added a separate Quick Launch toolbar that you could dock to the taskbar. The Quick Launch toolbar could be configured with buttons for your favorite apps, which could then be quickly launched from the toolbar—which, when docked, appeared to be part of the taskbar. In Windows XP, the Quick Launch toolbar was activated by default; it was still around in Windows Vista, but not automatically displayed.

Well, in Windows 7, the taskbar takes on the attributes of the traditional taskbar plus the old Quick Launch toolbar—and a little more. That is, the Win7 taskbar includes buttons (actually, just icons—no text) not just for running applications and documents, but also for your favorite applications. Click an icon to launch an app, or click an icon to switch to an open window; taskbar icons exist for both.

Deciphering Taskbar Icons

If you've used previous versions of Windows, you'll notice immediately that the Windows 7 taskbar looks a bit different. It's more glass-like than older taskbars, a little taller as well, and it displays icons, not buttons. There are no labels on the icons, just the icon graphic.

The advantage to this new design is both visual (a much cleaner look) and practical (the new icons—while larger than the icons on the old text buttons—take up less space on the taskbar). It's easier to see what's what while at the same time displaying more items in the same amount of screen real estate.

Because of the multiple functions of these new taskbar icons, it's difficult to look at an icon in the taskbar and determine whether it represents an open or closed application or document. Difficult, yes, but not impossible. Here's the key.

As you can see in Figure 3.10, an icon for a not-yet-open application or document—essentially a shortcut to that app or doc—appears on the taskbar with no border. An icon for an open window has a slight border, while still appearing translucent. An icon for the currently selected open window also has a border but is less transparent. And if there is more than one document open for a given application (or more than one tab open in a web browser), that app's icon button appears "stacked" to represent multiple instances.

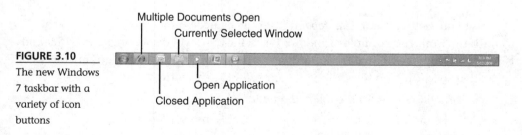

Multiple Documents Open
Currently Selected Window

FIGURE 3.10
The new Windows 7 taskbar with a variety of icon buttons

Open Application
Closed Application

Opening Applications and Switching Between Windows

Using the taskbar is simplicity itself. Click a shortcut icon to open the associated application or document. Click an open window icon to display that window front and center.

If you click a multiple-window icon, however, something interesting happens: Windows displays thumbnails for each of that application's open windows. (The same thing happens if you hover the cursor over any open-window icon, actually.) Move the cursor over a thumbnail, and that window temporarily displays on top of the stack on your desktop, no matter what its actual position. Click a thumbnail to switch to that window or click the red X on the thumbnail to close the window.

Using Jump Lists

The Windows 7 taskbar becomes even more useful with the addition of Jump Lists— kind of context-sensitive pop-up menus for each icon on the taskbar. To display an icon's Jump List, shown in Figure 3.11, right-click the icon.

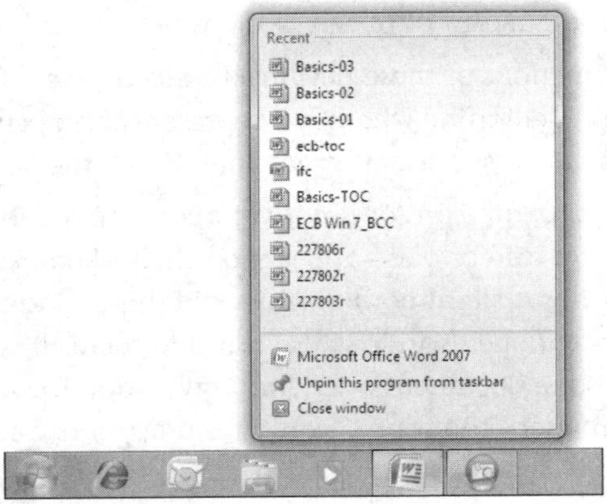

FIGURE 3.11

A Windows 7 taskbar Jump List.

What you see in a Jump List depends to some degree on the application associated with the icon. For example, Windows 7–specific apps will display more specific (and useful) Jump Lists than applications developed prior to Windows 7; an app has to be written specifically to take full advantage of this new feature.

Most Jump Lists contain the following items:

- The most recent documents opened in this application
- A link to open a new instance of this application
- An option to unpin this item from the taskbar (for shortcut icons)
- An option to close the current window (for open-window icons)

Win7–specific apps offer more application-appropriate items on their Jump Lists. For example, Windows Media Player 12 has a section for frequent playlists and albums, as well as a Tasks section with the most-recent program operations.

In short, Windows 7 taskbar Jump Lists are a lot like traditional right-click pop-up menus, but with more useful options. They make the new taskbar icons more useful than they would have been otherwise.

Managing Taskbar Buttons

Now that you know what the Windows 7 taskbar does, let's look a little at how to manage the new taskbar.

First, know that you have total control over the order of icons on the taskbar. Just drag and drop a taskbar icon from one position to another, and there it stays.

To add an application or document shortcut to the taskbar, just navigate to that item using the Start menu or Windows Explorer, right-click the item's icon, and select Pin to Taskbar. Alternatively, you can drag an icon from any folder to the taskbar. Either approach is quick and easy.

To remove an item from the taskbar, right-click it and select Unpin This Program from Taskbar from the Jump List.

Switching Between Programs

The taskbar is one way to switch between open programs, but it's not the only way. You can also do either of the following:

- Click any visible part of the application's window, which brings that window to the front.

- Hold down the Alt key and then press the Tab key repeatedly until the application window you want is selected. This is called *Windows Flip* and cycles through thumbnails of all open windows, as shown in Figure 3.12. When you're at the window you want, release the Alt key.

FIGURE 3.12
Use Windows Flip to select from thumbnails of all open programs.

- Hold down the Start button and then press the Tab key to activate the *Flip 3D* feature. This displays a three-dimensional stack of all open windows, as shown in Figure 3.13. Continue pressing the Tab key (or rotate the scroll button on your mouse) to cycle through the windows on the stack.

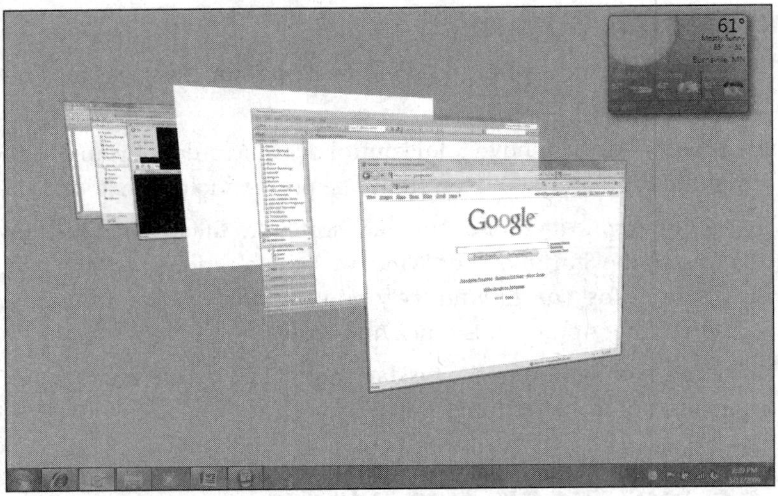

FIGURE 3.13
Flip 3D lets you flip through a three-dimensional stack of open windows.

Using Windows Explorer

In Windows 7, all the items stored on your computer—including programs, documents, and configuration settings—are accessible from *Windows Explorer*. This is a window that displays all the disk drives, folders, subfolders, and files on your computer system. You use Windows Explorer to find, copy, delete, launch, and even configure programs and documents.

You launch Windows Explorer from either the taskbar or the Start menu. Just click the Windows Explorer icon on the taskbar or select Documents from the Start menu.

Windows Explorer is also used to go directly to various types of documents on your hard drive. For example, when you click the Music icon on the Start menu, you open Windows Explorer looking directly at the open Music folder. When you click the Pictures icon on the Start menu, you open Windows Explorer looking directly at the open Pictures folder. And so forth.

Navigating Windows Explorer

When you open Windows Explorer, you see four icons. These icons let you go directly to all the Documents, Music, Pictures, and Videos stored on your hard drive. Double-click an icon to view the subfolders and files of that type.

On the left side of the Windows Explorer window is a Navigation pane, divided into several sections. The top section, Favorites, lists your most-used folders—Recently Changed, Public, Desktop, Downloads, Network, and Recent Places. Next is the Libraries section, which repeats the four icons in the main window—Documents, Music, Pictures, and Videos. Below that is a Homegroup section, which lets you access other computers on your network HomeGroup. The Computer section lets you access all the disk drives and devices connected to your computer. And the Network section lets you access all of your networked computers. Click any icon in the Navigation pane to view the contents of that item.

FIGURE 3.14

Navigating through your folders and subfolders with Windows Explorer.

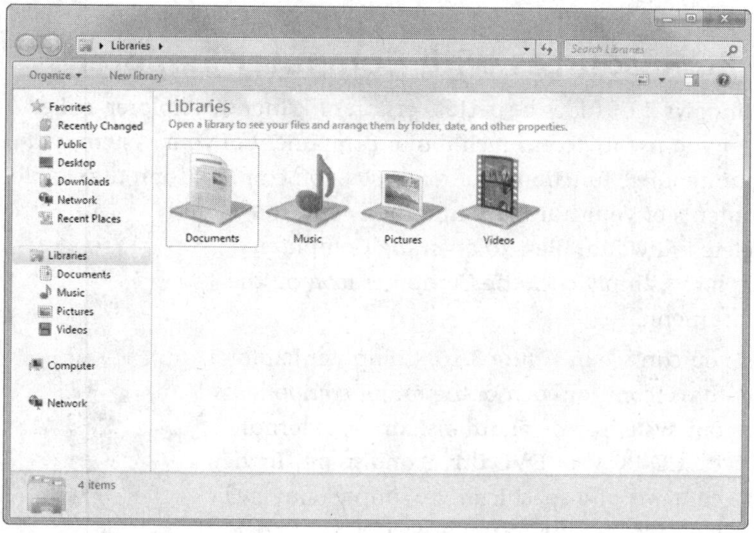

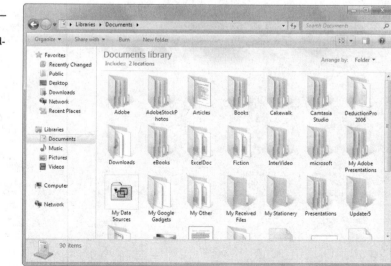

Let's examine how Windows Explorer works. Double-click the Documents icon in the main window (or click the Documents item in the Navigation pane), and you see a window full of folders, such as the one shown in Figure 3.15. Double-click a folder icon to view the contents of that folder—which could be individual files or additional folders (sometimes called *subfolders*). To launch a program or open a document, double-click that item's icon. To perform other tasks (copying, deleting, and so forth), right-click the icon and select an option from the pop-up menu.

FIGURE 3.15

Browsing through the folders and files stored on your system with Windows Explorer.

When you want to copy, delete, or otherwise manage files and folders, you use the Organize menu on the Windows Explorer toolbar. This menu includes most of the operations you need to manage your system's files and folders.

Managing PC Resources with Computer Explorer

Windows 7 includes a special version of Windows Explorer, called *Computer Explorer*, that you use to access each major component of your system and perform basic maintenance functions. For example, you can use Computer Explorer to "open" the contents of your hard disk and then copy, move, and delete individual files. To open the Computer Explorer, simply click the Computer icon on the Start menu.

As you can see in Figure 3.16, Computer Explorer contains icons for each of the major components of your system—your hard disk drive, external drives, CD-ROM or DVD drive, and so on. To view the contents of a specific drive, simply double-click the icon for that drive. You'll see a list of folders and files located on that drive; to view the contents of any folder, just double-click the icon for that folder.

> **note**
>
> In Windows XP, Computer Explorer was called My Computer.

FIGURE 3.16

Use Computer Explorer to manage your hard drive and other key components.

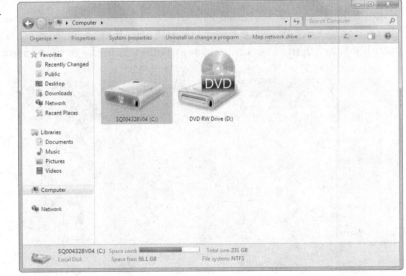

Managing Windows with the Control Panel

There's one more variation of Windows Explorer, similar to Computer Explorer, that you need to know about. This Explorer, called the *Control Panel*, is used to manage most of Windows' configuration settings. To open the Control Panel, click the Control Panel icon on the Start menu.

When the Control Panel opens, as shown in Figure 3.17, you can select a particular category you want to configure. Each item you select opens a window with a different set of options; just keep clicking until you find the specific item you want to configure.

note

To learn more about configuring various Windows settings, see Chapter 4.

FIGURE 3.17

The Windows 7 Control Panel— configuration tasks are organized by category.

Control Panel ▸

Search Control Panel

Adjust your computer's settings

View by: Category ▾

System and Security
Review your computer's status
Back up your computer
Find and fix problems

Network and Internet
View network status and tasks
Choose homegroup and sharing options

Hardware and Sound
View devices and printers
Add a device
Connect to a projector
Adjust commonly used mobility settings

Programs
Uninstall a program

User Accounts and Family Safety
Add or remove user accounts
Set up parental controls for any user

Appearance and Personalization
Change the theme
Change desktop background
Adjust screen resolution

Clock, Language, and Region
Change keyboards or other input methods
Change display language

Ease of Access
Let Windows suggest settings
Optimize visual display

All the Other Things in Windows

Windows is more than just a pretty desktop and some configuration utilities. Windows also includes many accessory programs and system tools you can use to perform basic system operations.

Built-In Applications and System Tools

Windows includes a number of single-function accessory programs, all accessible from the Start menu. These programs include a calculator, some games, two basic word processors (Notepad and WordPad), a drawing program (Paint), a player for audio and video files (Windows Media Player), a photo viewing program (Windows Photo Viewer), a DVD burning program (Windows DVD Maker), the Internet Explorer web browser, and more. You access all of these accessories from the Start menu and by selecting All Programs. Some programs are right on the All Programs menu; others are a level down on the Accessories menu.

Windows 7 also includes a handful of technical tools you can use to keep your system running smoothly. You can access all these tools by clicking the Start button and selecting All Programs, Accessories, System Tools.

note

To learn about the practical uses of these and other system tools, turn to Chapter 8, "Performing Routine Maintenance."

Downloading More Applications

In previous versions of Windows, Microsoft included even more built-in applications. In Windows 7, however, Microsoft decided to streamline the operating system a bit and make some of these applications optional. This is nice if you never use some of the applications, as they don't have to take up space on your hard drive.

Instead of including the applications in the operating system itself, Microsoft makes the applications available for free download as part of the Windows Live Essentials program. The applications you can download include the following:

- Windows Live Family Safety, for monitoring and controlling your children's Internet access
- Windows Live Mail, for sending and receiving email
- Windows Live Messenger, for instant messaging
- Windows Live Movie Maker, for editing digital movies
- Windows Live Photo Gallery, for viewing, organizing, and editing digital photos
- Windows Live Toolbar, for searching the Web (using Windows Live Search) directly from your web browser
- Windows Live Writer, for creating blog posts on Blogger, Wordpress, TypePad, and other blogging services

To download and install any or all of these applications, go to download.live.com and follow the directions there.

note

Most of the Windows Live Essentials applications were built into previous versions of Windows. Some computer manufacturers may still preload them onto their new PCs.

Getting Help in Windows

When you can't figure out how to perform a particular task, it's time to ask for help. In Windows 7, this is done through the Help and Support Center.

To launch the Help and Support Center, click the Start button and then select Help and Support. The Help and Support Center lets you search for specific answers to your problems, browse the table of contents, connect to another computer for remote assistance, go online for additional help, and troubleshoot any problems you may be having. Click the type of help you want and follow the onscreen instructions from there.

Shutting Down Windows—and Your Computer

You've probably already noticed that Windows starts automatically every time you turn on your computer. Although you will see lines of text flashing onscreen during the initial startup, Windows loads automatically and goes on to display the Windows desktop.

caution

Do *not* turn off your computer without shutting down Windows. You could lose data and settings that are temporarily stored in your system's memory.

Powering Down

When you want to turn off your computer, you do it through Windows. In fact, you don't want to turn off your computer any other way—you *always* want to turn off things through the official Windows procedure.

To shut down Windows and turn off your PC, click the Start button and then select Shut Down. If you have a desktop PC, you'll then want to manually turn off your monitor, printer, and other peripherals.

Putting Windows to Sleep

While you can totally power down your computer, you can also just put it to sleep, invoking Windows' special Sleep mode. When you enter Sleep mode, Windows saves all your open documents, applications, and data to both your PC's hard drive and memory; shuts down your PC's hard drive and monitor; and then enters a special power-saving mode. It doesn't turn off your computer—it simply puts it to sleep.

The advantage of using Sleep mode is that it makes it faster to turn your computer back on—or, more accurately, to wake it up. When you've put Windows in Sleep mode, pressing your computer's On button powers up your equipment, wakes up Windows from Sleep mode, and quickly retrieves all open documents and applications from system memory. It's a lot faster than rebooting from a power-off condition.

To invoke Sleep mode, click the Start button; then click the right-arrow button next to the Shut Down button and select Sleep from the pop-up menu.

THE ABSOLUTE MINIMUM

This chapter gave you a lot of background about Windows 7—your new PC's operating system. Here are the key points to remember:

- You use Windows to manage your computer system and run your software programs.
- Most functions in Windows are activated by clicking or double-clicking an icon or a button.
- All the programs and accessories on your system are accessed via the Start menu, which you display by clicking the Start button.
- Use Windows Explorer (and Computer Explorer) to view and manage the contents of your computer system.
- Use the Control Panel to manage Windows' configuration settings.
- When you can't figure out how to do something, click the Start button and select Help and Support.

4

PERSONALIZING WINDOWS

When you first turn on your new computer system, you see the Windows desktop as Microsoft (or your computer manufacturer) set it up for you. If you like the way it looks, great. If not, you can change it.

Windows presents a lot of different ways to personalize the look and feel of your desktop. In fact, one of the great things about Windows is how quickly you can make the desktop look like *your* desktop, different from anybody else's.

Getting to Know the Windows Control Panel

Virtually all of Windows' settings are configured via the Control Panel. You open the Control Panel by clicking the Start button and selecting Control Panel.

Figure 4.1 shows the Windows 7 Control Panel. You can click a major category, such as System and Security or Network and Internet, to access related configuration settings. Or you can click one of the key settings under a major heading to go directly to that setting.

FIGURE 4.1

The Windows 7 Control Panel.

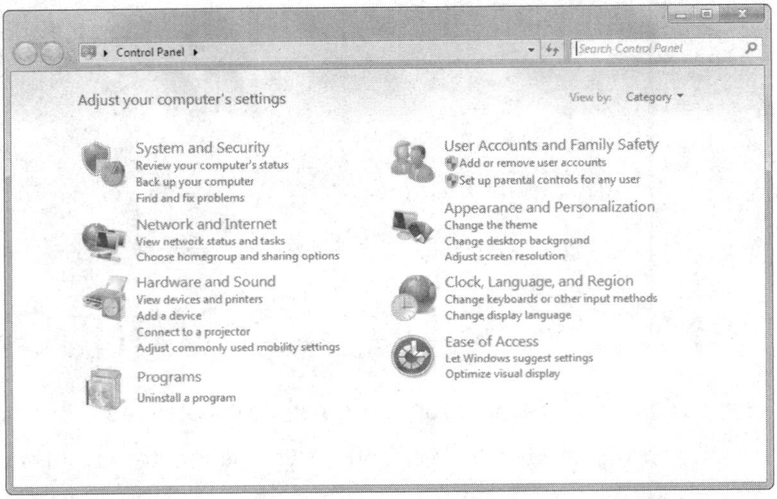

After you click through the various links, you eventually end up with a specific configuration utility displayed onscreen. Each type of configuration setting uses a different utility; you may see a full-fledged window full of controls, or a smaller dialog box with a few options to check. Whatever you see onscreen, select the options you want; then click OK. This applies the settings you selected.

Changing the Look of Your Desktop

One of the first things that most users want to personalize is the look of the Windows desktop. Read on to learn how.

Personalizing the Desktop Theme

In Windows 7, desktop backgrounds, window colors, sounds, and screensavers are organized

tip

Some styles include desktop slideshows, where multiple desktop backgrounds are displayed in order.

together into *themes*. Windows 7 includes a number of these preconfigured themes—and you can create your own, as well.

To choose a preexisting theme, follow these steps:

1. Right-click anywhere on the desktop and click Personalize from the pop-up menu.

2. When the Personalization window appears, as shown in Figure 4.2, click the new style you want to apply.

FIGURE 4.2

Use the Personalization window to change Windows' theme, desktop background, window colors, sounds, and screensaver.

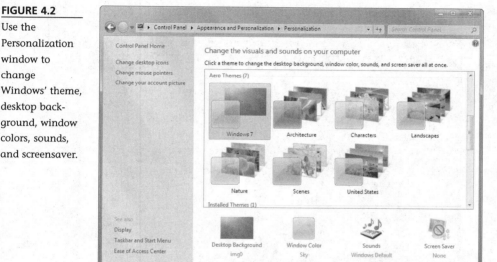

To create a new theme, start by applying the background, colors, sounds, and screensaver you want. Your choices now appear in the Personalization window as an Unsaved Theme. Right-click this theme in the window and select Save Theme. When prompted, give the theme a name and click the Save button. This new theme now appears in the Personalization window for you to select in the future.

tip

You can also open the Personalization window from the Windows Control Panel. Just select Change the Theme (in the Appearance and Personalization section).

Personalizing the Desktop Background

You don't have to change the entire theme to personalize Windows. Windows 7 lets you change each element of the theme individually, starting with the desktop background.

Windows 7 offers a wide selection of pictures you can use for your desktop background; you can also opt to have a plain-colored background, or choose any other picture on your PC. All you have to do is follow these steps:

1. Right-click anywhere on the desktop and click Personalize from the pop-up menu.

2. When the Personalization window appears, click Desktop Background.

3. This opens the Desktop Background window, shown in Figure 4.3. Click the Picture Location list and select what kind of background you want—Windows Desktop Backgrounds, Pictures Library, Top Rated Photos, or Solid Colors.

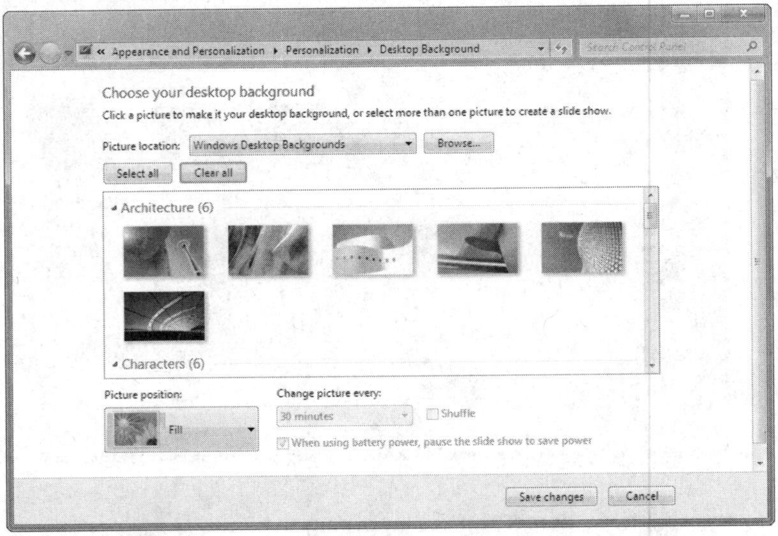

FIGURE 4.3

Choosing a new background for your Windows desktop.

4. Scroll through the list of options until you find the background you want. Select the background by clicking it; this automatically applies the background to your desktop.

5. To determine how the picture fills your desktop, click the Picture Position list and select Fill, Fit, Stretch, Tile, or Center.

6. Click Save Changes.

tip

To select another picture stored elsewhere on your computer, click the Browse button and browse for the picture you want.

Creating a Desktop Slideshow

Prior to Windows 7, you could only select one picture for the desktop background. Windows 7, however, lets you have multiple desktop backgrounds displayed one after another in a desktop slideshow. It's a great way to view all your favorite photos—without having to manually switch backgrounds.

To create a desktop slideshow, follow these steps:

1. Right-click anywhere on the desktop and click Personalize from the pop-up menu.
2. When the Personalization window appears, click Desktop Background.
3. From the Desktop Background window, click the Picture Location list and select what kind of background you want.
4. Hold down the Ctrl key and click the background images you want to include in the slideshow.
5. To determine how long each background displays, select a value from the Change Picture Every list.
6. To display background images in a random order, click the Shuffle option.
7. Click Save Changes.

The result is an ever-changing desktop background—great for displaying all your favorite images.

Changing the Color Scheme

The Windows 7 interface is called Aero, and it's a nice combination of translucent (see-through) colors. You can change the color scheme, however, as well as the level of translucency used in windows and other onscreen elements.

To change the color and translucency in Windows 7, follow these steps:

1. Right-click anywhere on the desktop and click Personalize from the pop-up menu.
2. When the Personalization window appears, click Window Color.
3. When the Window Color and Appearance window appears, as shown in Figure 4.4, click the color scheme you want. Alternatively, you can click the Show Color Mixer button to fine-tune the selected hue, saturation, and brightness.

note

If your PC doesn't have enough graphics horsepower, it can't display the translucent Aero interface. In this instance, you'll see the Windows 7 Basic interface instead—which looks similar but doesn't have the translucency or many of the three-dimensional effects. (The Basic interface is also what you'll see if you're running the Windows 7 Starter edition, which doesn't include the Aero interface.)

4. To make the onscreen windows more transparent, move the Color Intensity slider to the left. To make the windows more solid, move the slider to the right.

5. Click Save Changes.

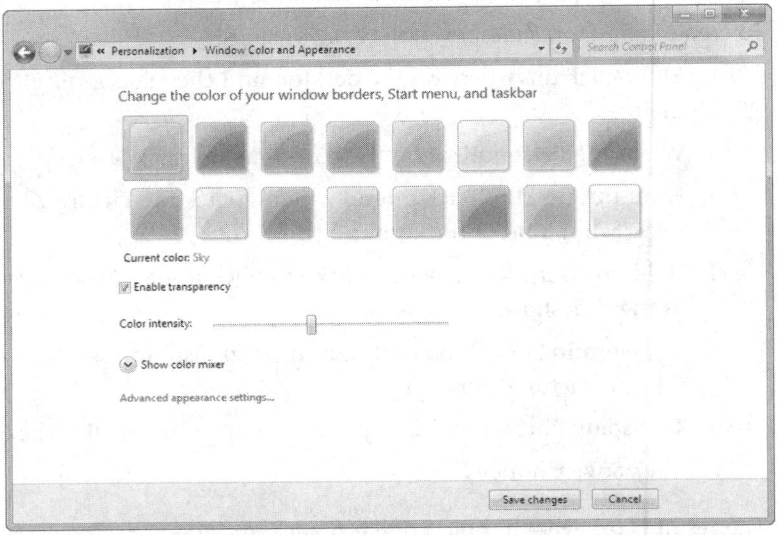

FIGURE 4.4

Choosing a new color scheme and transparency for your Windows desktop.

Changing the Desktop Size

You can also configure your computer's display so that the desktop is larger or smaller than normal. A larger desktop lets you view more things onscreen at the same time—even though each item is smaller than before. A smaller desktop displays fewer items, but they're larger. (This is great if your eyesight is less than perfect.)

Changing the size of the desktop is accomplished by changing Windows' *screen resolution*. You do this by following these steps:

1. Right-click anywhere on the desktop and click Screen Resolution from the pop-up menu.

2. When the Screen Resolution window appears, as shown in Figure 4.5, click the Resolution button.

3. Move the slider to the top to set a higher resolution (and display more items on the desktop); move it to the bottom to set a lower resolution.

4. Click OK to apply your changes.

tip

To best use all the features of Windows 7, go for a 1024×768 or higher resolution. If this setting makes things look too small (a problem if you have a smaller monitor), try the 800×600 resolution.

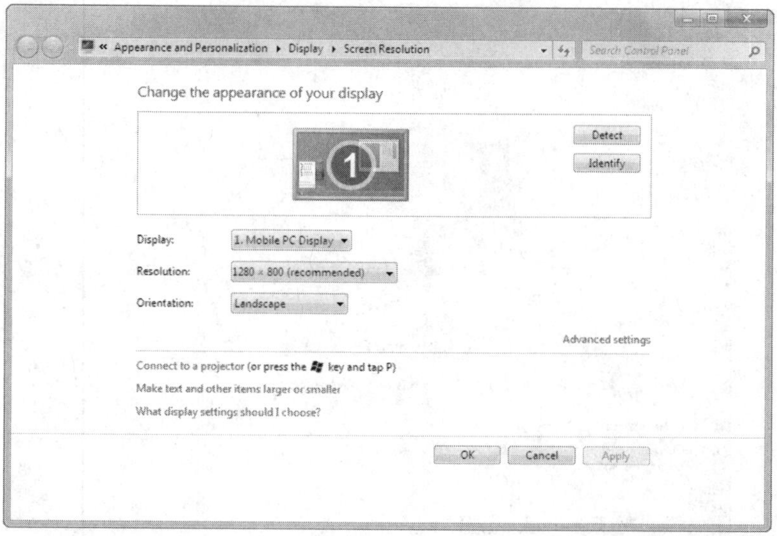

FIGURE 4.5

Use the Screen Resolution window to configure Windows' display settings.

Choosing a Screen Saver

Screen savers display moving designs on your computer screen when you haven't typed or moved the mouse for a while. This prevents static images from burning into your screen—and provides some small degree of entertainment if you're bored at your desk.

To activate one of the screensavers included with Windows 7, follow these steps:

1. Right-click anywhere on the desktop and click Personalize from the pop-up menu.

2. When the Personalization window appears, click Screen Saver.

3. When the Screen Saver Settings dialog box appears, as shown in Figure 4.6, select a screensaver from the Screen Saver drop-down list. (You can preview any selected screensaver by clicking the Preview button.)

4. Click the Settings button to configure that screensaver's specific settings (if available).

5. Click OK when you're done.

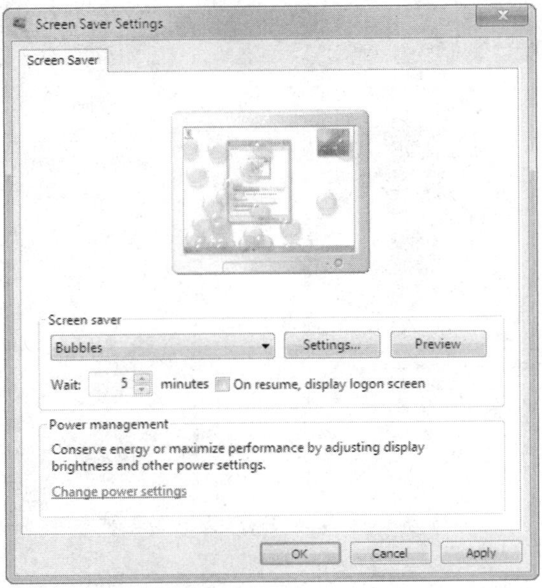

FIGURE 4.6

Selecting a Windows screen-saver.

Adding Desktop Gadgets

Windows 7 lets you add a variety of *gadgets* to the desktop. These gadgets, like the ones shown in Figure 4.7, are actually small utility applications that perform a single simple function. For example, the Clock gadget displays the current time, the Weather gadget reports the current weather conditions and forecast for your area, and so on.

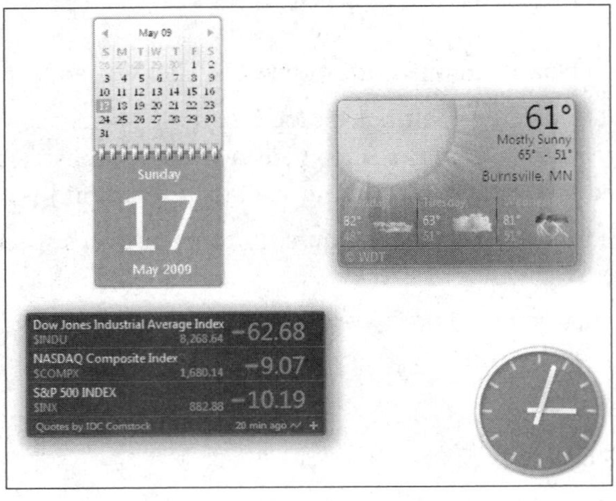

FIGURE 4.7

Gadgets on the Windows desktop.

To add gadgets to your desktop, follow these steps:

1. Right-click anywhere on the desktop; then select Gadgets from the pop-up menu.

2. When the Gadgets window appears, as shown in Figure 4.8, double-click the gadget you wish to add.

3. To view a larger selection of gadgets, click Get More Gadgets Online.

FIGURE 4.8
Adding new
gadgets.

Once you've added a gadget to the desktop, you can position it anywhere you want by clicking and dragging the gadget with your mouse. To remove a gadget from your desktop, hover over the gadget and then click the X.

Some gadgets have options for how they're displayed. For example, you can enter your own location into the Weather gadget to display your local weather conditions and forecast. To configure the options for a gadget, right-click it and select Options.

tip

You can also change how much the desktop shows through a gadget's background. Just right-click the gadget, select Opacity, and then select a percent.

Organizing Shortcut Icons

Windows lets you display a variety of shortcut icons—those little pictures on your desktop that function as shortcuts for starting applications and opening documents. Placing a shortcut on your desktop is an alternative to launching items from the Start menu.

Creating New Shortcuts on the Desktop

To put a new shortcut on your desktop, follow these steps:

1. Use Windows Explorer to navigate to the application or document for which you want to create a shortcut.

2. Right-click the file icon and then select Send To, Desktop (Create Shortcut).

To remove a shortcut icon from the desktop, just drag it into the Recycle Bin.

tip

You can also create a shortcut by right-dragging a file icon directly to the desktop, or by right-clicking on the desktop and selecting New, Shortcut from the pop-up menu.

Changing the Name of a Shortcut

When you create a new shortcut icon, the word "Shortcut" is automatically added to the icon's name. You can get rid of this if you want.

To change the name of a shortcut, follow these steps:

1. Right-click the shortcut on your desktop.

2. When the pop-up menu appears, select Rename.

3. The shortcut's name is now highlighted on your desktop. Use the Delete or Backspace keys to erase parts of the existing name and then type a new name. Press Enter when you've finished entering the new name.

Arranging Icons on the Desktop

All those desktop icons let you quickly open your most-used programs, but they can really clutter up the look of your Windows desktop. To better arrange your icons, right-click a blank area of the desktop, select Sort By, and choose from one of the following options:

- **Name**—Sorts items alphabetically by filename
- **Size**—Sorts items by file size, from smallest to largest
- **Item Type**—Sorts items by file type so that files with the same extension are grouped together
- **Date Modified**—Sorts items by date, from oldest to most recent

In addition, you can force all the icons on your desktop to snap to an invisible grid. Just right-click the desktop, click View, and then select Auto Arrange Icons.

Changing the Way the Start Menu Works

You use the Start menu every time you launch a program. Windows offers a few ways for you to customize the way the Start menu works for you.

Displaying Fewer Programs on the Start Menu

By default, the Start menu displays the ten most-recent applications you've run. If this is too much for you, you can reconfigure the Start menu to display fewer applications at a time.

To display fewer programs, follow these steps:

1. Right-click the Start button and select Properties from the pop-up menu.
2. When the Taskbar and Start Menu Properties dialog box appears, select the Start Menu tab.
3. Click the Customize button to display the Customize Start Menu dialog box.
4. Select a new number from the Number of Recent Programs to Display list.
5. Click OK when finished.

Adding a Program to the Start Menu—Permanently

If you're not totally comfortable with the way programs come and go from the Start menu, you can add any program to the Start menu—*permanently*. All you have to do is follow these steps:

1. Click the Start button to display the Start menu.
2. Click All Programs to open the Programs menu.
3. Navigate to a specific program.
4. Right-click that program to display the pop-up menu.
5. Select Pin to Start Menu.

> **tip**
>
> You can also "pin" programs to the Windows 7 taskbar. Just right-click an application on the All Programs list and select Pin to Taskbar.

The program you selected now appears on the Start menu, just below the browser and email icons.

To remove a program you've added to the Start menu, right-click its icon and select Unpin from Start Menu.

Resetting the Time and Date

The time and date for your system should be automatically set when you first turn on your computer. If you find that you need to change or reset the time or date settings, all you have to do is follow these steps:

1. Click the time display in the notification area of the taskbar; then select Change Date and Time Settings.

2. When the Date and Time dialog box appears, select the Date and Time tab.

3. Click the Change Date and Time button.

4. When the Date and Time Settings dialog box appears, select the correct month and year; then use the clock control to set the correct time.

5. Click OK when finished; then click OK to close the preceding dialog box.

While you're in the Date and Time dialog box, you can also set your time zone. Just click the Change Time Zone button and select your time zone from the pull-down list.

Setting Up Additional Users

Chances are you're not the only person using your computer; it's likely that you'll be sharing your PC to some degree with your spouse and kids. Fortunately, you can configure Windows so that different people using your computer sign on with their own custom settings—and access to their own personal files.

You should assign each user in your household his own password-protected *user account*. Anyone trying to access another user's account and files without the password will then be denied access.

You can establish two different types of user accounts on your computer—computer administrator and standard user. Only an administrator account can make system-wide changes to your PC, install software, and access all the files on the system.

When you first configured Windows on your PC, you were set up as an administrator. The other members of your household should be set up with standard accounts; they'll be able to use the computer and access their own files, but they won't be able to install software or mess up the main settings.

tip

You can have more than one administrator account per PC, so you might want to set up your spouse with an administrator account, too.

Creating a New Account

Only the computer administrator can add a new user to your system. To set up a new account in Windows 7, follow these steps:

1. From the Start menu, select Control Panel.

2. When the Control Panel opens, select Add or Remove User Accounts (in the User Accounts and Family Safety section).

3. When the next window appears, click Create a New Account.

4. When prompted, enter a name for the new account; then select whether this account is for a standard user or an account administrator.

5. Click the Create Account button.

Windows now creates the new account and randomly assigns a picture that will appear next to the username.

Changing an Account

If you don't like the picture assigned to an account, you can change this picture at any time by opening the Control Panel and selecting Add or Remove User Accounts. When the Manage Accounts window appears, as shown in Figure 4.9, select the account you want to change; then select the Change the Picture option.

FIGURE 4.9
Managing user accounts.

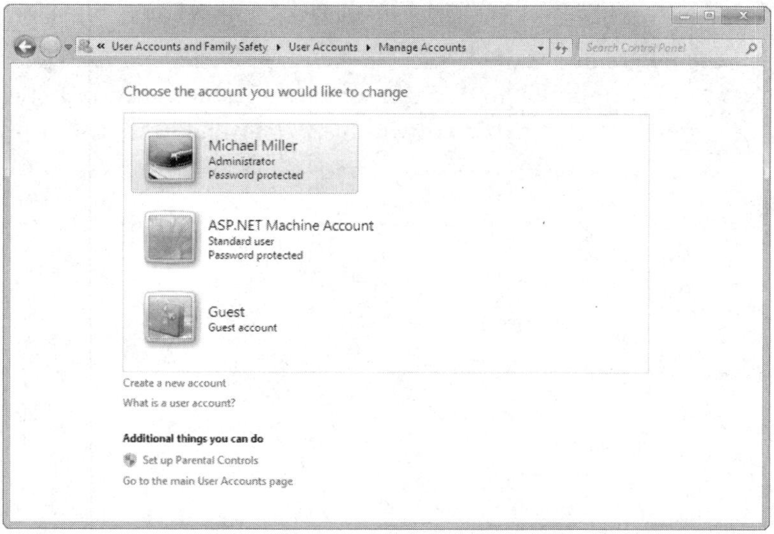

By default, no password is assigned to the new account. If you want to assign a password, return to the Manage Accounts window, select the account, and then select the Create a Password option.

caution

If you create a password for your account, you'd better remember it. You won't be able to access Windows—or any of your applications and documents—if you forget the password!

THE ABSOLUTE MINIMUM

Here are the key points to remember from this chapter:

- Most Windows settings are configured via the Control Panel.

- Windows 7 lets you change the desktop theme, desktop background, color scheme, window transparency, and screensaver.

- You can also change how many programs are displayed on the Start menu and which programs are permanently "pinned" to the menu.

- If you have multiple users in your household, you can create a user account for each person and assign each user his own password. (Just make sure that you remember your password—or you won't be able to log in to Windows!)

5

WORKING WITH FILES, FOLDERS, AND DISKS

Managing the data stored on your computer is vitally important. After you've saved a file, you may need to copy it to another computer, move it to a new location on your hard drive, rename it, or even delete it. You have to know how to perform all these operations—which means learning how to work with Windows' files, folders, and disks.

Understanding Files and Folders

All the information on your computer is stored in *files*. A file is nothing more than a collection of digital data. The contents of a file can be a document (such as a Word memo or Excel spreadsheet), a digital photo or music track, or the executable code for a software program.

Every file has its own unique name. A defined structure exists for naming files, and its conventions must be followed for Windows to understand exactly what file you want when you try to access one. Each filename must consist of two parts, separated by a period—the *name* (to the left of the period) and the *extension* (to the right of the period). A filename can consist of letters, numbers, spaces, and characters and looks something like this: **filename.ext**.

Windows stores files in *folders*. A folder is like a master file; each folder can contain both files and additional folders. The exact location of a file is called its *path* and contains all the folders leading to the file. For example, a file named **filename.doc** that exists in the **system** folder, that is itself contained in the **windows** folder on your **C:** drive, has a path that looks like this: **C:\windows\system\filename.doc**.

Learning how to use files and folders is a necessary skill for all computer users. You might need to copy files from one folder to another or from your hard disk to a floppy disk. You certainly need to delete files every now and then.

> **tip**
>
> By default, Windows hides the extensions when it displays filenames. To display extensions in Windows 7, open the Control Panel, select Appearance and Personalization, and then select Folder Options. When the Folder Options dialog box appears, select the View tab; then, in the Advanced Settings list, *uncheck* the Hide Extensions for Known File Types option. Click OK when finished.

Viewing Files and Folders

In Windows 7, you use Windows Explorer to view the files and folders on your system. While there are numerous ways to open Windows Explorer, the easiest is to click the Windows Explorer icon on the taskbar. (Other ways to explore your files: Open the Documents, Pictures, Music, or Computer folders from the Start menu.)

As you can see in Figure 5.1, Windows Explorer displays not only individual files but also other folders—called *subfolders*—that that contain more files. You can perform most file-related operations by clicking the Organize button to display the Organize menu, or by right-clicking a file icon to display the context-sensitive pop-up menu.

FIGURE 5.1

Manage your files and folders with Windows Explorer.

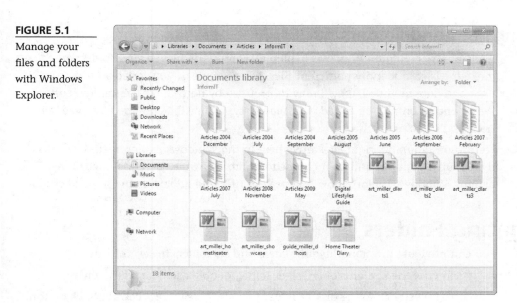

Changing the Way Files Are Displayed

You can choose to view the contents of a folder in a variety of ways. To change the file view, click the right arrow next to the Views button at the top left of the Explorer toolbar; this displays a pull-down menu with lots of viewing options. You can then select from the available views: Extra Large Icons, Large Icons, Medium Icons, Small Icons, List, Details, Tiles, or Content. You change views—which also changes the size of the file icons—by moving the slider up and down.

tip

Any of the icon views are good for working with graphics files or for getting a quick thumbnail glance at a file's contents. The Details view is better if you're looking for files by date or size.

Sorting Files and Folders

When viewing files in Window Explorer, you can sort your files and folders in a number of ways. To do this, right-click anywhere in the Windows Explorer window, select the Sort By option, and then choose to sort by Name, Date Modified, Type, Size, or Tags. You can also choose to sort the items in either ascending or descending order.

If you want to view your files in alphabetical order, choose to sort by Name. If you want to see all similar files grouped together, choose to sort by Type. If you want to sort your files by the date and time they were last edited, choose the Date Modified option. And if you want to sort by a user-applied file tag (assuming you've done this in the file's host program), choose the Tags option.

Grouping Files and Folders

You can also configure Windows Explorer to group the files in your folder, which can make it easier to identify particular files. For example, if you sorted your files by time and date modified, they'll now be grouped by date (Today, Yesterday, Last Week, and so on). If you sorted your files by type, they'll be grouped by file extension, and so on.

To turn on grouping, right-click anywhere in the Windows Explorer window, select the Group By option, and then choose to group by Name, Date Modified, Type, Size, or Tags. Windows Explorer now groups your files and folders by the selected criteria.

Navigating Folders

You can navigate through all your folders and subfolders in several ways:

- To view the contents of a disk or folder, double-click the selected item.
- To move back to the disk or folder previously selected, click the Back button on the toolbar.
- To choose from the history of disks and folders previously viewed, click the down arrow in the Address bar at the top of the Windows Explorer window and select a disk or folder.
- If you've moved back through multiple disks or folders, you can move forward to the next folder by clicking the Forward button on the toolbar.
- Go directly to any disk or folder by entering the path in the Address bar (in the format **x:\folder\subfolder**) and pressing Enter.
- Move backward through the "bread crumb" path in the Address bar. Click any previous folder location (separated by arrows) to display that particular folder.

tip

Click any arrow between locations in the Address bar to view additional paths from that location.

You can also go directly to key locations by using the list of locations in the Navigation pane on the left side of the Windows Explorer window. This pane displays the most common locations for files on your system. The top part of the pane displays your Favorite Links, while the Computer section on the bottom of the pane displays all the contents of your system in a treelike outline. Click any section of the tree to display that item's contents.

Working with Libraries

New to Windows 7 is the concept of *libraries*, which is a new way to manage your files. A library is kind of a virtual folder; it doesn't physically exist on your hard disk but instead points to the subfolders and files you place within it.

If you've opened Windows Explorer, you've already seen four libraries. That's because the Documents, Music, Pictures, and Videos icons don't point to specific folders, but rather to libraries of files of a given type, wherever they're located on your hard disk. That's right, double-clicking doesn't open the Documents folder itself (although that folder does exist); it opens a virtual collection of documents.

So Windows 7 displays all your documents, no matter which folder they're really stored in, in the Documents library. All your digital music files are displayed in the Music library, all your digital photos in the Pictures library, and all your digital video files in the Video library.

In addition to these four default libraries, you can create your own libraries to virtually organize files from any folder on your hard disk. You can use your own user-created libraries to organize files stored in various folders across your hard disk. For example, you could create a library for a project that has Word documents stored in one folder, Excel spreadsheets in another, and photos in still another.

To create a new library, open Windows Explorer and follow these steps:

1. Click the New Library button on the Windows Explorer toolbar.
2. When the new library icon appears, type a name for the new library.
3. Double-click the icon for the new library.
4. When the next screen appears, click the Include a Folder button.
5. When the Include Folder in New Library dialog box appears, navigate to and click the folder you wish to include in the library; then click the Include Folder button.

To add more folders to the library, open the library and click the "X Folder" link under the library name. When the New Library Locations window appears, click the Add button. From the next window, navigate to the folder you want to include, then click the Include Folder button. Repeat these steps to add even more folders.

Searching for Files

As organized as you might be, you may not always be able to find the specific files you want. Fortunately, Windows 7 offers an easy way to locate difficult-to-find files, via the new Instant Search function. Instant Search indexes all the files stored on your hard disk (including email messages) by type, title, and contents. So you can search for a file by extension, filename, or keywords within the document.

To use the Instant Search feature, follow these steps:

1. From within Windows Explorer, locate the search box at the top right of the window, as shown in Figure 5.2.

2. Enter one or more keywords into the search box.

3. Press Enter.

tip

You can also search for files from the Instant Search box on the Windows Start menu.

FIGURE 5.2

The search box in Windows Explorer.

Windows now displays a list of files that match your search criteria. Double-click any icon to open that file.

Creating New Folders

The more files you create, the harder it is to organize and find things on your hard disk. When the number of files you have becomes unmanageable, you need to create more folders—and subfolders—to better categorize your files.

To create a new folder, follow these steps:

1. Navigate to the drive or folder where you want to place the new folder.

2. Click the New Folder button on the toolbar.

3. A new, empty folder now appears within the Windows Explorer window, with the filename **New Folder** highlighted.

4. Type a name for your folder (which over-writes the **New Folder** name) and press Enter.

caution

Folder and filenames can include up to 255 characters—including many special characters. Some special characters, however, are "illegal," meaning that you *can't* use them in folder or file-names. Illegal characters include the following: \ / : * ? " < > |.

caution

The one part of the file-name you should never change is the exten-sion—the part that comes after the "dot." That's because Windows and other software programs recognize differ-ent types of program files and doc-uments by their extension. This is why, by default, Windows hides these file extensions—so you can't change them by mistake.

Renaming Files and Folders

When you create a new file or folder, it helps to give it a name that somehow describes its contents. Sometimes, however, you might need to change a file's name. Fortunately, Windows makes it relatively easy to rename an item.

To rename a file (or folder), follow these steps:

1. Click the file or folder you want to rename.

2. Click the Organize button and then select Rename from the pull-down menu (or just press the F2 key on your keyboard); this highlights the filename.

3. Type a new name for your file or folder (which overwrites the current name) and press Enter.

Copying Files

Now it's time to address the most common things you do with files—copying and moving them from one location to another.

It's important to remember that copying is different from moving. When you *copy* an item, the original item remains in its original location—plus you have the new copy. When you *move* an item, the original is no longer present in the original location—all you have is the item in the new location.

The Easy Way to Copy

To copy a file or a folder from within Windows Explorer, follow these steps:

1. Select the item you want to copy.

2. Click the Organize button and select Copy from the pull-down menu.

3. Use Windows Explorer to navigate to the new location for the item.

4. Click the Organize button and select Paste from the pull-down menu.

That's it. You've just copied the file from one location to another.

Other Ways to Copy

The method just presented is only one of many ways to copy a file. Windows 7 provides several other methods, including

■ Right-click a file and select Copy from the pop-up menu, and then paste to the new location.

■ Right-click a file and select Send To from the pop-up menu, and then select a location from the choices listed.

- Hold down the Ctrl key and then use your mouse to drag the file or folder from one location to another within Windows Explorer.

- Drag the file or folder while holding down the right mouse button. When you drop the file into a new location, you see a pop-up menu that asks whether you want to move it or copy it. Select the copy option.

Moving Files

Moving a file (or folder) is different from copying it. Moving cuts the item from its previous location and places it in a new location. Copying leaves the original item where it was *and* creates a copy of the item elsewhere.

In other words, when you copy something you end up with two of it. When you move something, you only have the one.

The Easy Way to Move

To move a file, follow these steps:

1. Select the item you want to move.
2. Click the Organize button and select Cut from the pull-down menu.
3. Use Windows Explorer to navigate to the new location for the item.
4. Click the Organize button and select Paste from the pull-down menu.

Other Ways to Move a File

Just as Windows provides several other ways to copy a file, you also have a choice of alternative methods for moving a file, including the following:

- Right-click a filename and select Cut from the pop-up menu; then paste it to the new location.

- Use your mouse to drag the file from one location to another.

- Drag the file or folder while holding down the right mouse button. When you drop the file into a new location, you see a pop-up menu that asks whether you want to move it or copy it. Select the move option.

Deleting Files

Too many files eat up too much hard disk space—which is a bad thing because you only have so much disk space. (Music and video files, in particular, can chew up big chunks of your hard drive.) Because you don't want to waste disk space, you should periodically delete those files (and folders) you no longer need.

The Easy Way to Delete

Deleting a file is as easy as following these two simple steps:

1. Select the file.

2. Click the Organize button and select Delete from the pull-down menu.

This simple operation sends the file to the Windows Recycle Bin, which is kind of a trash can for deleted files. (It's also a trash can that periodically needs to be dumped—as discussed later in this activity.)

Other Ways to Delete a File

As you might expect, there are other ways to delete files in Windows 7. In particular, you can do the following:

- Highlight the file and press the Del key on your keyboard.
- Drag the file from Windows Explorer onto the Recycle Bin icon on your desktop.

Restoring Deleted Files

Have you ever accidentally deleted the wrong file? If so, you're in luck. For a short period of time, Windows stores the files you delete in the Recycle Bin. The Recycle Bin is actually a special folder on your hard disk; if you've recently deleted a file, it should still be in the Recycle Bin folder.

To "undelete" a file from the Recycle Bin, follow these steps:

1. Double-click the Recycle Bin icon on your desktop (shown in Figure 5.3) to open the Recycle Bin folder.

2. Click the file(s) you want to restore.

3. Click the Restore This Item button on the toolbar.

This copies the deleted file back to its original location, ready for continued use.

FIGURE 5.3

The Recycle Bin, where all your deleted files end up.

Recycle Bin

Managing the Recycle Bin

Deleted files do not stay in the Recycle Bin indefinitely. When you've deleted enough files to exceed the space allocated for these files, the oldest files in the Recycle Bin are automatically and permanently deleted from your hard disk.

If you'd rather dump the Recycle Bin manually (and thus free up some hard disk space), follow these steps:

1. Double-click the Recycle Bin icon on your desktop to open the Recycle Bin folder.

2. Click the Empty the Recycle Bin button on the toolbar.

3. When the confirmation dialog box appears, click Yes to completely erase the files, or click No to continue storing the files in the Recycle Bin.

Working with Compressed Folders

Really big files can be difficult to move or copy. They're especially difficult to transfer to other users, whether by email or portable disk drive.

Fortunately, Windows includes a way to make big files smaller. *Compressed folders* take big files and compress their size, which makes them easier to copy or move. After the file has been transferred, you can then uncompress the file back to its original state.

Compressing a File

Compressing one or more files is a relatively easy task from within any Windows folder. Just follow these steps:

1. Select the file(s) you want to compress.

2. Right-click the file(s) to display the pop-up menu.

3. Select Send to, Compressed (zipped) Folder.

Windows now creates a new folder that contains compressed versions of the file(s) you selected. (This folder is distinguished by a little zipper on the folder icon, as shown in Figure 5.4.) You can now copy, move, or email this folder, which is a lot smaller than the original file(s).

note

The compressed folder is actually a file with a .ZIP extension, so it can be used with other compression/decompression programs, such as WinZip.

Extracting Files from a Compressed Folder

The process of decompressing a file is actually an *extraction* process. That's because you *extract* the original file(s) from the compressed folder.

In Windows 7, this process is eased by the use of the Extraction Wizard. Follow these steps:

1. Right-click the compressed folder to display the pop-up menu.
2. Select Extract All.
3. When the Extraction Wizard launches, select a location for the extracted files and then click the Extract button to complete the process.

Copying Files to Another Computer

Of course, you're not limited to copying and moving files from one location to another on a single PC. You can also copy files to other PCs via either a network connection or some sort of portable disk drive.

Copying Files over a Network

We talk more about network operations in Chapter 7, "Setting Up a Home Network." For now, it's important to know that if your PC is connected to a network and has file sharing activated, you can copy and move files from one network computer to another just as you can within folders on a single computer.

In Windows Vista, you access the other computers on your network by opening Windows Explorer and clicking Network in the Navigation pane. As you can see in Figure 5.5, each computer on your network is now displayed; double-click a PC's icon to view the public (sharable) folders on this computer. You can then copy files to or from any public folder on your network.

FIGURE 5.5

Viewing all the PCs on your home network.

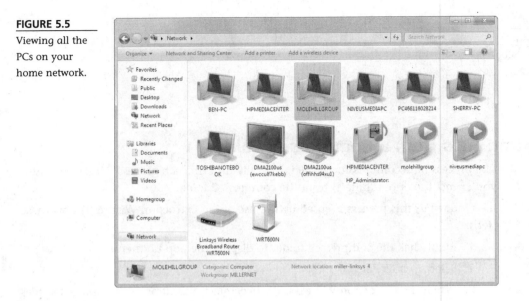

Copying Files with a Portable Drive

If you're not on a network, you can use a portable drive to transport files from one computer to another. The most popular type of portable drive today is the USB drive, such as the one shown in Figure 5.6, which stores computer data in flash memory. You can find USB drives with capacities up to 32GB—more than big enough to hold even your biggest files.

FIGURE 5.6

Use a USB drive to transport files from one computer to another.

To use a USB drive, simply insert the device into an open USB port on your computer. Once inserted, the drive appears as a new drive in the Computer Explorer window. Double-click the USB drive icon to view the contents of the drive; you can then copy and paste files from your hard drive to the USB drive and vice versa. When you're finished copying files, just remove the USB device. It's that simple.

Copying Files via Email

Another popular way to send files from one computer to another is via email. You can send any file as an email *attachment*; a file is literally attached to an email message. When the message is sent, the recipient can open or save the attached file when reading the message.

To learn how to send files as email attachments, turn to Chapter 28, "Sending and Receiving Email."

Backing Up Your Important Files

Then there's the issue of protecting your files. What do you do if your computer crashes or your hard disk dies? Are all your important files and documents totally lost?

Not if you're prescient enough to back up your key files on a regular basis. The easiest way to do this is by connecting an external hard disk drive to your computer. Get a big enough external disk (about the same size as your main hard disk), and you can copy your entire hard disk to the external drive. Then, if your system ever crashes, you can restore your backed-up files from the external drive to your computer's system unit.

Learn more about Windows Backup in Chapter 8, "Performing Routine Maintenance."

External hard drives can be purchased for around $100 and are easy to connect via either USB or FireWire. You can use the proprietary backup software that comes with most external drives, or use the Windows Backup utility. Whichever program you use, you should back up your data at least weekly—if not daily. That way you won't lose much fresh data if the worst happens.

THE ABSOLUTE MINIMUM

Here are the key points to remember from this chapter:

- You manage your files and folders from Windows Explorer; most of the operations you'll want to perform are accessible from the Organize pull-down menu.

- If you accidentally delete a file, you may be able to recover it by opening the Recycle Bin window.

- If you need to share a really big file, consider compressing it into a compressed folder (also called a .ZIP file).

- To copy a file to another PC, you can copy the file over a network, send the file as an email attachment, or copy the file to a portable USB drive.

- You should back up your important files to an external hard drive, using Windows Backup or a similar backup utility.

PART III

UPGRADING AND MAINTAINING YOUR SYSTEM

6

ADDING NEW HARDWARE AND DEVICES TO YOUR SYSTEM

If you just purchased a brand-new, right-out-of-the-box personal computer, it probably came equipped with all the components you could ever want—or so you think. At some point in the future, however, you might want to expand your system by adding a second printer, a scanner, an external hard drive, better speakers, a different mouse or keyboard, or something equally new and exciting.

Adding new hardware to your system is relatively easy if you know what you're doing. That's where this chapter comes in.

Most Popular Peripherals

When it comes to adding stuff to your PC, what are the most popular peripherals? Here's a list of hardware you can add to or upgrade on your system:

- **Hard drive**—To add more storage capacity to your system or to perform periodic backups from your main hard disk. The easiest type of hard drive to add is an external unit, which can connect via either USB or FireWire and cost just a hundred bucks or so. If you have a desktop PC, you may also be able to add a second internal drive, but that's a lot more work.

- **Memory card reader**—So you can read data from devices (such as digital cameras) that use various types of flash memory cards.

- **USB memory device**—To provide gigabytes of removable storage; you can transport the USB memory device from one computer to another, connecting to each PC's USB port.

- **Monitor**—To replace or supplement the built-in display on a notebook computer or replace the existing monitor on a desktop system (typically with a larger screen).

- **Video card**—On desktop PCs, to upgrade your system's video playback and graphics, typically for video editing or playing visually demanding PC games.

- **Sound card**—On desktop PCs, to improve the audio capabilities of your system; this is particularly important if you're playing state-of-the-art PC games, watching surround-sound DVD movies, or mixing and recording your own digital audio.

- **Speakers**—To upgrade the quality of your computer's sound system. (Surround-sound speaker systems with subwoofers are particularly popular, especially with PC gamers.)

- **Keyboard**—To replace a notebook's built-in keyboard with a larger, more fully featured model or to upgrade the capabilities of a desktop's included keyboard.

- **Mouse**—To provide a more traditional input in place of notebook PC's touchpad or to upgrade the capabilities of a desktop system's mouse. (For example, many users like to upgrade from wired to wireless mice.)

- **Joystick or other game controller**—To get better action with your favorite games.

- ■ **Broadband modem**—To obtain high-speed DSL or cable Internet service.
- ■ **CD/DVD drive (burner)**—To add recordable/rewritable capabilities to your system.
- ■ **Printer**—To improve the quality of your printouts, to add color to your printouts, or to add photo-quality printing to your system. You can even add specialty label printers, which are great if you do a lot of mailing or eBay shipping.
- ■ **Scanner**—So that you can scan photographs and documents into a digital format to store on your computer's hard drive.
- ■ **Webcam**—So that you can send real-time video to friends and family.
- ■ **Network card**—So that you can connect your computer to other computers in a small home network via Ethernet cable.
- ■ **Wireless router**—So that you can create a wireless network in your home and share your broadband Internet connection among multiple computers.
- ■ **Wireless network adapter**—So that you can connect your computer to any wireless network.

Understanding Ports

Everything that's hooked up to your PC is connected via some type of *port*. A port is simply an interface between your PC and another device—either internally (inside your PC's system unit) or externally (via a connector on the back of the system unit).

Internal ports are automatically assigned when you plug a new card into its slot inside a desktop PC's system unit. Both desktop and notebook PCs also have lots of external ports of various types—each optimized to send and receive specific types of data. Different types of hardware connect via different types of ports.

The most common types of external ports are shown in Table 6.1.

TABLE 6.1   External Ports

Connector	Type	Uses	Description
	USB	Almost anything—iPods, other portable audio players, digital cameras, webcams, printers, scanners, WiFi adapters, modems, external sound cards, mice, keyboards, joysticks, external hard drives, external CD/DVD drives, and USB memory devices	The most common type of connector in use today; USB is a faster, more intelligent form of the older serial port. USB devices can be added while your computer is still running, which you can't do with older types of ports.
	FireWire	Digital camcorders, external hard drives, external CD/DVD burners, and professional digital audio workstations	Also called IEEE 1394, the FireWire interface enables hot pluggable, high-speed data transmission.
	Keyboard/ Mouse	Keyboards, mice, and other input devices	Sometimes called a PS/2 port, used to connect both wired and wireless input devices.
	Parallel	Printers, scanners	An older type of port, still used for some types of printers, that enables communications going in two directions at once.
	Serial	Modems, printers, mice	No longer widely used, serial ports enable communication one bit at a time, in one direction at a time.
	Gameport	Joysticks and other game controllers, as well as MIDI devices and musical instruments	This port is typically used to connect gaming controllers; it can also function as a MIDI port with the appropriate adapter.
	SCSI	Hard drives, CD/DVD drives	The *small computer system interface* (SCSI) port is a high-speed parallel interface, typically used for fast external data storage.

Adding New External Hardware

The easiest way to add a new device to your system is to connect it externally—which saves you the trouble of opening your PC's case. (And, of course, if you have a notebook PC, the *only* way to add new hardware is externally; you can't get inside the notebook case to add anything else!)

The most common external connector today is the USB port. USB is a great concept (and truly "universal") in that virtually every type of new peripheral comes in a USB version. Want to add a second hard disk? Don't open the PC case; connect an external drive via USB. Want to add a new printer? Forget the older parallel port connection; get a USB printer instead. Want to connect to a home network? Don't bother with Ethernet cards; get a USB-compatible wireless adapter.

USB is popular because it's so easy to use. When you're connecting a USB device, not only do you not have to open your PC's case, but you don't even have to turn off your system when you add the new device. That's because USB devices are *hot swappable*. That means you can just plug the new device into the port, and Windows will automatically recognize it in real time.

The original USB standard, version 1.1, has been around for awhile and is what you'd find on PCs made more than five or six years ago. The newer USB 2.0 protocol is much faster than USB 1.1 and is standard on all newer computers. For what it's worth, newer USB 2.0 ports are fully backward compatible with older USB 1.1 devices, so if you're connecting an older peripheral, you're okay. You want to use newer USB 2.0 connections when you're installing devices that transfer a lot of data, such as external hard drives.

Then there's FireWire. Like USB devices, FireWire devices are hot swappable and easy to connect. Like USB 2.0, FireWire is a very fast standard, which makes it ideal for connecting devices that move a lot of data, such as hard drives and camcorders. (It's also a little more expensive, which is why USB is still preferred for most devices.)

note

No matter how you're connecting a new device, make sure to read the installation instructions for the new hardware and follow the manufacturer's instructions and advice.

tip

If you connect too many USB devices, it's possible to run out of USB connectors on your PC. If that happens to you, buy an add-on USB hub, which lets you plug multiple USB peripherals into a single USB port.

To connect a new USB or FireWire device, follow these steps:

1. Find a free USB or FireWire port on your system unit and connect the new peripheral, as shown in Figure 6.1.

FIGURE 6.1
Connecting an external device via USB.

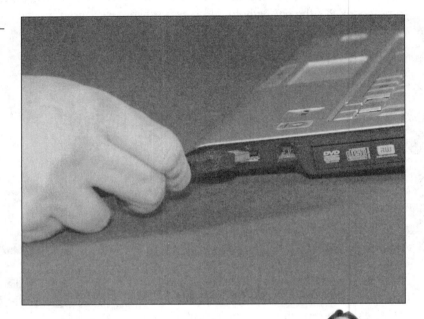

2. Windows should automatically recognize the new peripheral and either install the proper device driver automatically or prompt you to provide a CD or disk containing the driver file. Follow the onscreen instructions to finish installing the driver.

That's it! The only variation on this procedure is if the peripheral's manufacturer recommends using its own installation program, typically provided on an installation CD. If this is the case, follow the manufacturer's instructions to perform the installation and setup.

Connecting Portable Devices to Your PC

These days, a lot of the devices you connect to your PC really aren't computer peripherals.

note

A device driver is a small software program that enables your PC to communicate with and control a specific device. Windows includes built-in device drivers for many popular peripherals. If Windows doesn't include a particular driver, you typically can find the driver on the peripheral's installation disk or on the peripheral manufacturer's website.

Instead, they are gadgets that you use on their own but plug into your PC to share files.

What kinds of portable devices are we talking about? Here's a short list:

- Portable music players, such as Apple's popular iPod and iPhone
- Digital cameras
- Digital camcorders
- USB keychain memory devices

Most of these devices connect to a USB port on your PC; some camcorders use a FireWire connection instead. As you remember, both USB and FireWire ports are hot-swappable, which means that all you have to do is connect the device to the proper port—no major configuration necessary. In most cases, the first time you connect your device to your PC, you'll need to run some sort of installation utility to install the device's software on your PC's hard drive. Each subsequent time you connect the device, your PC should recognize it automatically and launch the appropriate software program.

Once your portable device is connected to your PC, what you do next is up to you. Most of the time, you'll be transferring files either from your PC to the portable device, or vice versa. Use the device's software program to perform these operations, or use Windows Explorer to copy files back and forth.

For example, you can use a USB memory device as a removable and portable memory storage system. One of these USB drives is smaller than a pack of chewing gum and can hold several gigabytes' worth of data in electronic flash memory. Plug a USB memory device into your PC's USB port, and your PC recognizes it just as if it were another disk drive. You can then copy files from your PC to the USB drive to take your work (or your digital music or photo files) with you.

For more detailed information, see the instructions that came with your portable device.

> **note**
>
> Learn more about connecting a digital camera in Chapter 32, "Organizing and Editing Your Digital Photos." Learn more about connecting a portable music player in Chapter 36, "Using Your PC with an iPod or iPhone."

THE ABSOLUTE MINIMUM

Here's what you need to know if you're adding new equipment to your computer system:

- The easiest way to connect a new peripheral is via an external USB or FireWire connection.

- When you're installing an internal card, make sure that you turn off your PC before you open the system unit's case.

- In most cases, Windows automatically recognizes your new hardware and automatically installs all the necessary drivers.

- Connecting a portable device, such as a portable music player or digital camera, is typically done via an external USB port.

7

SETTING UP A HOME NETWORK

When you need to connect two or more computers, you need to create a computer *network*.

Why would you want to connect two computers? Maybe you want to transfer files or digital photos from one computer to another. Maybe you want to share an expensive piece of hardware (such as a printer) instead of buying one for each PC. Maybe you want to connect all your computers to the same Internet connection. Whatever your reasons, it's easy to set up and configure a simple home network. Read on to learn how!

How Networks Work

When it comes to physically connecting your network, you have two ways to go—wired or wireless. A wireless network is more convenient (no wires to run), but a wired network is faster. Which you choose depends on how you use the computers you network.

If you use your network primarily to share an Internet connection or a printer or to transfer the occasional word processing file, wireless should work just fine. However, if you plan on transferring a lot of big files from one PC to another or using your network for multiplayer gaming, you'll want to stick to a faster wired network.

Wired Networks

A *wired network* is the kind that requires you to run a bunch of cables from each PC to a central hub or router. In a wired network, you install a *network interface card* (NIC) in each PC and connect the cards via Ethernet cable. (Note that many new PCs come with built-in Ethernet capability, so you don't have to purchase an additional card.) Although this type of network is fast and easy enough to set up, you still have to deal with all those cables—which can be a hassle if your computers are in different areas of your house.

The speed you get from a wired network depends on the type of Ethernet technology used by each piece of equipment. The oldest Ethernet technology transfers data at just 10Mbps; Fast Ethernet transfers data at 100Mbps; and the newer Gigabit Ethernet transfers data at 1 gigabit per second (1,000Mbps). Either Fast Ethernet or Gigabit Ethernet are fine for transferring really big files between computers or for playing real-time PC games.

note How quickly data is transferred across a network is measured in megabits per second, or Mbps. The bigger the Mbps number, the faster the network—and faster is always better than slower.

Wireless Networks

The alternative to a wired network is a *wireless network*. Wireless networks use radio frequency (RF) signals to connect one computer to another. The advantage of wireless, of course, is that you don't have to run cables. This is a big plus if you have a large house with computers on either end or on different floors.

note WiFi is short for *wireless fidelity*.

The most popular wireless networks use the WiFi standard. The original WiFi standard, known as 802.11b, transferred data at 11Mbps—slower than Fast Ethernet, but fast enough for most practical purposes. Next up was 802.11g, which transferred data at 54Mbps—more than fast enough for most home networking needs.

Even faster is the new 802.11n standard (not yet finalized, but available in some "pre-n" or "draft n" equipment now on the market), which delivers a blazing 600Mbps data transmission with a substantially longer range than older equipment. Current 802.11b and g equipment has a range of about 100 feet between transmitter and receiver; 802.11n promises a 160-foot range, with less interference from other wireless household devices.

note

The 600Mbps rate for 802.11n networks is the theoretical maximum. In practice, expect rates between 200Mbps and 300Mbps.

In addition, you can combine wired and wireless technologies into a single network. Some PCs can connect directly to a wireless router via Ethernet, while others can connect via wireless WiFi signals. This type of mixed network is quite common.

Connecting and Configuring

Whether you're going wired or wireless, the setup is surprisingly easy. You have to assemble the appropriate cards, cables, and hubs and then install and connect them all. After everything is hooked up properly, you then have to configure all the PCs on your network. The configuration can be made from within Windows or via the configuration utility provided with your network router or wireless adapter. You run this utility on each computer you connect to your network and then configure the network within Windows.

Setting Up a Wired or Wireless Network

Connecting multiple computers in a wired network is actually fairly simple. Just make sure that you do the proper planning beforehand and buy the appropriate hardware and cables; everything else is a matter of connecting and configuration.

How It Works

If you're setting up a wired network, you'll need to install a NIC in each computer you intend to connect. Each NIC then connects, via Ethernet cable, to the network *router*, which is a simple device that functions like the hub of a wheel and serves as the central point in your network. Then, after you make the physical connections, each computer has to be configured to function as part of the network and to share designated files, folders, and peripherals.

In a wireless network, the hub function is performed by a *wireless router*. This device can make both wireless and wired connections; most base stations include four or more Ethernet connectors in addition to wireless capabilities.

You still need to connect your broadband modem and your main PC to the router via Ethernet cables, at least for the initial configuration, but all the other PCs on your network will connect wirelessly, via wireless adapters. These devices function as mini-transmitters/receivers to communicate with the base station. Most notebook PCs come with built-in wireless adapters; you can add a wireless adapter to a desktop PC via a simple USB connection.

When complete, your network should look something like the one in Figure 7.1.

FIGURE 7.1

A typical wire-
less network.

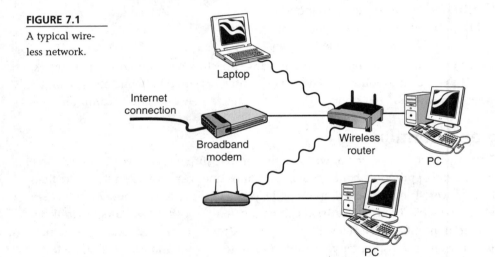

What You Need

Here's the specific hardware you'll need to set up your network:

- Network interface cards—typically built into most new PCs (on a wired net-work, one for each PC; on a wireless network, just one for the main PC)

- Network router (one for the entire network; use a wireless router for a wireless network)

- Ethernet cables (on a wired network, one for each PC and another for your broadband modem; on a wireless network, one for the main PC and a second for the broadband modem)

- Wireless network adapters (one for each client PC; these may already be built into notebook PCs)

Making the Connections

Naturally, you should follow the instructions that come with your networking hardware to properly set up your network. In general, however, here are the steps to take:

1. Run an Ethernet cable from your broadband modem to your router and connect to the port on your router labeled "Internet."

2. Run an Ethernet cable from the router to your main computer.

3. Connect your network router to a power source.

4. If you're connecting a wired network, connect each of the other computers to your network router via Ethernet cables.

5. If you're connecting a wireless network, move on to the second computer in your network and install a wireless networking adapter if it doesn't have built-in wireless networking.

6. Connect the second PC to your new wireless network, using the built-in wireless networking utility.

7. Repeat steps 4–6 for each additional computer on your wireless network.

After you've connected all the computers on your network, you can proceed to configure any devices (such as printers) you want to share over the network. For example, if you want to share a single printer over the network, it connects to one of the network PCs (*not* directly to the router) and then is shared through that PC.

Configuring Windows for Your New Network

After your network hardware is all set up, you have to configure Windows to recognize and

note

If your host PC does not have built-in Ethernet networking, you need to install an internal network interface card or external Ethernet-to-USB device.

tip

When you first connect a new router to your network, you should configure the router using the software that came with the device. Follow the manufacturer's directions to configure the network and wireless security.

caution

Some DSL and cable modems include a built-in router and firewall that might interfere with your regular wireless router. You may need to disable the router capabilities of your modem or reconfigure your wireless router to avoid the conflict. Consult with your broadband Internet service provider and router manufacturer if you run into problems.

work with your new network. If you're running Windows 7 or Windows Vista, this is a painless and practically transparent step.

Configuring Windows 7 and Windows Vista

Configuring Windows 7 and Windows Vista PCs for a new network is quite easy. In fact, if you're connecting via Ethernet, you don't have to do a thing; Windows will recognize your new network and start using it automatically.

If you're connecting via a wireless connection, configuration is only slightly more involved. Click the Network icon in the notification area of the taskbar; then select your network from the Jump List and click the Connect button. When prompted to select a network location, select Home. That's all there is to it.

Configuring Windows XP

Configuring an older computer running Windows XP for your new network is a little more complicated—although the task is made easier via the Network Setup Wizard. You start by opening the Control Panel and clicking Network and Internet Connections. When prompted, select Set Up or Change Your Home or Small Office Network. This launches the Network Setup Wizard.

Click the Next button to move through the introductory screens. When the Select a Connection Method screen appears, select This Computer Connects to the Internet Through a Residential Gateway or Through Another Computer on My Network and then click Next. When the next screen appears, enter a description for this PC (make and model is good), along with a unique name (such as "Main Computer"); then click Next. When the next screen appears, enter a name for your network and then click Next. Finally, on the next screen, check Turn On File and Printer Sharing. Continue clicking Next to finish the wizard, and Windows will be properly configured.

Setting Up Wireless Security

One of the issues with a wireless network is that all your data is just out there, broadcast over the air via radio waves, for anyone to grab. Fortunately, to keep outsiders from tapping into your wireless network, you can add wireless security to your network. This is done by assigning a fairly complex encryption code to your network; in order to tap into the network, a computer must know the code.

You can assign security codes to all the PCs in your network in one of several ways. First, most wireless hubs, routers, and adapters come with configuration utilities that let you activate this type of wireless security. If your wireless equipment has this type of configuration utility, use it.

Otherwise, you can use Windows' built-in wireless security. To enable wireless security in Windows 7, follow these steps:

1. Click the Network icon in the taskbar notification area and select Open Network and Sharing Center.

2. From the Network and Sharing Center, click Set Up a New Connection or Network.

3. When the next window opens, select Set Up a New Network and click Next.

4. Windows should now automatically detect your network hardware and settings. Follow the onscreen instructions to enter your network's SSID name, and then either automatically assign or manually enter a network key. The type and length of the key you choose depends on the type of encryption you choose; the strongest encryption comes from a 26-character WEP key.

note

SSID stands for *Service Set Identifier*, which is a set of letters or numbers that identify a particular wireless network. You create the SSID when you initially install and configure your router.

After the network key is assigned, write it down. You'll need to run this wizard on all the other PCs on the network and manually enter this same key for each computer. (Alternatively, Windows lets you save the key to a USB drive, which you can then transfer to your other PCs.) After all the work is done, only those PCs that have been assigned this specific key can connect to your wireless network—which means no more neighbors leeching off your wireless connection.

Sharing Files and Printers Across the Network

After you have your network up and running, it's time to take advantage of it—by copying or moving files from one computer to another, and by connecting all your computers to a single network printer. To do all this, you first have to enable file and printer sharing on each of your computers.

caution

Be cautious about turning on file sharing. When you allow a folder to be shared, anyone accessing your network can access the contents of the folder.

Enabling File and Printer Sharing in Windows 7

For machines running Windows 7, activating file printer sharing is a snap. Here's what you do:

1. Click the Network icon in the taskbar notification area and select Open Network and Sharing Center.

2. From the Network and Sharing Center, click Choose Homegroup and Sharing Options.

3. In the next window, click Change Advanced Sharing Options.

4. On the next screen, shown in Figure 7.2, click the down arrow next to Home or Work.

5. Click Turn On File and Printer Sharing.

6. Click Turn On Sharing So Anyone with Network Access Can Read and Write Files in the Public Folders.

7. Click Save Changes.

note

You only have to enable printer sharing for the computer to which the printer is physically connected. Once printer sharing is enabled on that PC, the printer will be visible from all other computers connected to your network.

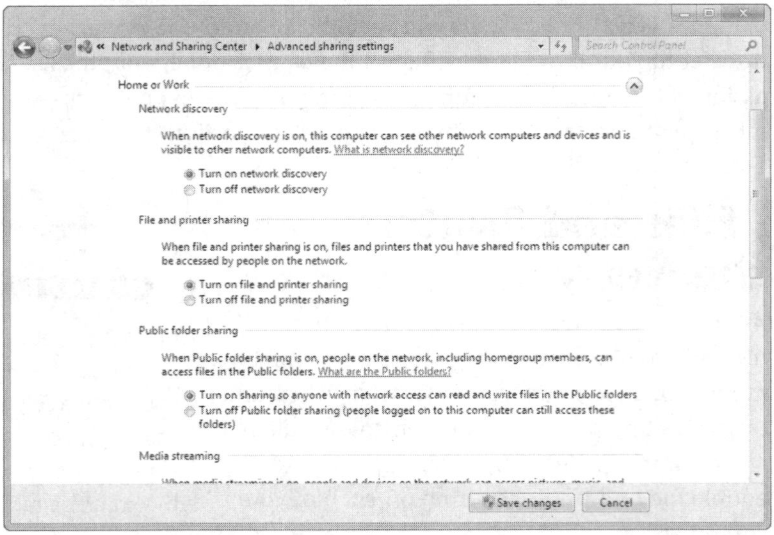

FIGURE 7.2

Enabling file and printer sharing.

Enabling File and Printer Sharing in Windows Vista

Windows Vista is similar enough to Windows 7 that file/printer sharing activation is similarly easy. To turn on file sharing, you open the Windows Vista Network and Sharing Center, click the down arrow next to the Public Folder Sharing option in the

Sharing and Discovery section, and then check the Turn On File Sharing option. To turn on printer sharing, click the down arrow next to the Printer Sharing option and then check the Turn On Printer Sharing option.

Enabling File and Printer Sharing in Windows XP

Activating file and printer sharing on older Windows XP computers is a different process. Since you may have older PCs connected to your network, we'll go over that process in brief here.

With Windows XP, you can share files stored in the Shared Documents folder or in any other folder you specify. By default, file sharing is turned on for the Shared Documents folder; you have to manually activate file sharing for any other folder you want to use. You do this by using My Computer to navigate to the folder that contains the file you want to share. Right-click the folder icon and select Sharing and Security from the pop-up menu. When the Properties dialog box appears, select the Sharing tab, check the Share This Folder on the Network option, and then click OK.

In Windows XP, the process is slightly more involved than with Windows 7. From the Control Panel, double-click Printers and Other Hardware, and then select View Installed Printers or Fax Printers. When the Printers and Faxes window opens, select the printer that you want to share; then click Share This Printer in the Printer Tasks panel. When the printer Properties dialog box appears, select the Sharing tab and check the Share This Printer option. Edit the name of the printer if you want and then click OK.

Accessing Other Computers on Your Network

To access other computers on your network, click the Windows Explorer icon on the Windows taskbar. When Windows Explorer opens, click Network in the Favorites list; this displays all your network computers. Double-click any networked computer to view its shared folders and files.

tip

On most systems, shared files are stored in the Public folder. Look in this folder first for the files you want.

Installing a Network Printer on Other PCs

After you've enabled printer sharing on your main PC, you have to install that network printer on all the other computers on your network. In Windows 7, you do so by following these steps:

1. Click the Start button on the Windows taskbar.
2. From the Start menu, select Devices and Printers.

3. When the Devices and Printers window opens, as shown in Figure 7.3, click Add a Printer from the toolbar.

4. When the Add a Printer window opens, click Add a Network, Wireless or Bluetooth Printer; then click Next.

5. Select your printer from the list; then click Next.

6. When the next screen appears, click Next.

7. If you want this printer to be your default printer, click Set as the Default Printer.

8. Click Finish.

FIGURE 7.3

Getting ready to install a network printer on a remote PC.

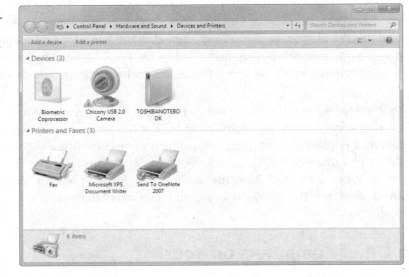

After the network printer is installed, it should appear in the list of available printers whenever you choose to print a document or photo from this PC.

Adding Your Computer to a HomeGroup

Windows 7 adds a new *HomeGroup* feature that makes it easier to network multiple home computers. A HomeGroup is kind of a simplified network that consists of other computers running Windows 7. All computers connected to the HomeGroup can automatically share files and printers.

To create a new HomeGroup, follow these steps:

1. Click the Network icon in the taskbar notification area and select Open Network and Sharing Center.

2. From the Network and Sharing Center, click Choose HomeGroup and Sharing Options.

3. When the HomeGroup window appears, click Create a HomeGroup.

4. On the next screen, shown in Figure 7.4, check those types of items you wish to share across your network: Pictures, Music, Videos, Documents, or Printers, then Click Next.

5. Click Create Now.

6. Write down the HomeGroup password so that you can enter it when configuring other computers on the network.

7. Click Finish.

note

Only PCs running Windows 7 can be part of a HomeGroup. PCs running older versions of Windows do not have the HomeGroup feature and must use the normal networking functions instead. For that reason, it makes sense to enable HomeGroups only on networks consisting solely of Windows 7 computers.

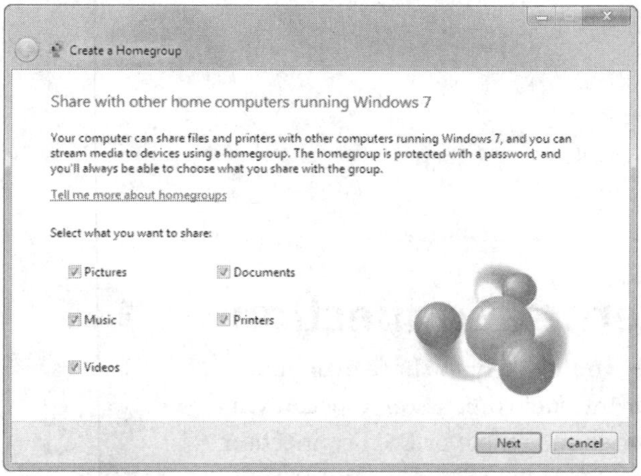

FIGURE 7.4
Creating a new HomeGroup.

Managing Your Network

In Windows 7, all network functions can be monitored and managed via the Network and Sharing Center. You've already seen the Network and Sharing Center when you configured various aspects of your new network; there's more that it can do, however.

To open the Network and Sharing Center, shown in Figure 7.5, click the Network button on the taskbar; then click Open Network and Sharing Center. From there, you can configure network discovery (to see other PCs on your network), file sharing, public folder sharing, printer sharing, password-protected sharing, and media sharing (for music, video, and picture files).

tip

To display a map of all the computers on your network, click the See Full Map link.

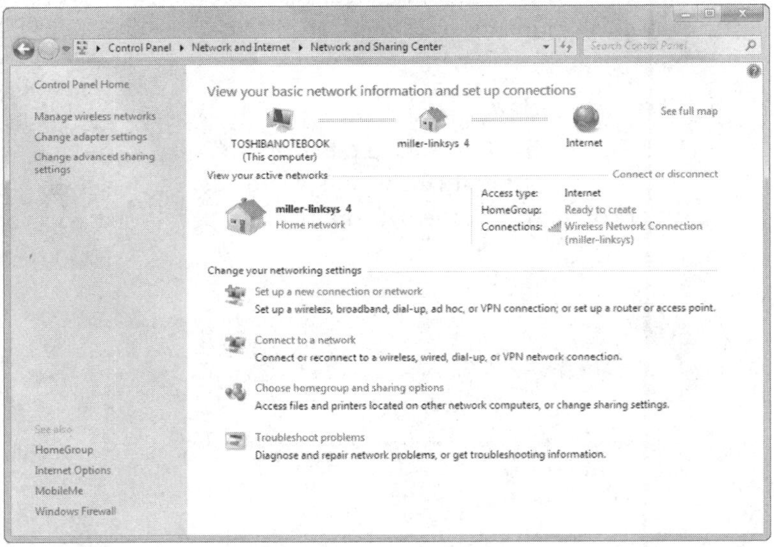

FIGURE 7.5

The Windows 7 Network and Sharing Center.

Sharing an Internet Connection

The other thing you're likely to share over your network is your Internet connection, especially if you have a broadband (cable or DSL) connection. For many users, this is the primary—and sometimes the sole—reason to set up a home network.

Sharing an Internet connection is easy in Windows 7. When you connect your computer to the network router, the Internet connection should be automatically available (assuming you have your broadband modem connected to your router, of course). There's no special configuration necessary.

note

Learn more about sharing an Internet connection in Chapter 16, "Connecting to the Internet—at Home and on the Road."

THE ABSOLUTE MINIMUM

Here are the key things to remember about creating a home network:

- To share information or hardware between two or more computers, you have to connect them in a network.

- There are two basic types of networks: wired and wireless (WiFi).

- If you've set up a wireless network, you should add wireless security to protect the network from outside intruders.

- To share folders and printers between computers on your network, enable Windows' file and printer sharing feature.

- You can also share your broadband Internet connection over your home network, so all your computers have Internet access.

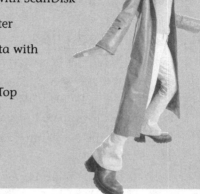

8

PERFORMING ROUTINE MAINTENANCE

"An ounce of prevention is worth a pound of cure."

That old adage might seem trite and cliché, but it's also true—especially when it comes to your computer system. Spending a few minutes a week on preventive maintenance can save you from costly computer problems in the future.

To make this chore a little easier, Windows includes several utilities to help you keep your system running smoothly. You should use these tools as part of your regular maintenance routine—or if you experience specific problems with your computer system.

Free Up Disk Space by Deleting Unnecessary Files and Programs

Even with today's enormous hard disks, you can still end up with too many useless files and programs taking up too much hard disk space. Fortunately, Windows makes it easy to delete those items you don't use any more.

Cleaning Up Unused Files

Fortunately, Windows includes a utility that identifies and deletes unused files. The Disk Cleanup tool is what you want to use when you need to free up extra hard disk space for more frequently used files.

To use Disk Cleanup, follow these steps:

1. Click the Start button to display the Start menu.

2. Select All Programs, Accessories, System Tools, Disk Cleanup.

3. If prompted, select the drive you want to clean up.

4. Disk Cleanup automatically analyzes the contents of your hard disk drive. When it's finished analyzing, it presents its results in the Disk Cleanup dialog box, shown in Figure 8.1.

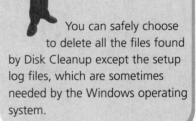

note

You can safely choose to delete all the files found by Disk Cleanup except the setup log files, which are sometimes needed by the Windows operating system.

FIGURE 8.1

Use Disk Cleanup to delete unused files from your hard disk.

Disk Cleanup for SQ004328V04 (C:)

Disk Cleanup

You can use Disk Cleanup to free up to 947 MB of disk space on SQ004328V04 (C:).

Files to delete:

☑ 🖼 Downloaded Program Files	23.6 MB
☑ 📄 Temporary Internet Files	2.33 MB
☐ 📄 Offline Webpages	41.4 KB
☐ 📄 Debug Dump Files	267 MB
☑ 📄 Microsoft Office Temporary Files	430 KB

Total amount of disk space you gain: 47.4 MB

Description

Downloaded Program Files are ActiveX controls and Java applets downloaded automatically from the Internet when you view certain pages. They are temporarily stored in the Downloaded Program Files folder on your hard disk.

Clean up system files   View Files

How does Disk Cleanup work?

OK   Cancel

5. You now have the option of permanently deleting various types of files: downloaded program files, temporary Internet files, offline web pages, deleted files in the Recycle Bin, and so forth. Select which files you want to delete.

6. Click OK to begin deleting.

Removing Unused Programs

Another way to free up valuable hard disk space is to delete those programs you never use. This is accomplished using Windows' Uninstall or Change a Program utility. Follow these steps:

tip

Most brand-new PCs come with unwanted programs and trial versions installed at the factory. Many users choose to delete these "bloatware" programs when they first run their PCs.

1. From the Windows Control Panel, click Uninstall a Program (in the Programs section).

2. When the next screen appears, as shown in Figure 8.2, click the program you wish to delete.

3. Click Uninstall.

FIGURE 8.2

Uninstall any program you're no longer using.

Make Your Hard Disk Run Better by Defragmenting

If you think that your computer is taking longer than usual to open files or notice that your hard drive light stays on longer than usual, you might need to *defragment* your hard drive.

File fragmentation is sort of like taking the pieces of a jigsaw puzzle and storing them in different boxes along with pieces from other puzzles. The more dispersed the pieces are, the longer it takes to put the puzzle together. Spreading the bits and pieces of a file around your hard disk occurs whenever you install, delete, or run an application or when you edit, move, copy, or delete a file.

If you notice that your system takes longer and longer to open and close files or run applications, it's because these file fragments are spread all over the place. You fix the problem when you put all the pieces of the puzzle back in the right boxes— which you do by defragmenting your hard disk.

To defragment your hard disk, use Windows' Disk Defragmenter utility. In Windows 7, Disk Defragmenter runs periodically in the background, automatically defragging your hard disk whenever your computer is turned on. You can also choose to run the utility manually, to affect more immediate results.

To run Disk Defragmenter manually, follow these steps:

1. Click the Start button to display the Start menu.
2. Select All Programs, Accessories, System Tools, Disk Defragmenter to open the Disk Defragmenter utility.
3. If prompted, select the drive you want to defragment, typically drive **C:**.
4. Click Defragment Disk.

Defragmenting your drive can take awhile, especially if you have a large hard drive or your drive is really fragmented. So you might want to start the utility and let it run overnight while you're sleeping.

Perform a Hard Disk Checkup with ScanDisk

Any time you run an application, move or delete a file, or accidentally turn the power off while the system is running, you run the risk of introducing errors to your hard disk. These errors can make it harder to open files, slow down your hard disk, or cause your system to freeze when you open or save a file or an application.

Fortunately, you can find and fix most of these errors directly from within Windows. All you have to do is run the built-in ScanDisk utility.

To find and fix errors on your hard drive, follow these steps:

1. Click the Start button to display the Start menu.
2. Select Computer to open the Computer Explorer.
3. Click the icon for the drive you want to scan.
4. Click the Properties button on the toolbar.
5. When the Properties dialog box appears, select the Tools tab.
6. Click the Check Now button in the Error-Checking section.
7. When the Check Disk dialog box appears, check both the options (Automatically Fix File System Errors and Scan for and Attempt Recovery of Bad Sectors).
8. Click Start.

Windows now scans your hard disk and attempts to fix any errors it encounters. Note that you may be prompted to reboot your PC if you're checking your computer's C: drive.

Using the Windows Action Center

In Windows 7, the best way to manage your PC's maintenance and security is via the new Action Center utility. As you can see in Figure 8.3, the Action Center centralizes a lot of maintenance operations, error reporting, and troubleshooting operations.

FIGURE 8.3

Monitoring your system's maintenance with the Windows 7 Action Center.

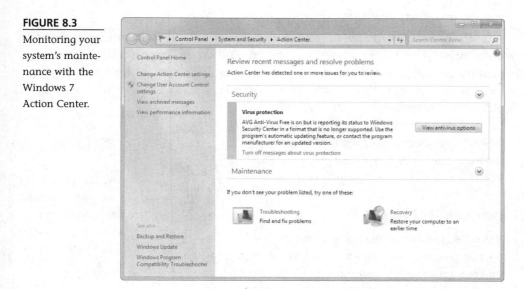

To access the Action Center, open the Windows Control Panel and select System & Security, and then Action Center. The Action Center will alert you to any action you need to take to protect and maintain your system.

Backing Up Your Important Data with Windows Backup

One more piece of maintenance can make or break the way you use your computer. I'm talking about the necessity of backing up your data files so that if your computer ever crashes or goes dead, you have backup copies of everything that's important to you—including your work documents, music files, digital photos, and the like.

caution

For many users, the scariest thing about a PC data disaster is losing all their valuable digital photographs. If you don't have backups of your digital files, you could lose several years' worth of photos if your hard disk crashes.

Choosing a Backup Device

The easiest way to back up your data files is to use an external hard disk. These days you can get a very large drive (500GB to 1TB in size) for around a hundred dollars or so, which makes not backing up fairly inexcusable. Make sure you get an external drive about the same size as your PC's internal hard disk.

Most external hard drives connect to your PC via USB; some bigger disks use the faster FireWire connection. Either type of connection is fine, and both are easy enough to connect and install.

After the external hard drive is connected, you need to run a software program that automates the backup process. Most external hard drives come with their own proprietary backup programs; these are typically easy to use and get the job done. You can also use one of the many third-party backup programs sold at your local computer or electronics store, such as Acronis True Image (www.acronis.com) or CMS Bounceback (www.cmsproducts.com/product_bounceback_software.htm). You'll typically pay from $50 to $100 for one of these programs.

tip

The easiest way to perform a backup is to use an external hard disk drive. These drives provide lots of storage space for a relatively low cost, and they connect to your PC via USB. There's no excuse not to do it!

Using Windows Backup

If your PC is running Windows 7, you have a backup program built into the operating system that lets you schedule automatic backups of your key data. Follow these steps to set up an automatic backup using the Windows Backup utility:

1. Open the Windows Control Panel and click Back Up Your Computer (in the System and Security section).

2. When the next window appears, click Set Up Backup.

3. This launches the Windows Backup program, shown in Figure 8.4. Select where you want to back up your data—to an external hard disk, to a CD or DVD disc, or to another computer on your network—and then click Next.

4. When the next screen appears, select Let Windows Choose and click Next.

5. On the final screen, click Save Settings and Run Backup to perform your first backup.

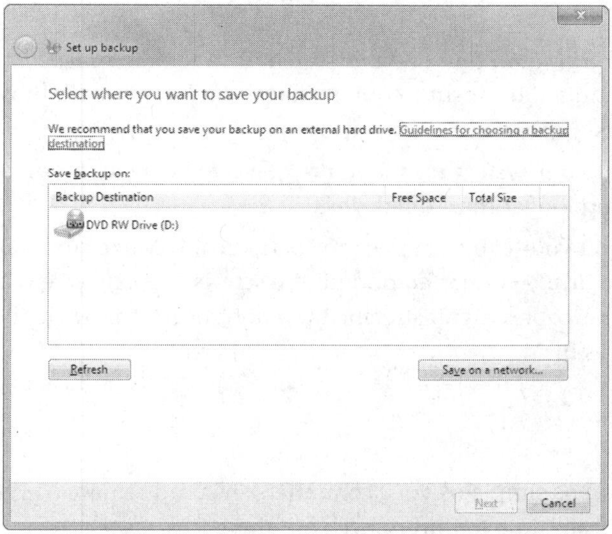

FIGURE 8.4

Use Windows Backup to back up your valuable data files.

Note that Windows Backup performs what is called an *incremental* backup. That is, it doesn't back up every file every time; it only backs up those files that are new or have changed since the last backup.

Keeping Your Hardware in Tip-Top Condition

There's also a fair amount of preventive maintenance you can physically perform on your computer hardware. It's simple stuff, but it can really extend the life of your PC.

tip

By default, Windows Backup will back up your data once a week (Sunday at 7:00 p.m.). To change the backup schedule, click Change Schedule and select how often, what day, and what time to back up.

System Unit

The system unit on a desktop PC—or the entire unit of a notebook computer—has a lot of sensitive electronics inside, from memory chips to disk drives to power supplies. Check out these maintenance tips to keep your system unit from flaking out on you:

- Position your computer in a clean, dust-free environment. Keep it away from direct sunlight and strong magnetic fields. In addition, make sure that your system unit and your monitor have plenty of air flow around them to keep them from overheating.

- Hook up your system unit to a surge suppressor to avoid damaging power spikes.

- Avoid turning on and off your system unit too often; it's better to leave it on all the time than incur frequent "power on" stress to all those delicate components. However...

- Turn off your system unit if you're going to be away for an extended period—anything longer than a few days.

- Check all your cable connections periodically. Make sure that all the connectors are firmly connected and all the screws properly screwed—and make sure that your cables aren't stretched too tight or bent in ways that could damage the wires inside.

Keyboard

Even something as simple as your computer keyboard requires a little preventive maintenance from time to time. Check out these tips:

- Keep your keyboard away from young children and pets—they can get dirt and hair and Silly Putty all over the place, and they have a tendency to put way too much pressure on the keys.

- Keep your keyboard away from dust, dirt, smoke, direct sunlight, and other harmful environmental stuff. You might even consider putting a dust cover on your keyboard when it's not in use.

- Use a small vacuum cleaner to periodically sweep the dirt from your keyboard. (Alternatively, you can use compressed air to *blow* the dirt away.) Use a cotton swab or soft cloth to clean between the keys. If necessary, remove the keycaps to clean the switches underneath.

- If you spill something on your keyboard, disconnect it immediately and wipe up the spill. Use a soft cloth to get between the keys; if necessary, use a screwdriver to pop off the keycaps and wipe up any seepage underneath. Let the keyboard dry thoroughly before trying to use it again.

Display

If you think of your computer display as a little television set, you're on the right track. Just treat your screen as you do your TV, and you'll be okay. That said, look at these preventive maintenance tips:

- As with all other important system components, keep your monitor away from direct sunlight, dust, and smoke. Make sure that it has plenty of ventilation, especially around the back; don't cover the rear cooling vents with paper or any other object, and don't set anything bigger than a small plush toy on top of the cabinet.

- Don't place strong magnets in close proximity to your monitor. (This includes external speakers.)

- With your monitor turned off, periodically clean the monitor screen. For an LCD flat-panel monitor, use water to dampen a lint-free cloth, and then wipe the screen; do not spray liquid directly on the screen. Do not use any cleaner that contains alcohol or ammonia; these chemicals may damage an LCD screen. (You can, however, use commercial cleaning wipes specially formulated for LCD screens.)

- Don't forget to adjust the brightness and contrast controls on your monitor every now and then. Any controls can get out of whack—plus, your monitor's performance will change as it ages, and simple adjustments can often keep it looking as good as new.

Printer

Your printer is a complex device with a lot of moving parts. Follow these tips to keep your printouts in good shape:

- Use a soft cloth, mini-vacuum cleaner, or compressed air to clean the inside and outside of your printer on a periodic basis. In particular, make sure that you clean the paper path of all paper shavings and dust.

- If you have an ink-jet printer, periodically clean the ink jets. Run your printer's cartridge cleaning utility, or use a small pin to make sure that they don't get clogged.

- If you have a laser printer, replace the toner cartridge as needed. When you replace the cartridge, remember to clean the printer cleaning bar and other related parts, per the manufacturer's instructions.

- Don't use alcohol or other solvents to clean rubber or plastic parts—you'll do more harm than good!

Maintaining a Notebook PC

All the previous tips hold for both desktop and notebook PCs. If you have a notebook PC, however, there are additional steps you need to take to keep everything working in tip-top condition.

Using the Windows Mobility Center

Let's start with all the various settings that are unique to a notebook PC—power plan, monitor brightness, wireless networking, and so forth. Windows 7 puts all these settings into a single control panel called the Windows Mobility Center. As you can see in Figure 8.5, you can use the Mobility Center to configure and manage just about everything that makes your notebook run better.

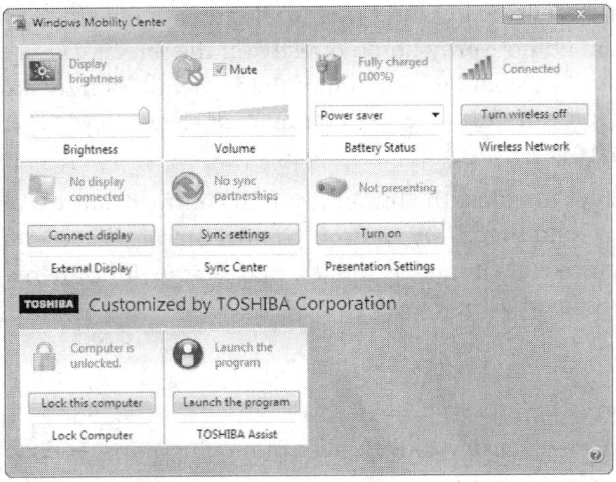

FIGURE 8.5

Manage key notebook PC settings with the Windows Mobility Center.

To access the Windows Mobility Center, click the Start button and select All Programs, Accessories, Windows Mobility Center. Click the button or adjust the slider for whichever option you need to change.

Conserving Battery Life

One of the key issues with a notebook PC is battery life. It's especially important if you use your notebook a lot on the road.

Any notebook, even a desktop replacement model, will give you at least an hour of operation before the battery powers down. If you need more battery life than that, here are some things you can try:

note

Some notebook manufacturers will add their own mobile configuration settings to the Windows Mobility Center.

- **Change your power scheme**—Windows includes several built-in power schemes that manage key functions to provide either longer battery life or better performance. (It's always a trade-off between the two.) You can switch power schemes from the Windows Mobility Center (in the Battery Status section) or by clicking the Power icon in the notification area of the Windows taskbar.

- **Dim your screen**—The brighter your screen, the more power your PC uses. Conserve on power usage by dialing down the brightness level of your notebook's screen.

- **Turn it off when you're not using it**—A PC sitting idle is still using power. If you're going to be away from the keyboard for more than a few minutes, turn off the notebook to conserve power—or put the PC into sleep or hibernation mode, which also cuts power use.

- **Don't do anything taxing**—Anytime you write or read a file from your notebook's hard disk, you use power. The same goes with using the CD or DVD drive; every spin of the drive drains the battery. If you use your notebook to watch DVD movies, don't expect the batteries to last as long as if you were just checking email or surfing the Web.

- **Buy a bigger battery**—Many notebook manufacturers sell batteries that have various capacities. You may be able to buy a longer-lasting battery than the one that came in the box.

- **Buy a second battery**—When the first battery is drained, remove it and plug in a fresh one.

- **Buy a smaller notebook**—Ultraportable models use less power and have longer battery life than do midsize notebooks, which in turn are less power-hungry than desktop replacement models. The smaller the screen and the less powerful the CPU, the longer the notebook's battery life.

If worse comes to worst, keep an eye out for an available power outlet. Most coffee shops and airport lounges have at least one seat next to a power outlet; just carry your notebook's AC adapter with you and be ready to plug in when you can.

Securing Your Notebook

One of the great things about a notebook PC is that it's small and easily portable. One of the bad things about a notebook PC is that's it's small and easily portable—which makes it attractive to thieves. Take care to protect your notebook when you're using it in public, which may mean investing in a notebook lock or some similar sort of antitheft device. Of course, just being vigilant helps; never leave your notebook unattended in a coffee shop or airport terminal.

In addition, be careful about transmitting private data over a public WiFi network. Avoid the temptation to do your online shopping (and transmit your credit card number) from your local coffee shop; wait until you're safely connected to your home network before you send your private data over the WiFi airwaves.

THE ABSOLUTE MINIMUM

Here are the key points to remember from this chapter:

- Dedicating a few minutes a week to PC maintenance can prevent serious problems from occurring in the future.
- To delete unused files from your hard disk, use the Disk Cleanup utility.
- To defragment a fragmented hard disk, use the Disk Defragmenter utility (which automatically runs in the background with Windows Vista).
- To find and fix hard disk errors, use the ScanDisk utility.
- Make sure that you keep all your computer hardware away from direct sunlight, dust, and smoke, and make sure that your system unit has plenty of ventilation.
- Protect your valuable files by backing them up to an external hard disk—using either a third-party backup program or, in Windows Vista, the Windows Backup utility.
- If you have a notebook PC, take appropriate steps to conserve battery life—and keep your PC safe from thieves!

9

DEALING WITH COMMON PROBLEMS

Computers aren't perfect. It's possible—although unlikely—that at some point in time, something will go wrong with your PC. It might refuse to start, it might freeze up, it might crash and go dead. Yikes!

When something goes wrong with your computer, there's no need to panic (even though that's what you'll probably feel like doing). Most PC problems have easy-to-find causes and simple solutions. The key thing is to keep your wits about you and attack the situation calmly and logically—following the advice you'll find in this chapter.

How to Troubleshoot Computer Problems

No matter what kind of computer-related problem you're experiencing, there are six basic steps you should take to track down the cause of the problem. Work through these steps calmly and deliberately, and you're likely to find what's causing the current problem—and then be in a good position to fix it yourself:

1. **Don't panic!**—Just because there's something wrong with your PC is no reason to fly off the handle. Chances are there's nothing seriously wrong. Besides, getting all panicky won't solve anything. Keep your wits about you and proceed logically, and you can probably find what's causing your problem and get it fixed.

2. **Check for operator errors**—In other words, something *you* did wrong. Maybe you clicked the wrong button, pressed the wrong key, or plugged something into the wrong jack or port. Retrace your steps and try to duplicate your problem. Chances are the problem won't recur if you don't make the same mistake twice.

3. **Check that everything is plugged into the proper place and that the system unit itself is getting power**—Take special care to ensure that all your cables are *securely* connected—loose connections can cause all sorts of strange results.

4. **Make sure you have the latest versions of all the software installed on your system**—While you're at it, make sure you have the latest versions of device drivers installed for all the peripherals on your system.

5. **Try to isolate the problem by when and how it occurs**—Walk through each step of the process to see if you can identify a particular program or driver that might be causing the problem.

6. **When all else fails, call in professional help**—If you think it's a Windows-related problem, contact Microsoft's technical support department. If you think it's a problem with a particular program, contact the tech support department of the program's manufacturer. If you think it's a hardware-related problem, contact the manufacturer of your PC or the dealer you bought it from. The pros are there for a reason—when you need technical support, go and get it.

caution

Not all tech support is free. Unless you have a brand new PC or brand new software, expect to pay a fee for technical support.

Troubleshooting in Safe Mode

If you're having trouble getting Windows to start, it's probably because some setting is wrong or some driver is malfunctioning. The problem is, how do you get into Windows to fix what's wrong, when you can't even start Windows?

The solution is to hijack your computer before Windows gets hold of it and force it to start *without* whatever is causing the problem. You do this by watching the screen as your computer boots up and pressing the F8 key just before Windows starts to load. This displays the Windows startup menu, where you select Safe mode.

Depending on the severity of your system problem, Windows might start in Safe mode automatically.

Safe mode is a special mode of operation that loads Windows in a very simple configuration. Once in Safe mode, you can look for device conflicts, restore incorrect or corrupted device drivers, or restore your system to a prior working configuration (using the System Restore utility, discussed later in this chapter).

What to Do When Windows Freezes

Probably the most common computer trouble is the freeze-up. That's what happens when your PC just stops dead in its tracks. The screen looks normal, but nothing works—you can't type onscreen, you can't click any buttons, nothing's happening.

If your system happens to freeze up, the good news is that there's probably nothing wrong with your computer hardware. The bad news is that there's probably something funky happening with your operating system.

This doesn't mean your system is broken. It's just a glitch. And you can recover from glitches. Just remember not to panic and to approach the situation calmly and rationally.

What Causes Windows to Freeze?

If Windows up and freezes, what's the likely cause? There can be many different causes of a Windows freeze, including the following:

- You might be running an older software program or game that isn't compatible with your version of Windows. If so, upgrade the program.

- A memory conflict might exist between applications or between an application and Windows. Try running fewer programs at once or running problematic programs one at a time to avoid potential memory conflicts.

- You might not have enough memory installed on your system. Upgrade the amount of memory in your PC.

- You might not have enough free hard disk space on your computer. Delete any unnecessary files from your hard drive.

- Your hard disk might be developing errors or bad sectors. Check your hard disk for errors. (See the "Perform a Hard Disk Checkup with ScanDisk" section in Chapter 8, "Performing Routine Maintenance.")

Dealing with Frozen Windows

When Windows freezes, you need to get it unfrozen and up and running again. The way to do this is to shut down your computer. You may be able to do this by pressing Ctrl+Alt+Del to display the Windows Task Manager, and then selecting Shut Down from the toolbar. If that doesn't work, press and hold down your computer's power button until your system shuts off. You can then start up your computer again; chances are everything will be working just fine this time around.

If your system crashes or freezes frequently, however, you should call in a pro. These kinds of problems can be tough to track down by yourself when you're dealing with Windows.

Dealing with a Frozen Program

Sometimes Windows works fine, but an individual software program freezes. Fortunately, recent versions of Windows present an exceptionally safe environment; when an individual application crashes or freezes, it seldom messes up your entire system. You can use a utility called the Windows Task Manager to close the problem application without affecting other Windows programs.

When a Windows application freezes or crashes, press Ctrl+Alt+Del; this opens the Windows Task Manager, shown in Figure 9.1. Select the Applications tab and then select the frozen application from the list. Now click the End Task button. After a few seconds, a Wait/Shutdown window appears; confirm that you want to shut down the selected application; then click the End Task button.

This closes the offending application and lets you continue your work in Windows.

If you have multiple applications that crash on a regular basis, the situation can often be attributed to insufficient memory. See your computer dealer about adding more RAM to your system.

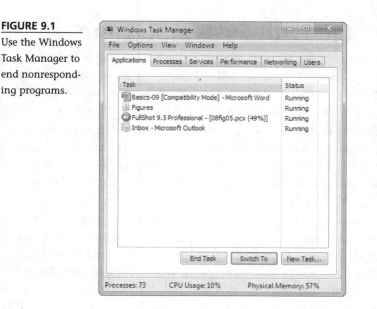

Dealing with a Major Crash

Perhaps the worst thing that can happen to your computer system is that it crashes—completely shuts down, without warning. If this happens to you, start by not panicking. Stay calm, take a few deep breaths, and then get ready to get going again.

You should always wait about 60 seconds after a computer crashes before you try to turn on your system again. This gives all the components time to settle down and—in some cases—reset themselves. Just sit back and count to 60 (slowly); then press your system unit's "on" button.

Nine times out of ten, your system will boot up normally, as if nothing unusual has happened. If this is what happens for you, great! If, on the other hand, your system doesn't come back up normally, you'll need to start troubleshooting the underlying problem, as discussed later in this chapter.

Even if your system comes back up as usual, the sudden crash might have done some damage. A system crash can sometimes damage any software program that was running at the time, as well as any documents that were open when the crash occurred. You might have to reinstall a damaged program or recover a damaged document from a backup file.

Undoing the Damage with System Restore

Perhaps the best course of action when your system crashes is to use Microsoft's System Restore utility. This utility can automatically restore your system to the state it was in before the crash occurred—and save you the trouble of reinstalling any damaged software programs. It's a great safety net for when things go wrong.

System Restore works by monitoring your system and noting any changes that are made when you install new applications. Each time it notes a change, it automatically creates what it calls a *restore point*. A restore point is basically a "snapshot" of key system files (including the Windows Registry) just before the new application is installed.

If something in your system goes bad, you can run System Restore to set things right. Pick a restore point before the problem occurred (such as right before a new installation), and System Restore will undo any changes made to monitored files since the restore point was created. This restores your system to its preinstallation—that is, *working*—condition.

To restore your system from a restore point, follow these steps:

1. Click the Start button to display the Start menu.
2. Select All Programs, Accessories, System Tools, System Restore to open the System Restore window.
3. When the System Restore window appears, click Next.
4. When the next window appears, as shown in Figure 9.2, you can choose to restore to Windows' recommended restore point or to a different restore point. (Check the Show More Restore Points option.) Make your choice and click Next.
5. When the confirmation screen appears, click the Finish button.

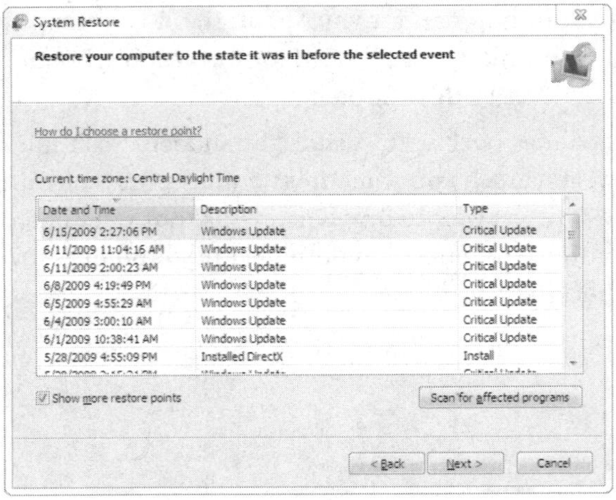

FIGURE 9.2

Use the System Restore utility to restore damaged programs or system files.

Windows now starts to restore your system. You should make sure that all open programs are closed because Windows will need to be restarted during this process.

When the process is complete, your system should be back in tip-top shape. Note, however, that it might take a half-hour or more to complete a system restore—so you'll have time to order a pizza and eat dinner before the operation is done!

> **caution**
>
> System Restore will help you recover any damaged programs and system files, but it won't help you recover damaged documents or data files.

THE ABSOLUTE MINIMUM

Here are the key points to remember from this chapter:

- If something strange happens to your computer system, the first thing to do is *not panic!*

- Most so-called computer problems are actually caused by operator error, so back up and do whatever it is you did one more time—carefully, this time.

- You can shut down frozen programs from the Windows Task Manager, which you display by pressing Ctrl+Alt+Del.

- You can also use the Windows Task Manager to manually reboot your computer—and if this doesn't work, simply press and hold down the power button on your PC's system unit.

- Some problems can be fixed from Windows Safe mode; to enter Safe mode, restart your computer and press F8 before the Windows start screen appears.

- If your system misbehaves after installing new software or hardware, use the System Restore utility to return your system to its preinstallation state.

10

PROTECTING YOUR PC FROM VIRUSES, SPAM, AND OTHER ONLINE NUISANCES

When you connect your computer to the Internet, you open a whole new can of worms—literally. Computer worms, viruses, spyware, spam, and the like can attack your computer and cause it to run slowly or not at all. In addition to these malicious software programs (called *malware*) that can infect your computer, you're likely to come across all manner of inappropriate content that you'd probably rather avoid. It can be a nasty world online, if you let it.

Fortunately, it's easy to protect your computer and your family from these dangers. All you need are a few software utilities—and a lot of common sense!

Safeguarding Your System from Computer Viruses

A *computer virus* is a malicious software program designed to do damage to your computer system by deleting files or even taking over your PC to launch attacks on other systems. A virus attacks your computer when you launch an infected software program, launching a "payload" that oftentimes is catastrophic.

Signs of Infection

How do you know whether your computer system has been infected with a virus?

In general, whenever your computer starts acting different from normal, it's possible that you have a virus. You might see strange messages or graphics displayed on your computer screen or find that normally well-behaved programs are acting erratically. You might discover that certain files have gone missing from your hard disk or that your system is acting sluggish—or failing to start at all. You might even find that your friends are receiving emails from you (that you never sent) that have suspicious files attached.

If your computer exhibits one or more of these symptoms—especially if you've just downloaded a file from the Internet or received a suspicious email message—the prognosis is not good. Your computer is probably infected.

note

Many computer attacks today are executed using personal computers compromised by a computer virus. These so-called *zombie computers* are operated via remote control in an ad hoc attack network called a *botnet*. A firewall program protects against incoming attacks and botnet controllers.

How to Catch a Virus

Whenever you share data with another computer or computer user (which you do all the time when you're connected to the Internet), you risk exposing your computer to potential viruses. There are many ways you can share data and many ways a virus can be transmitted:

- Opening an infected file attached to an email message or instant message
- Launching an infected program file downloaded from the Internet
- Sharing a data CD, USB memory drive, or floppy disk that contains an infected file
- Sharing over a network a computer file that contains an infected file

Of all these methods, the most common means of virus infection is via email—with instant messaging close behind. Whenever you open a file attached to an email message or instant message, you stand a good chance of infecting your computer system with a virus—even if the file was sent by someone you know and trust. That's because many viruses "spoof" the sender's name, thus making you think the file is from a friend or colleague. The bottom line is that no email or instant message attachment is safe unless you were expressly expecting it.

Practicing Safe Computing

Because you're not going to completely quit doing any of these activities, you'll never be 100% safe from the threat of computer viruses. There are, however, some steps you can take to reduce your risk:

- Don't open email attachments from people you don't know—or even from people you *do* know if you aren't expecting them. That's because some viruses can hijack the address book on an infected PC, thus sending out infected email that the owner isn't even aware of. Just looking at an email message won't harm anything; the damage comes when you open a file attached to the email.

- Don't accept files sent to you via instant messaging; like email attachments, files sent via IM can be easily infected with viruses and spyware.

- Download files only from reliable file archive websites, such as Download.com (www.download.com) and Tucows (www.tucows.com).

- Don't access or download files from music and video file-sharing networks, which are notoriously virus- and spyware-ridden. Instead, download music and movies from legitimate sites, such as the iTunes Store and Amazon MP3 downloads.

- Don't execute programs you find in Usenet newsgroups or posted to web message boards or blogs.

- Don't click links sent to you from strangers via instant messaging or in a chat room.

- Share disks and files only with users you know and trust.

- Use antivirus software—and keep it up-to-date with the most recent virus definitions.

These precautions—especially the first one about not opening email attachments—should provide good insurance against the threat of computer viruses.

caution

If you remember nothing else from this chapter, remember this: Never open an unexpected file attachment. Period!

Disinfecting Your System with Antivirus Software

Antivirus software programs are capable of detecting known viruses and protecting your system against new, unknown viruses. These programs check your system for viruses each time your system is booted and can be configured to check any programs you download from the Internet. They're also used to disinfect your system if it becomes infected with a virus.

The most popular antivirus programs include

- AVG Anti-Virus (www.avg.com)
- Avira AntiVir (www.free-av.com)
- Kaspersky Anti-Virus (www.kaspersky.com)
- McAfee VirusScan (www.mcafee.com)
- Norton AntiVirus (www.symantec.com)
- Trend Micro AntiVirus + AntiSpyware (www.trendmicro.com)
- Microsoft Security Essentials (www.microsoft.com/security_essentials/)

All of these programs do a good job—although their prices vary considerably. For example, AVG Anti-Virus and Avira AntiVir are available for free (and do a great job), while Norton AntiVirus and McAfee VirusScan each cost $39.99 for a one-year subscription.

Whichever antivirus program you choose, you'll need to go online periodically to update the virus definition database the program uses to look for known virus files. Because new viruses are created every week, this file of known viruses must be updated accordingly.

caution

Your antivirus software is next to useless if you don't update it at least weekly. An outdated antivirus program won't be capable of recognizing—and protecting against—the very latest computer viruses.

Hunting Down Spyware

Even more pernicious than computer viruses is the proliferation of *spyware*. A spyware program installs itself on your computer and then surreptitiously sends information about the way you use your PC to some interested third party. Spyware typically gets installed in the background when you're installing another program. Peer-to-peer music-trading networks (*not* legitimate online music stores, such as the iTunes Store) are one of the biggest sources of spyware; when you install the file-trading software, the spyware is also installed.

Having spyware on your system is nasty—almost as bad as being infected with a computer virus. Some spyware programs will even hijack your computer and launch pop-up windows and advertisements when you visit certain web pages. If there's spyware on your computer, you definitely want to get rid of it.

Unfortunately, most antivirus programs won't catch spyware because spyware isn't a virus. To track down and uninstall these programs, then, you need to run an anti-spyware utility, such as Windows Defender (shown in Figure 10.1), which is included free with Windows 7—and available as a free download for older computers systems.

FIGURE 10.1

Finding hidden spyware pro-grams with Windows Defender.

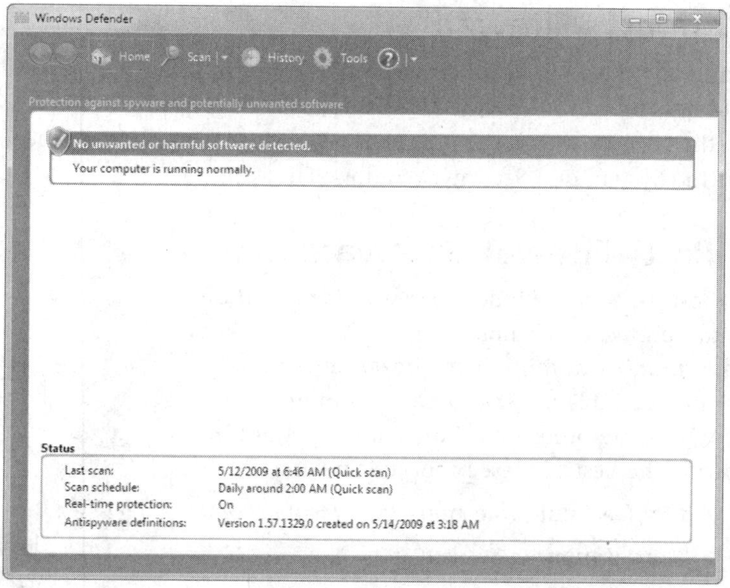

Here are some of the best of these spyware fighters:

- Ad-Aware (www.lavasoftusa.com)
- Spybot Search & Destroy (www.safer-networking.org)
- Webroot Spy Sweeper (www.webroot.com)
- Windows Defender
  (www.microsoft.com/windows/products/winfamily/defender/)

In addition, some of the major Internet security suites, such as Norton Internet Security and the McAfee Internet Security Suite, include anti-spyware modules. Check the program's feature list before you buy.

Defending Against Computer Attacks

Connecting to the Internet is a two-way street—not only can your PC access other computers online, but other computers can also access *your* PC. Which means that unless you take proper precautions, malicious hackers can read your private data, damage your system hardware and software, and even use your system (via remote control) to cause damage to other computers.

You protect your system against outside attack by blocking the path of attack with a *firewall*. A firewall is a software program that forms a virtual barrier between your computer and the Internet. The firewall selectively filters the data that is passed between both ends of the connection and protects your system against outside attack.

Using the Windows Firewall

Fortunately for all of us, Microsoft builds a firewall utility into Windows 7. The Windows Firewall is activated by default, although you can always check to make sure that it's up and working properly. You do this by opening the Control Panel and selecting System and Security, Windows Firewall.

Using Third-Party Firewall Software

For most users, the Windows Firewall is more than enough protection against computer attacks. That said, a number of third-party firewall programs also are available, most of which are more robust and offer more protection than Windows' built-in firewall. The best of these programs include

note

If you're running a third-party firewall program, you may need to turn off the Windows Firewall.

- McAfee Total Protection (www.mcafee.com)
- Norton Internet Security (www.symantec.com)
- ZoneAlarm Free Firewall (www.zonelabs.com)

Fighting Email Spam

If you're like most users, well over half the messages delivered to your email inbox are unsolicited, unauthorized, and unwanted—in other words, *spam*. These spam messages are the online equivalent of the junk mail you receive in your postal mailbox, and it's a huge problem.

Although it's probably impossible to do away with 100% of the spam you receive (you can't completely stop junk mail, either), there are steps you can take to reduce the amount of spam you have to deal with. The heavier your spam load, the more steps you can take.

Protecting Your Email Address

Spammers accumulate email addresses via a variety of methods. Some use high-tech methods to harvest email addresses listed on public web pages and message board postings. Others use the tried-and-true approach of buying names from list brokers. Still others automatically generate addresses using a "dictionary" of common names and email domains.

One way to reduce the amount of spam you receive is to limit the public use of your email address. It's a simple fact: The more you expose your email address, the more likely it is that a spammer will find it—and use it.

To this end, you should avoid putting your email address on your web page or your company's web page. You should also avoid including your email address in post-ings you make to web-based message boards or Usenet newsgroups. In addition, you should most definitely not include your email address in any of the conversations you have in chat rooms or via instant messaging.

Another strategy is to actually use *two* email addresses. Take your main email address (the one you get from your ISP) and hand it out only to a close circle of friends and family; do *not* use this address to post public messages or to register at websites. Then obtain a second email address (you can get a free one at www.hotmail.com, mail.yahoo.com, or gmail.google.com) and use that one for all your public activity. When you post on a message board or newsgroup, use the second address. When you order something from an online mer-chant, use the second address. When you regis-ter for website access, use the second address. Over time, the second address will attract the spam; your first email address will remain pri-vate and relatively spam-free.

> **tip**
>
> If you do have to leave your email address in a pub-lic forum, you can insert a spamblock into your address—an unexpected word or phrase that, although easily removed, will confuse the software spam-mers use to harvest addresses. For example, if your email address is johnjones@myisp.com, you might change the address to read johnSPAMBLOCKjones@myisp.com . Other users will know to remove the SPAMBLOCK from the address before emailing you, but the spam harvesting software will be foiled.

Blocking Spammers in Your Email Programs

Most email software and web-based email serv-ices include some sort of spam filtering. For example, Windows Live Mail automatically sends suspected spam to the Junk E-mail folder. (And if a spam message gets through the filter, just select it and click the Junk button to manu-ally send it to the Junk E-mail folder.) You should always enable the anti-spam features in

> **tip**
>
> It's a good idea to review messages in your spam folder periodically to make sure no legitimate messages have been accidentally sent there.

your email, which should block most of the unwanted messages you might otherwise receive.

Using Anti-Spam Software

If the amount of spam in your Inbox becomes particularly onerous, you might want to consider using an anti-spam software program. Most anti-spam software uses some combination of spam blocking or content filtering to keep spam messages from ever reaching your Inbox; their effectiveness varies, but they will decrease the amount of spam you receive to some degree.

The most popular anti-spam software includes

- ANT 4 MailChecking (www.ant4.com)
- iHateSpam (www.sunbeltsoftware.com)
- MailWasher (www.mailwasher.net)

In addition, many antivirus and content filtering programs include anti-spam modules. If you're already using an antivirus program or security suite, check whether it offers spam email filtering.

Resisting Phishing Scams

Phishing is a technique used by online scam artists to steal your identity by tricking you into disclosing valuable personal information, such as passwords, credit card numbers, and other financial data. If you're not careful, you can mistake a phishing email for a real one—and open yourself up to identity theft.

A phishing scam typically starts with a phony email message that appears to be from a legitimate source, such as your bank, eBay, or PayPal. (Figure 10.2 shows just such a fake message.) When you click the link in the phishing email, you're taken to a fake website masquerading as the real site, complete with logos and official-looking text. You're encouraged to enter your personal information into the forms on the web page; when you do so, your information is sent to the scammer, and you're now a victim of identity theft. When your data falls into the hands of criminals, it can be used to hack into your online accounts, make unauthorized charges on your credit card, and maybe even drain your bank account.

Until recently, the only guard against phishing scams was common sense. That is, you should never click through a link in an email message that asks for any type of personal information—whether that be your bank account number or eBay password. Even if the email *looks* official, it probably isn't; legitimate institutions and websites never include this kind of link in their official messages. Instead, you should access your personal information only by using your web browser to go directly to the website in question. Don't link there!

FIGURE 10.2

A phony phishing message—it looks just like the real thing!

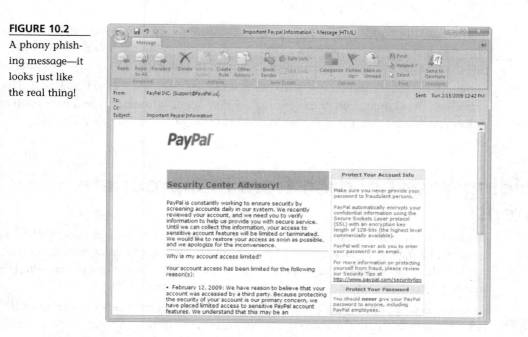

Fortunately, Windows 7 offers some protection against phishing scams. For example, Internet Explorer 8 includes a new SmartScreen Filter that alerts you to potential phishing sites. As you can see in Figure 10.3, when you attempt to visit a known or suspected phishing site, the browser displays a warning message. Do not enter information into these suspected phishing sites—return to your home page, instead!

FIGURE 10.3

An anti-phishing alert in Internet Explorer 8.

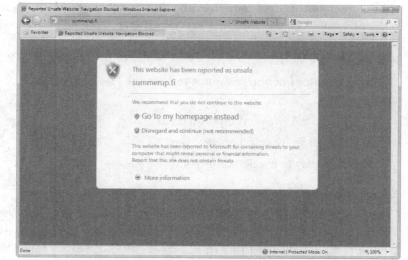

In addition, the Windows Live Mail program (downloadable for free as part of Windows Live Essentials) includes a similar anti-phishing filter. If you receive a suspected phishing message, the program displays a message alerting you to that fact.

But whatever programs you use, you also need to use your head. Don't click through suspicious email links, and don't give out your personal information and passwords unless you're sure you're dealing with an official (and not just an official-looking) site!

Shielding Your Children from Inappropriate Content

The Internet contains an almost limitless supply of information on its tens of billions of web pages. Although most of these pages contain useful information, it's a sad fact that the content of some pages can be quite offensive to some people—and that there are some Internet users who prey on unsuspecting youths.

As a responsible parent, you want to protect your children from any of the bad stuff (and bad people) online, while still allowing access to all the good stuff. How do you do this?

Using Content-Filtering Software

If you can't trust your children to always click away from inappropriate web content, you can choose to install software on your computer that performs filtering functions for all your online sessions. These safe-surfing programs guard against either a preselected list of inappropriate sites or a preselected list of topics—and then block access to sites that meet the selected criteria. Once you have the software installed, your kids won't be able to access the really bad sites on the Web.

The most popular filtering programs include the following:

- CyberPatrol (www.cyberpatrol.com)
- CYBERsitter (www.cybersitter.com)
- Net Nanny (www.netnanny.com)

Microsoft also offers a Family Safety utility as part of its free Windows Live Essential suite of programs. You can download this utility for free from get.live.com. In addition, many of the big Internet security suites (such as those from McAfee and Norton/Symantec) offer built-in content-filtering modules.

note

The Family Safety utility (then called Parental Controls) was built into Windows Vista but unbundled from the core operating system in Windows 7.

Kids-Safe Searching

If you don't want to go to all the trouble of using content-filtering software, you can at least steer your children to some of the safer sites on the Web. The best of these sites offer kid-safe searching so that all inappropriate sites are filtered out of the search results.

The best of these kids-safe search and directory sites include

tip

A kids-safe search site is often good to use as the start page for your children's browser because it is a launching pad to guaranteed safe content.

- AltaVista—AV Family Filter (www.altavista.com; go to the Settings page and click the Family Filter link)
- Ask Kids (www.askkids.com)
- Fact Monster (www.factmonster.com)
- Google SafeSearch (www.google.com; go to the Preferences page and then choose a SafeSearch Filtering option)
- Yahoo! Kids (kids.yahoo.com)

Encouraging Safe Computing

Although using content-filtering software and kids-safe websites are good steps, the most important thing you can do, as a parent, is to create an environment that encourages appropriate use of the Internet. Nothing replaces traditional parental supervision, and at the end of the day, you have to take responsibility for your children's online activities. Provide the guidance they need to make the Internet a fun and educational place to visit—and your entire family will be better for it.

Here are some guidelines you can follow to ensure a safer surfing experience for your family:

- Make sure that your children know never to give out identifying information (home address, school name, telephone number, and so on) or to send their photos to other users online. This includes not putting overly personal information (and photos!) on their MySpace and Facebook pages.
- Provide each of your children with an online pseudonym so they don't have to use their real names online.
- Don't let your children arrange face-to-face meetings with other computer users without parental permission and supervision. If a meeting is arranged, make the first one in a public place and be sure to accompany your child.
- Teach your children that people online might not always be who they seem; just because someone says that she's a 10-year-old girl doesn't necessarily mean that she really is 10 years old, or a girl.

- Consider making Internet surfing an activity you do together with your younger children—or turn it into a family activity by putting your kids' PC in a public room (such as a living room or den) rather than in a private bedroom.

- Set reasonable rules and guidelines for your kids' computer use. Consider limiting the number of minutes/hours they can spend online each day.

- Monitor your children's Internet activities. Ask them to keep a log of all websites they visit or check their browser history; oversee any chat sessions they participate in; check out any files they download; even consider sharing an email account (especially with younger children) so that you can oversee their messages.

- Don't let your children respond to messages that are suggestive, obscene, belligerent, or threatening—or that make them feel uncomfortable in any way. Encourage your children to tell you if they receive any such messages, and then report the senders to your ISP.

- Install content-filtering software on your PC and set up one of the kid-safe search sites (discussed earlier in this section) as your browser's start page.

Teach your children that Internet access is not a right; it should be a privilege earned by your children and kept only when their use of it matches your expectations.

THE ABSOLUTE MINIMUM

Here are the key points to remember from this chapter:

- Avoid computer viruses by not opening unsolicited email attachments and by using an anti-spam software program.

- Use anti-spyware tools, such as Windows Defender, to track down and remove spyware programs from your computer.

- Protect your computer from an Internet-based attack by turning on the Windows Firewall or using a third-party firewall program.

- Fight email spam by keeping your email address as private as possible, upgrading to a newer or more fully featured mail program, and using anti-spam software.

- Avoid falling for phishing scams characterized by fake—but official-looking—email messages.

- To protect against inappropriate content on the Internet, install content-filtering software—and make sure that your children use kid-safe websites.

PART IV

USING COMPUTER SOFTWARE

11

INSTALLING NEW SOFTWARE

Your new computer system probably came with a bunch of programs preinstalled on its hard disk. As useful as these programs are, at some point you're going to want to add something new. Maybe you want to upgrade from Microsoft Works to the more full-featured Microsoft Office. Maybe you want to add some educational software for the kids or a productivity program for yourself. Maybe you just want to play some new computer games.

Whatever type of software you're considering, installing it on your computer system is easy. In most cases software installation is so automatic you don't have to do much more than stick a disc in the CD/DVD drive and click a few onscreen buttons. Even when it isn't that automatic, Windows will walk you through the installation process step-by-step—and you'll be using your new software in no time!

Automatic Installation

Almost all software programs have their own built-in installation programs. Installing the software is as easy as running this built-in program.

If the program you're installing comes on a CD-ROM or DVD, just insert the program's main or installation CD/DVD in your computer's CD/DVD drive. You'll probably see a notification window like the one in Figure 11.1; click the install or setup option.

FIGURE 11.1
You'll see this window when you insert a software installation disc in your computer's CD/DVD drive.

AutoPlay

DVD RW Drive (D:) Home Studio 7

Always do this for software and games:

Install or run program from your media

Run Autorun.exe
Publisher not specified

General options

Open folder to view files
using Windows Explorer

View more AutoPlay options in Control Panel

The program's installation program should then start automatically. All you have to do from here is follow the onscreen instructions—and, if instructed, reboot your computer at the end of the installation process.

Manual Installation

If the installation program *doesn't* start automatically when you insert an installation disc, you have to launch it manually. To do this, click the Start button, select Computer, and then double-click the icon for your CD/DVD drive. This opens the drive and displays the contents of the installation disc. Look for a file called **setup.exe** or **install.exe**; then double-click that file's icon. This launches the software's installation program; follow the onscreen instructions from there.

Installing Software from the Internet

Nowadays, many software publishers make their products available via download from the Internet. Some users like this because they can get their new programs immediately, without having to make a trip to the store.

When you download a program from a major software publisher, the process is generally easy to follow. You probably have to read a page of do's and don'ts, agree to the publisher's licensing agreements, and then click a button to start the download. If you're purchasing a commercial program online, you'll also need to provide your credit card information, of course. Then, after you specify where (which folder on your hard disk) you want to save the downloaded file, the download begins.

When the download is complete, you should be notified via an onscreen dialog box. When prompted, choose to run the program you just downloaded. Follow the onscreen instructions from there.

Sometimes, programs you download from the Internet require the use of ActiveX controls—something that Internet Explorer normally blocks for security reasons. If you go to install a program and nothing happens, look for a message underneath your browser's address bar. If you're sure that this is a legitimate part of the program you're installing, click the message and select Install ActiveX Control from the pop-up menu. The installation should proceed normally from this point.

tip

Most software publishers that offer downloadable software also let you order CD versions of their software—although you might have to pay extra to get a physical copy.

caution

Unless you're downloading a program from a trusted download site, the downloaded file could contain a computer virus. See Chapter 10, "Protecting Your PC from Viruses, Spam, and Other Online Nuisances," for more information.

THE ABSOLUTE MINIMUM

Here are the key points to remember from this chapter:

- Most programs come with their own built-in installation programs; the installation should start automatically when you insert the program's installation CD.

- If the installation program doesn't start automatically, you can launch the program manually by opening your CD/DVD drive from Computer Explorer.

- You also can download some programs from the Internet—just be careful about catching a computer virus!

THE SUITE SPOT: WORKING WITH MICROSOFT WORKS AND MICROSOFT OFFICE

When you first turned on your new PC, you might have been surprised to see your desktop already populated with a bunch of shortcut icons for different programs. These are the programs that were preinstalled by your PC's manufacturer. Which particular programs were pre-installed on your PC depends on what sort of arrangements the PC manufacturer made with the software publishers.

Many PC manufacturers preinstall some sort of software "suite," which is basically a bundle of useful productivity programs. For many users, this suite of programs will be all you need to perform basic computer tasks such as letter writing and number crunching.

The two most popular software suites today are Microsoft Works and Microsoft Office. Some lower-priced computers come with Works pre-installed, while many new computers also come with a trial version of Office—which is a more fully featured suite than the simpler Microsoft Works. We'll take a quick look at both.

Working with Works

Microsoft Works is a suite of five basic applications, all tied together by an interface called the Task Launcher. The key components of Works are

- **Works Word Processor**—A simple word processing program you can use to write letters, memos, and notes.

- **Works Spreadsheet**—A simple spreadsheet program that lets you enter rows and columns of numbers and other data, and then performs basic calculations and analysis on those numbers.

- **Works Database**—A simple database program that functions more-or-less like a giant electronic filing cabinet.

- **Works Calendar**—A schedule management program.

- **Address Book**—An all-purpose contact manager you can use to store names, addresses, phone numbers, and email addresses.

Microsoft's goal with Microsoft Works is to provide an easy-to-use interface to its most-used applications. To that end, when you launch Microsoft Works, the Works Task Launcher appears onscreen. Along the top of the Task Launcher are buttons that link to five different pages; each page represents a different way to enter a program or document.

The Task Launcher's main pages include

- **Home**—The Home page, shown in Figure 12.1, is what you see when you first launch Works Suite. The Home page includes tabs to view your Calendar and Contacts, as well as a Quick Launch bar that lets you launch any Works Suite application directly.

- **Templates**—Use the Templates page to identify a particular type of document you want to create—select the template, and the Task Launcher will launch the appropriate program, with the appropriate template already loaded.

- **Programs**—Use the Programs page to launch a specific Works Suite program—then select the task you want that program to perform.

- **Projects**—Use the Tasks page to create large-scale projects or open preexisting projects—select the project, and the Task Launcher will launch the appropriate program along with a step-by-step wizard to get you started.

- **History**—Use the History page to reload any document you've recently edited with any Works Suite application.

FIGURE 12.1

The Home page of the Works Task Launcher.

When Task Launcher is launched, select a page, select a program or task, and then you're ready to work!

Launching a Program

You use the Programs page to launch individual Works applications. Just follow these steps:

1. From the Works Task Launcher, select the Programs page.

2. From the Choose a Program list, select a program.

3. From the tasks displayed for that program, click a task.

The Task Launcher now launches the program you selected with the appropriate task-based template or wizard loaded.

Creating a New Document

To create a specific type of document—and have Works load the right program for that task, automatically—you use the Templates page, as shown in Figure 12.2. Just follow these steps:

1. From the Works Task Launcher, select the Templates page.

2. From the Choose a Category list, select a particular type of template.

3. From the templates displayed for that category, click a specific template.

note

In older versions of Works, the Templates page is called the Tasks page.

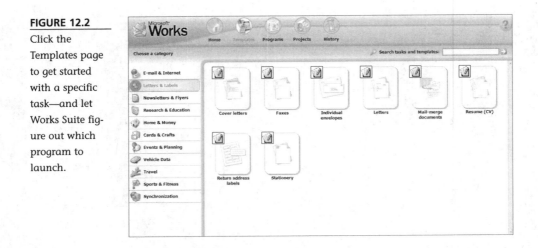

The Task Launcher now launches the appropriate program for your selected template with that template already loaded.

Opening an Existing Document

If you've been working with Works for a while, you can use the History page to reopen documents you previously created.

The History page lists all your recently used files, newest files first. For each file, the Task Launcher includes the filename, the date it was originally created, the type of template it's based on (when known), and the program associated with that file. You can re-sort the list of files by any column by clicking the column header. For example, if you wanted to sort files by name, you would click the Name header; click a second time to sort in the reverse order.

To open a file listed in the History pane, just click its name. Task Launcher will launch the program associated with that file and then load the selected file into the program.

tip

If the file you want isn't listed on the History tab, Task Launcher lets you search for that file. When you click the Find Files and Folders link, Task Launcher displays a Windows file/folder window with the search function enabled. You can use this window to search your entire system for specific files.

Managing a Big Project

Moving? Planning a party? Getting ready for the holidays? Microsoft Works helps you with many big projects by offering a ready-made project planner, complete with suggested tasks for each project. Here's what you do:

1. From the Works Task Launcher, open the Projects page, shown in Figure 12.3.

2. Click the button for the project you want to start.

3. When the individual page appears, click an item in the To Do list to set a Due Date.

4. Click the New To Do button to add new items to the To Do list.

tip

If a specific type of project isn't listed on the Projects page, click the Blank Project button to build your own custom project and To Do list.

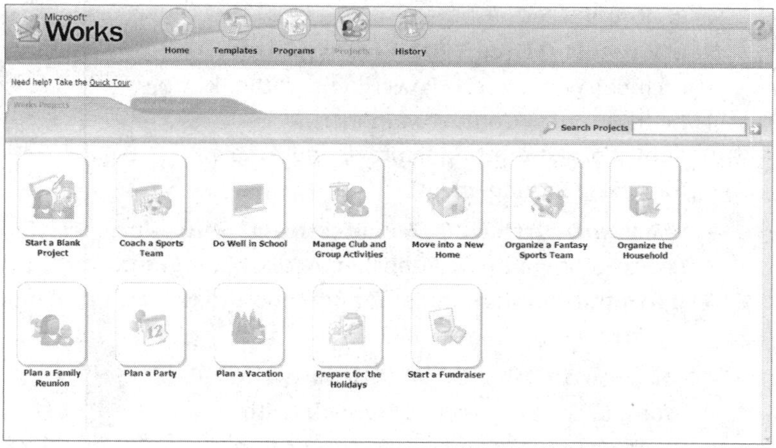

FIGURE 12.3

Open the Projects page to create and manage big projects.

Introducing Microsoft Office

Microsoft Works isn't the only software suite available today. Some manufacturers opt to include other software suites with their new PCs; you can also buy these other applications in standalone versions.

The most-used software suite, especially in the corporate environment, is Microsoft Office, a suite of professional-level applications that are more fully featured than the ones in Works. The latest version of Microsoft Office is Office 2007, although the older Office 2003 version is still widely used.

Office Editions

If you're looking to upgrade to Microsoft Office, know that Microsoft sells several different "editions" of the suite. Each edition contains a different bundle of programs; which Office programs you get depends on the edition of Office you have:

■ **Microsoft Office 2007 Basic**—Includes Microsoft Word (word processor), Excel (spreadsheet), and Outlook (email and scheduling)

- **Microsoft Office 2007 Standard**—Includes Word, Excel, Outlook, and PowerPoint (presentations)

- **Microsoft Office 2007 Home and Student**—Includes Word, Excel, PowerPoint, and OneNote (note organizer)

- **Microsoft Office 2007 Small Business**—Includes Word, Excel, PowerPoint, Outlook (with Business Contact Manager), Publisher (desktop publishing), and Accounting Express (small-business accounting)

- **Microsoft Office 2007 Professional**—Includes Word, Excel, PowerPoint, Outlook (with Business Contact Manager), Publisher, Accounting Express, and Access (database management)

- **Microsoft Office 2007 Professional Plus**—Includes Word, Excel, PowerPoint, Outlook, Publisher, Access, Communicator (instant messaging), InfoPath (information gathering), and server-based content and forms management

- **Microsoft Office 2007 Ultimate**—Includes Word, Excel, PowerPoint, Outlook (with Business Contact Manager), Accounting Express, Publisher, Access, InfoPath, Groove (workgroup collaboration), OneNote, and various enterprise-oriented tools

- **Microsoft Office 2007 Enterprise**—Includes Word, Excel, PowerPoint, Outlook, Publisher, Access, InfoPath, Groove, OneNote, Communicator, and various enterprise-oriented tools

If your new PC comes with Office 2007 chances are it's the Basic or Standard edition. You can always update to another version to obtain additional Office applications.

note

Another office suite you might find preinstalled on some PCs is Corel's WordPerfect suite, which includes the WordPerfect word processor, Quattro Pro spreadsheet, and Paradox database program.

note

Many new PCs come with a trial version of Office (typically the Standard edition) pre-installed. You can use this version for 90 days at no charge; at that point, you have the option of purchasing the software or having the trial version deactivated.

The New Office 2007 Interface

Although Microsoft Office doesn't have a unified launch page, as Works does, all the Office applications share a common interface. In the older Office 2003, this interface looked a lot like that of most other Windows applications. But in Office 2007, Microsoft has upped the ante and provided a completely revamped program interface.

As you can see in Figure 12.4, all Office 2007 interfaces do away with toolbars and menu bars, instead offering a collection of function buttons in a context-sensitive *Ribbon*. Each Ribbon has a series of tabs; select a different tab to view a different collection of function buttons. The Ribbon changes automatically depending on what type of task you're currently performing, so the most common operations should always be at the top of the screen. And all the Office 2007 applications feature a similar Ribbonized experience; whether you use Word, Excel, PowerPoint, or Outlook, the operation is pretty much the same.

FIGURE 12.4

The Office 2007 interface (in Excel), complete with context-sensitive Ribbon.

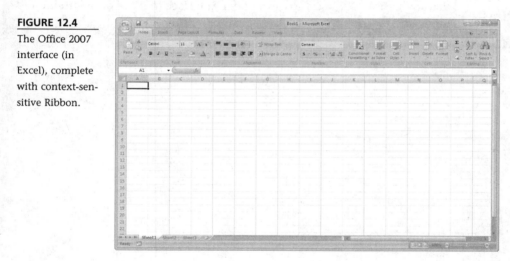

If you're used to Office 2003, the Ribbon approach might be a little confusing at first because almost everything is in a different place. For example, where's the much-used File menu? Well, in Office 2007, most of the File menu functions are found somewhere on the Ribbon, or by clicking the round Office button in the top-left corner. In fact, the menu that's displayed when you click the Office button is pretty much the same as the old File menu—although it's probably just as easy to access the operations directly from the Ribbon.

After you get used to the new interface, using Office 2007 applications is much the same as using their Office 2003 counterparts. And whichever version you're using, Office is a lot more fully featured than Microsoft Works. So if you're using Works but find it somewhat limiting (that is, you can't always get it to do what you want), consider making the upgrade to Office—it's probably worth the money.

THE ABSOLUTE MINIMUM

Here are the key points to remember from this chapter:

- Most new PCs come with a suite or bundle of applications preinstalled—the most popular of which are Microsoft Works and Microsoft Office.

- Works' Task Launcher lets you launch individual programs, create new documents by choosing a particular template or project, open old documents you've worked on, or create and manage big projects.

- If Works can't do what you need it to, upgrade to Microsoft Office—which is Microsoft's more fully featured office suite.

- Different editions of Office include different sets of programs; the Basic edition, preinstalled on most new PCs, includes Microsoft Word, Excel, and Outlook.

- Microsoft Office 2007 sports a new Ribbon interface in place of the traditional menus and toolbars.

13

LETTERS, MEMOS, AND MORE: WORKING WITH MICROSOFT WORD

When you want to write a letter, fire off a quick memo, create a report, or create a newsletter, you use a type of software program called a *word processor*. For most computer users, Microsoft Word is the word processing program of choice. Word is a full-featured word processor, and it's included with Microsoft Office. You can use Word for all your writing needs—from basic letters to fancy newsletters, and everything in between.

Exploring the Word Interface

Before we get started, let's take a quick tour of the Word workspace—so you know what's what and what's where.

You start Word from the Windows Start menu (select Start, All Programs, Microsoft Office, Microsoft Office Word 2007). When Word launches, a blank document appears in the Word workspace.

What's Where in Word

When you open a new document in Word 2007, you see a document contained within a workspace. The key features of the workspace, shown in Figure 13.1, include

- **Title bar**—This is where you find the filename of the current document, as well as buttons to minimize, maximize, and close the window for the current Word document.
- **Ribbon**—In Word 2007, Microsoft has abandoned the traditional menus, toolbars, and sidebars found in previous versions of the program. Instead, it puts all of its functions on what it calls the Ribbon, which is a collection of buttons and controls that run along the top of the Word workspace. Different tabs on the Ribbon display different collections of functions.
- **Document**—This main space displays your current Word document.
- **Scrollbars**—The scrollbar at the bottom of the page lets you scroll left and right through the current page; the scrollbar along the side of the workspace lets you scroll through a document from top to bottom.

Viewing a Word Document—in Different Ways

Word can display your document in one of five different *views*. You select a view by clicking one of the View buttons at the bottom of the Word window.

Each view is a particular way of looking at your document:

- **Draft**—This is primarily a text-based view because certain types of graphics objects—backgrounds, headers and footers, and some pictures—aren't displayed. This is not a good view for laying out the elements on your page.
- **Print Layout**—This is the view you use to lay out the pages of your document—with all elements visible, including graphics and backgrounds.

FIGURE 13.1

The Word 2007 workspace—all functions are found on the Ribbon.

- **Full Screen Reading**—This view makes it easier to read documents that you don't need to edit by hiding all toolbars and resizing the text for better viewing.

- **Web Layout**—This is the view you use when you're creating a document to be displayed on the Web. In this view all the elements in your document (including graphics and backgrounds) are displayed as they would be if viewed by a web browser.

- **Outline**—This is a great view for looking at the structure of your document, presenting your text (but not graphics!) in classic outline fashion. In this view you can collapse an outlined document to see only the main headings or expand a document to show all (or selected) headings and body text.

Zooming to View

If Word displays a document too large or too small for your tastes, it's easy to change the size of the document display using the Zoom slider at the bottom-right corner of the screen. Choose the setting that fits as much of the document onscreen as you want.

Working with Documents

Anything you create with Word is called a *document*. A document is nothing more than a computer file that can be copied, moved, and deleted—or edited—from within Word.

Creating a New Document

Any new Word document you create is based on what Word calls a *template*. A template combines selected styles and document settings—and, in some cases, prewritten text or calculated fields—to create the building blocks for a specific type of document. You can use templates to give yourself a head start on specific types of documents.

To create a new document based on a specific template, follow these steps:

1. Click the Office button and select New.

2. When the New Document window appears, as shown in Figure 13.2, select a type of template from the Templates list on the left side of the window. You can choose from Installed Templates on your PC or additional templates found on Microsoft Office Online.

3. Available templates for that category are now displayed in the middle pane of the window, and a sample document appears in the preview pane on the right. Double-click the template you want to use.

note

If you select a template from Microsoft Office Online, that template will be downloaded to your PC—which means you must be connected to the Internet to use the selected template.

If you don't know which template to use for your new document, just select Blank and Recent from the Templates list, and then select Blank Document. This opens a new document using Word's Normal template. This is a basic template, with just a few text styles defined—a good starting point for any new document.

Opening an Existing Document

To open a previously created document, click the Office button and select Open. When the Open dialog box appears, navigate to and select the file you want to open; then click the Open button.

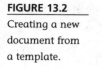

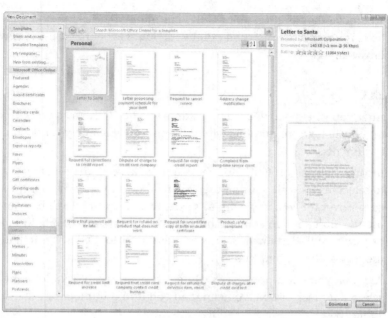

Saving the Document

Every document you make—that you want to keep—must be saved to a file.

The first time you save a file, you have to specify a filename and location. Do this by clicking the Office button and selecting Save As. When the Save As dialog box appears, select a file format, click the Browse Folders button to select a location to save the file, and then enter a filename and click the Save button.

When you make additional changes to a document, you must save those changes. Fortunately, after you've saved a file once, you don't need to go through the whole Save As routine again. To "fast save" an existing file, all you have to do is click the Save button on the Quick Access toolbar. Alternatively, you can click the Office button and then select Save.

Working with Text

Now that you know how to create and save Word documents, let's examine how you put specific words on paper—or, rather, onscreen.

Entering Text

You enter text in a Word document at the *insertion point*, which appears onscreen as a blinking cursor. When you start typing on your keyboard, the new text is added at the insertion point.

You move the insertion point with your mouse by clicking on a new position in your text. You move the insertion point with your keyboard by using your keyboard's arrow keys.

Editing Text

After you've entered your text, it's time to edit. With Word you can delete, cut, copy, and paste text—or graphics—to and from anywhere in your document or between documents.

Before you can edit text, though, you have to *select* the text to edit. The easiest way to select text is with your mouse; just hold down your mouse button and drag the cursor over the text you want to select. You also can select text using your keyboard; use the Shift key—in combination with other keys—to highlight blocks of text. For example, Shift+left arrow selects one character to the left; Shift+End selects all text to the end of the current line.

Any text you select appears as white text against a black highlight. After you've selected a block of text, you can then edit it in a number of ways, as detailed in Table 13.1.

TABLE 13.1   Word Editing Operations

Operation	Keystroke
Delete	Del
Copy	Ctrl+Ins or Ctrl+C
Cut	Shift+Del or Ctrl+X
Paste	Shift+Ins or Ctrl+V

Formatting Text

After your text is entered and edited, you can use Word's numerous formatting options to add some pizzazz to your document. It's easiest to edit text when you're working in Print Layout view because this displays your document as it will look when printed. To switch to this view, select the View Ribbon and click Print Layout.

Formatting text is easy—and most achievable from the Home Ribbon in Word 2007. Both of these items include buttons for bold, italic, and underline, as well as font, font size, and font color. To format a block of text, highlight the text and then click the desired format button.

Checking Spelling and Grammar

If you're not a great speller, you'll appreciate Word's automatic spell checking. You can see it right onscreen; just deliberately misspell a word, and you'll see a squiggly red line under the misspelling. That's Word telling you you've made a spelling error.

When you see that squiggly red line, position your cursor on top of the misspelled word and then right-click your mouse. Word now displays a pop-up menu with its suggestions for spelling corrections. You can choose a replacement word from the list or return to your document and manually change the misspelling.

Sometimes Word meets a word it doesn't recognize, even though the word is spelled correctly. In these instances, you can add the new word to Word's spelling dictionary by right-clicking the word and selecting Add from the pop-up menu.

Word also includes a built-in grammar checker. When Word identifies bad grammar in your document, it underlines the offending passage with a green squiggly line. Right-click anywhere in the passage to view Word's grammatical suggestions.

Printing a Document

When you've finished editing your document, you can instruct Word to send a copy to your printer.

Previewing Before You Print

It's a good idea, however, to preview the printed document onscreen before you print it—so you can make any last-minute changes without wasting a lot of paper.

To view your document with Word's Print Preview, click the Office button and select Print, Print Preview. The to-be-printed document appears onscreen with each page of the document presented as a small thumbnail. To zoom in or out of the preview document, click the Magnifier button and then click the magnifier cursor anywhere on your document. When you're done previewing your document, click the Close button.

Basic Printing

The fastest way to print a document is with Word's quick print option. You activate a fast print by clicking the Office button and selecting Print, Quick Print.

When you do a fast print of your document, you send your document directly to your default printer. This bypasses the Print dialog box (discussed next) and all other configuration options.

Changing Print Options

Sometimes fast printing isn't the best way to print. For example, you might want to print multiple copies or print to a different (nondefault) printer. For these and similar situations, you need to use Word's Print dialog box.

You open the Print dialog box, shown in Figure 13.3, by clicking the Office button and selecting Print, Print.

Select Your Printer

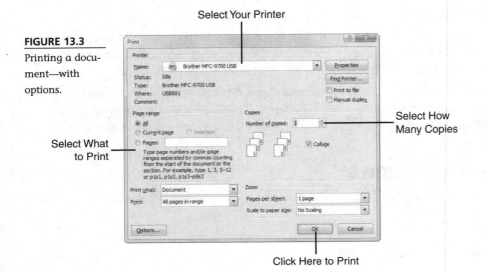

FIGURE 13.3
Printing a document—with options.

Select What to Print

Select How Many Copies

Click Here to Print

After you have the Print dialog box displayed, you can choose any one of a number of options specific to this particular print job. After you've made your choices, click the OK button to start printing.

Formatting Your Document

When you're creating a complex document, you need to format more than just a few words here and there.

Formatting Paragraphs

When you need to format complete paragraphs, you use the Page Layout Ribbon. Just click the Page Layout tab on the Ribbon, and you'll see all manner of page formatting options—margins, orientation, columns, page color, borders, and so forth.

Using Word Styles

If you have a preferred paragraph formatting you use over and over and over, you don't have to format each paragraph individually. Instead, you can assign all your formatting to a paragraph *style* and then assign that style to specific paragraphs throughout your document. Most templates come with a selection of predesigned styles; you can modify these built-in styles or create your own custom styles.

Styles include formatting for fonts, paragraphs, tabs, borders, numbering, and more. To apply a style to a paragraph, position the insertion point anywhere in the paragraph and then click the style you want in the Styles section of the Ribbon. You can select a different set of styles by clicking the Change Styles button, selecting Style Set, and then making a selection.

Working with an Outline

If you have a really long document, you might find it easier to work with the various sections in the form of an outline. For this purpose, Word lets you view your document in Outline view, as shown in Figure 13.4. Just click the Outline button at the bottom of the Word window.

FIGURE 13.4

Use Outline view to reorganize the sections of your document.

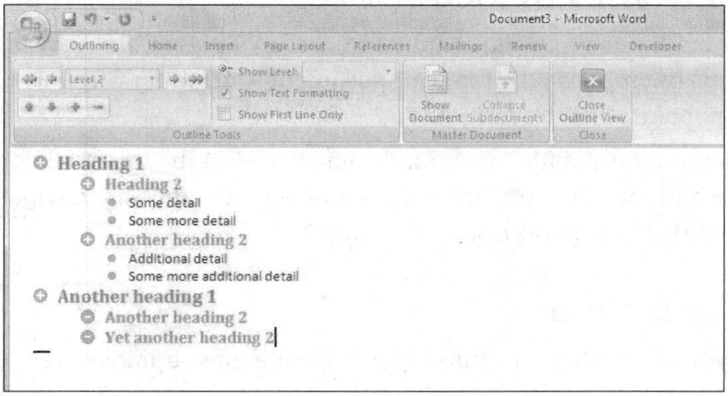

When you're in Outline view, Word displays your headings as different outline levels. Text formatted with the Heading 1 style appears as Level 1 headings in your outline, text formatted as Heading 2 appears as Level 2 headings, and so on.

To make your outline easier to work with, you can select how many levels of headings are displayed. (Just pull down the Outline Level list and select the appropriate level number.) You also can choose to expand or contract various sections of the outline by clicking the plus and minus icons to the side of each level text in your outline.

Outline view makes rearranging sections of your document extremely easy. When you're in Outline view, you can move an entire section from one place to another by selecting the Level heading and then clicking the up and down arrow buttons. (You also can drag sections from one position to another within the outline.)

Working with Pictures

Although memos and letters might look fine if they contain nothing but text, other types of documents—newsletters, reports, and so on—can be jazzed up with pictures and other graphics elements.

Inserting a Picture from the Clip Art Gallery

The easiest way to add a graphic to your document is to use Word's built-in Clip Art Gallery. The Clip Art Gallery is a collection of ready-to-use illustrations and photos, organized by topic, that can be pasted directly into your Word documents.

To insert a piece of clip art, select the Insert Ribbon and click the Clip Art button; this displays the Clip Art pane. Enter one or more keywords into the Search For box; then click Search. Pictures matching your criteria are now displayed in the pane. Double-click a graphic to insert it into your document.

Inserting Other Types of Picture Files

You're not limited to using graphics from the Clip Art Gallery. Word lets you insert any type of graphics file into your document—including GIF, JPG, BMP, TIF, and other popular graphics formats.

To insert a graphics file into your document, select the Insert Ribbon and click the Picture button. When the Insert Picture dialog box appears, navigate to and select the picture you want to insert; then click Insert.

Formatting the Picture

After you've inserted a picture in your document, you might need to format it for best appearance.

To format the picture, start by clicking the picture. This displays the Format Ribbon, shown in Figure 13.5. From here you can select different types of picture frames, change the picture's brightness and contrast, edit the position and text wrapping of the picture, and even crop the picture to a new size.

To move your picture to another position in your document, use your mouse to drag it to its new position. You also can resize the graphic by clicking the picture and then dragging a selection handle to resize that side or corner of the graphic.

FIGURE 13.5

Use the Format Ribbon to edit and format your picture.

THE ABSOLUTE MINIMUM

Here are the key points to remember from this chapter:

- Microsoft Word is a powerful word processing program included with Microsoft Office.

- The Word 2007 workspace replaces menus, toolbars, and sidebars with a tabbed Ribbon; this Ribbon contains buttons and controls for all program functions.

- You can view a Word document in several different ways. The most useful views are the Draft (Normal) and Print Layout views; you can also use the Outline view to display your document as a hierarchical outline.

- If you reuse similar formatting throughout your document, consider using a Word style to apply similar formatting to multiple paragraphs.

- Insert clip art or graphics files by using the Insert Ribbon; you can edit the graphic by using the Format Ribbon.

14

CRUNCHING NUMBERS: WORKING WITH MICROSOFT EXCEL

When you're on your computer and want to crunch some numbers, you use a program called a *spreadsheet*. There are several different spreadsheet programs available for your personal computer, but by far the most popular spreadsheet among both casual and serious number crunchers is Microsoft Excel. Excel is included as part of the Microsoft Office suite and is the spreadsheet program we'll examine in this chapter.

Understanding Spreadsheets

A spreadsheet is nothing more than a giant list. Your list can contain just about any type of data you can think of—text, numbers, and even dates. You can take any of the numbers on your list and use them to calculate new numbers. You can sort the items on your list, pretty them up, and print the important points in a report. You can even graph your numbers in a pie, line, or bar chart!

All spreadsheet programs work in pretty much the same fashion. In a spreadsheet, everything is stored in little boxes called *cells*. Your spreadsheet is divided into lots of these cells, each located in a specific location on a giant grid made of *rows* and *columns*. Each cell represents the intersection of a particular row and column.

> **note**
>
> This chapter covers Microsoft Excel 2007. If you have an older version of Excel, some operations might be slightly different.

As you can see in Figure 14.1, each column has an alphabetic label (A, B, C, and so on). Each row, on the other hand, has a numeric label (1, 2, 3, and so on). The location of each cell is the combination of its column and row locations. For example, the cell in the upper-left corner of the spreadsheet is in column A and row 1; therefore, its location is signified as A1. The cell to the right of it is B1, and the cell below A1 is A2. The location of the selected, or *active*, cell is displayed in the Name box.

FIGURE 14.1

An Excel spreadsheet—divided into many rows and columns.

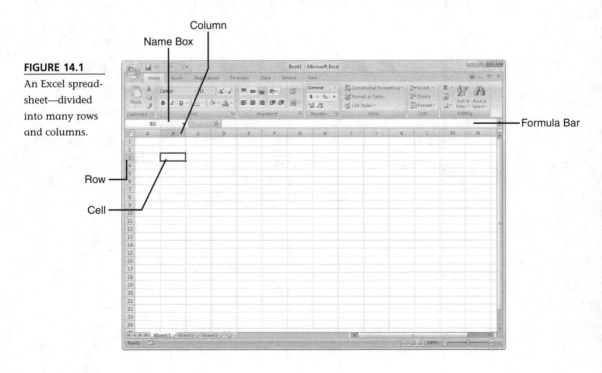

Column

Name Box

Formula Bar

Row

Cell

Next to the Name box is the Formula bar, which echoes the contents of the active cell. You can type data directly into either the Formula bar or active cell.

Entering Data

Entering text or numbers into a spreadsheet is easy. Just remember that data is entered into each cell individually—then you can fill up a spreadsheet with hundreds or thousands of cells filled with their own data.

To enter data into a specific cell, follow these steps:

1. Select the cell you want to enter data into.
2. Type your text or numbers into the cell; what you type will be echoed in the Formula bar at the top of the screen.
3. When you're done typing data into the cell, press Enter.

Inserting and Deleting Rows and Columns

Sometimes you need to go back to an existing spreadsheet and insert some new information.

Insert a Row or Column

To insert a new row or column in the middle of your spreadsheet, follow these steps:

1. Click the row or column header *that directly follows* where you want to make the insertion.
2. Go to the Cells section of the Ribbon and click the down arrow below the Insert button; then select either Insert Sheet Rows or Insert Sheet Columns.

Excel now inserts a new row or column either above or to the left of the row or column you selected.

Delete a Row or Column

To delete an existing row or column, follow these steps:

1. Click the header for the row or column you want to delete.
2. Go to the Cells section of the Ribbon and click the Delete button.

The row or column you selected is deleted, and all other rows or columns move up or over to fill the space.

Adjusting Column Width

If the data you enter into a cell is too long, you'll only see the first part of that data— there'll be a bit to the right that looks cut off. It's not cut off, of course; it just can't be seen since it's longer than the current column is wide.

You can fix this problem by adjusting the column width. Wider columns allow more data to be shown; narrow columns let you display more columns per page.

To change the column width, move your cursor to the column header and position it on the dividing line on the right side of the column you want to adjust. When the cursor changes shape, click the left button on your mouse and drag the column divider to the right (to make a wider column) or to the left (to make a smaller column). Release the mouse button when the column is the desired width.

tip

To make a column the exact width for the longest amount of data entered, position your cursor over the dividing line to the right of the column header and double-click your mouse. This makes the column width automatically "fit" your current data.

Using Formulas and Functions

Excel lets you enter just about any type of algebraic formula into any cell. You can use these formulas to add, subtract, multiply, divide, and perform any nested combination of those operations.

Creating a Formula

Excel knows that you're entering a formula when you type an equal sign (=) into any cell. You start your formula with the equal sign and enter your operations *after* the equal sign.

For example, if you want to add 1 plus 2, enter this formula into a cell: **=1+2**. When you press Enter, the formula disappears from the cell—and the result, or *value*, is displayed.

Basic Operators

Table 14.1 shows the algebraic operators you can use in Excel formulas.

TABLE 14.1 Excel Operators

Operation	Operator
Add	+
Subtract	–
Multiply	*
Divide	/

So if you want to multiply 10 by 5, enter **=10*5**. If you want to divide 10 by 5, enter **=10/5**.

Including Other Cells in a Formula

If all you're doing is adding and subtracting numbers, you might as well use a calculator. Where a spreadsheet becomes truly useful is when you use it to perform operations based on the contents of specific cells.

To perform calculations using values from cells in your spreadsheet, you enter the cell location into the formula. For example, if you want to add cells A1 and A2, enter this formula: **=A1+A2**. And if the numbers in either cell A1 or A2 change, the total will automatically change, as well.

An even easier way to perform operations involving spreadsheet cells is to select them with your mouse while you're entering the formula. To do this, follow these steps:

1. Select the cell that will contain the formula.
2. Type =.
3. Click the first cell you want to include in your formula; that cell location is automatically entered in your formula.
4. Type an algebraic operator, such as +, –, *, or /.
5. Click the second cell you want to include in your formula.
6. Repeat steps 4 and 5 to include other cells in your formula.
7. Press Enter when your formula is complete.

Quick Addition with AutoSum

The most common operation in any spreadsheet is the addition of a group of numbers. Excel makes summing up a row or column of numbers easy via the AutoSum function.

All you have to do is follow these steps:

1. Select the cell at the end of a row or column of numbers, where you want the total to appear.

2. Click the AutoSum button in the Editing section of the Ribbon, as shown in Figure 14.2.

Excel automatically sums all the preceding numbers and places the total in the selected cell.

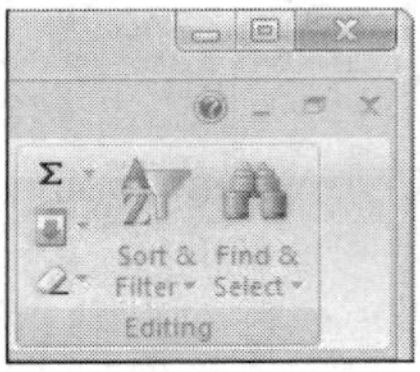

FIGURE 14.2

Click the AutoSum button to automatically add a row or column of numbers.

Other AutoSum Operations

Excel's AutoSum also includes a few other automatic calculations. When you click the down arrow on the side of the AutoSum button, you can perform the following operations:

- **Average**, which calculates the average of the selected cells
- **Count Numbers**, which counts the number of selected cells
- **Max**, which returns the largest value in the selected cells
- **Min**, which returns the smallest value in the selected cells

tip

When you're referencing consecutive cells in a formula, you can just enter the first and last number or the series separated by a colon. For example, cells A1 through A4 can be entered as A1:A4.

Using Functions

In addition to the basic algebraic operators previously discussed, Excel includes a variety of *functions* that replace the complex steps present in many formulas. For example, if you wanted to total all the cells in column A, you could enter the formula **=A1+A2+A3+A4**. Or, you could use the SUM function, which lets you sum a column or row of numbers without having to type every cell into the formula. (And when you use AutoSum, it's simply applying the SUM function.)

In short, a function is a type of prebuilt formula.

You enter a function in the following format: **=function(argument)**, where **function** is the name of the function and **argument** is the range of cells or other data you want to calculate. Using the last example, to sum cells A1 through A4, you'd use the following function-based formula: **=sum(A1,A2,A3,A4)**.

Excel includes hundreds of functions. You can access and insert any of Excel's functions by following these steps:

1. Select the cell where you want to insert the function.

2. Select the Formulas Ribbon, shown in Figure 14.3.

3. From here you can click a function category to see all the functions of a particular type, or you can click the Insert Function button to display the Function dialog box. Select the function you want.

4. If the function has related arguments, a Function Arguments dialog box is now displayed; enter the arguments and click OK.

5. The function you selected is now inserted into the current cell. You can now manually enter the cells or numbers into the function's argument.

FIGURE 14.3

Choose from hundreds of functions on the Formulas Ribbon.

Sorting a Range of Cells

If you have a list of either text or numbers, you might want to reorder the list for a different purpose. Excel lets you sort your data by any column, in either ascending or descending order.

To sort a range of cells, follow these steps:

1. Select all the cells you want to sort.

2. Click the Sort & Filter button in the Ribbon; then select how you want to sort—A to Z, Z to A, or in a custom order (Custom Sort).

3. If you select Custom Sort, you'll see the Sort dialog box, shown in Figure 14.4. From here you can select various levels of sorting; select which column to sort by and the order from which to sort. Click the Add Level button to sort on additional columns.

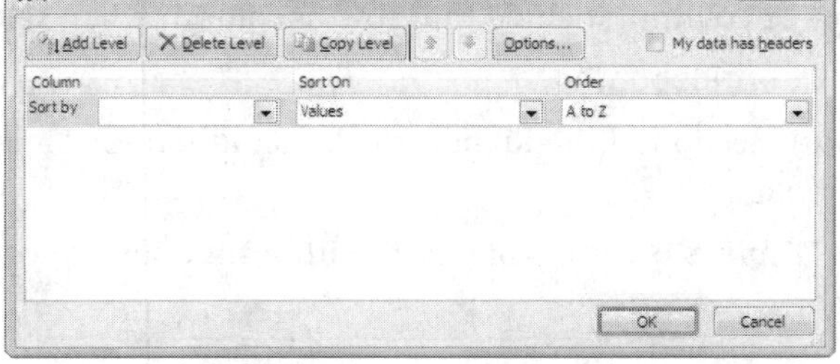

FIGURE 14.4

Sort your list by any column in any order.

Formatting Your Spreadsheet

You don't have to settle for boring-looking spreadsheets. You can format how the data appears in your spreadsheet—including the format of any numbers you enter.

Applying Number Formats

When you enter a number into a cell, Excel applies what it calls a "general" format to the number—it just displays the number, right-aligned, with no commas or dollar signs. You can, however, select a specific number format to apply to any cells in your spreadsheet that contain numbers.

All of Excel's number formatting options are in the Number section of the Ribbon. Click the dollar sign button to choose an accounting format, the percent button to choose a percentage format, the comma button to choose a comma format, or the General button to choose from all available formats. You can also click the Increase Decimal and Decrease Decimal buttons to move the decimal point left or right.

Formatting Cell Contents

You can also apply a variety of other formatting options to the contents of your cells. You can make your text bold or italic, change the font type or size, or even add shading or borders to selected cells.

These formatting options are found in the Font and Alignment sections of the Ribbon. Just select the cell(s) you want to format; then click the appropriate formatting button.

Creating a Chart

Numbers are fine, but sometimes the story behind the numbers can be better told through a picture. The way you take a picture of numbers is with a *chart*, such as the one shown in Figure 14.5.

You create a chart based on numbers you've previously entered into your Excel spreadsheet. It works like this:

1. Select the range of cells you want to include in your chart. (If the range has a header row or column, include that row or column when selecting the cells.)
2. Select the Insert Ribbon.
3. In the Charts section of the Ribbon, click the button for the type of chart you want to create.
4. Excel now displays a variety of charts within that general category. Select the type of chart you want.

FIGURE 14.5

Some numbers are better represented via a chart.

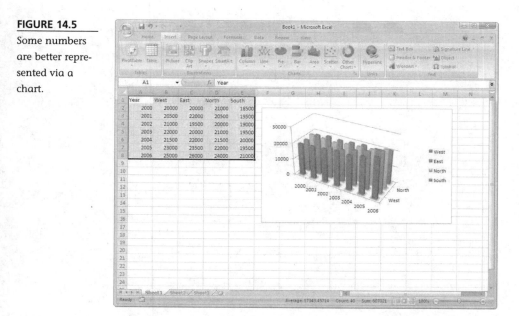

5. When the chart appears in your worksheet, select the Design Ribbon to edit the chart's type, layout, and style; or select the Layout Ribbon to edit the chart's labels, axes, and background.

THE ABSOLUTE MINIMUM

Here are the key points to remember from this chapter:

- Excel is by far the most widely used spreadsheet program today.

- A spreadsheet is composed of rows and columns; the intersection of a specific row and column is called a cell.

- Each cell can contain text, numbers, or formulas.

- You start an Excel formula with an = sign and follow it up with specific numbers (or cell locations) and operators—such as +, –, *, and /.

- To graphically display your spreadsheet data, use Excel 2007's Insert Ribbon.

15

Presenting Yourself: Working with Microsoft PowerPoint

When you need to present information to a group of people, the hip way to do it is with a PowerPoint presentation. Whether you use an overhead projector, traditional slides, or a computer projector, PowerPoint can help you create great-looking graphic and bullet-point presentations.

If you work in an office, you probably see at least one PowerPoint presentation a week—if not one a day. Teachers use PowerPoint to present lesson materials in class. Kids even use PowerPoint to prepare what used to be oral reports.

So get with the program—and learn how to create your own great-looking presentations with PowerPoint!

Understanding Microsoft PowerPoint

Microsoft PowerPoint is a presentation program included with most versions of Microsoft Office. We'll look at the latest version of the program, PowerPoint 2007.

The PowerPoint Workspace

As you can see in Figure 15.1, PowerPoint 2007 looks like most other Office 2007 applications. The workspace is dominated by the Ribbon at the top of the screen, with the current slide displayed in the middle.

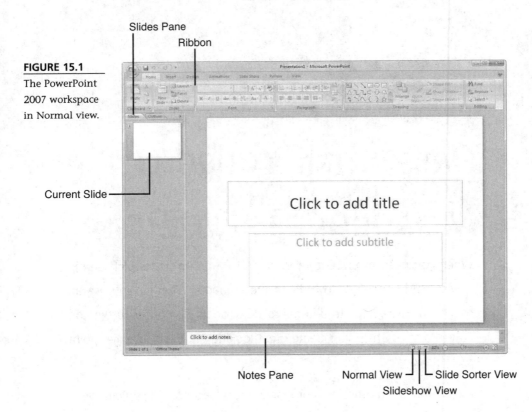

FIGURE 15.1
The PowerPoint 2007 workspace in Normal view.

On the left side of the workspace is something unique to PowerPoint—the Slides/Outline pane, which displays all the slides in your presentation in either text (Outline) or graphic (Slides) views. Below the current slide is a Notes pane, which lets you enter presentation notes. And at the very bottom of the window, near the right-hand corner, are the View buttons, which you use to switch between different views of your presentation.

Changing Views

The default view of the PowerPoint workspace is called, not surprising, Normal view. PowerPoint offers three different ways to view your presentation, all selectable from either the View buttons or the View menu. These views include

- **Normal**, which is the default view complete with Outline/Slides and Notes panes.
- **Slide Sorter**, which displays thumbnails of all the slides in your presentation.
- **Slide Show**, which launches a live full-screen "slideshow" of your entire presentation.

Creating a New Presentation

When you launch PowerPoint, a blank presentation is loaded and ready for your input. If you'd rather create a presentation based on a predesigned template (more on these next), click the Office button and select New; this displays the New Presentation window, which lets you choose from a list of available templates. Click a template to get started.

Applying a Theme

You don't have to reinvent the wheel when it comes to designing the look of your presentation. PowerPoint 2007 includes a number of slide *themes* that you can apply to any presentation, blank or otherwise. A theme specifies the color scheme, fonts, layout, and background for each slide you create in your presentation.

To apply a new theme to your current presentation, select the Design Ribbon (shown in Figure 15.2) and select a new theme from the Themes section. Make sure that you scroll through all available themes; you can also choose to apply only color, font, and effect schemes by using the controls to the right of the Themes section.

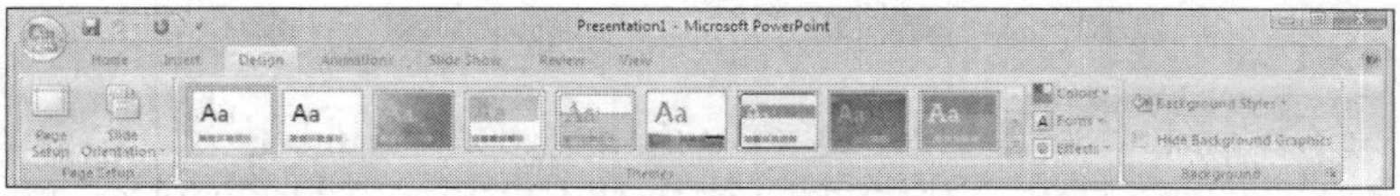

FIGURE 15.2
Use the Design Ribbon to apply a new theme to your presentation.

It's that simple. All the colors, fonts, and everything else from the theme are automatically applied to all the slides in your presentation—and every new slide you add will also carry the selected design.

Inserting New Slides

When you create a new presentation, PowerPoint starts with a single slide—the *title slide*. Naturally, you'll need to insert additional slides to create a complete presentation. PowerPoint lets you insert different types of slides, with different types of layouts for different types of information.

To insert a new slide, follow these steps:

1. Click the down button below the New Slide button on the Ribbon.

2. A variety of different slide layouts are now displayed in a drop-down visual menu; click the type of slide you want to insert.

Continue adding as many slides as you need to complete your presentation.

Working from an Outline

Rather than creating a presentation one slide at a time, some people find it easier to outline their entire presentation in advance. To this end, PowerPoint offers the Outline pane, located at the left of the workspace. Select the Outline tab, and PowerPoint displays each slide of your presentation in outline fashion.

To enter text for an outline level, all you have to do is type. To add another slide in your outline, press the Enter key. To add bullet text to a slide, press the Tab key. To add a sub-bullet, press Tab again. When you're done entering bullets, press Shift+Tab to move up the hierarchy and create a new slide.

Adding Text

As you've just seen, one way to add text to your slides is via the Outline pane. You can also enter text directly into each slide. When PowerPoint creates a new slide, the areas for text entry are designated with boilerplate text—"Click to add title" (for the slide's title) or "Click to add text" (for regular text or bullet points). Adding text is as easy as clicking the boilerplate text and then entering your own words and numbers. Press Enter to move to a new line or bullet. To enter a sub-bullet, press the Tab key first; to back up a level, press Shift+Tab.

Formatting Your Slides

You've already seen how to use design templates to format your entire presentation in one go. You can also format slides individually.

Formatting Text

Formatting text on a slide is just like formatting text in a word processing document. Select the text you want to format, and then click the appropriate button in the Font section of the Ribbon.

Changing Backgrounds

Don't like the slide background from the current template? Then change it! You can create single-color backgrounds, backgrounds that gradate between two different colors, and even backgrounds that incorporate a graphic or photograph.

To apply a new background to all the slides in your PowerPoint 2007 presentation, simply select the Design Ribbon and click the Background Styles button. This displays a variety of different backgrounds; select the one you want, and it will be applied to your entire presentation.

If you want even more background options, click the Background Styles button and then select the Format Background option. This displays the Format Background dialog box, shown in Figure 15.3, where you can choose from various types of fill and picture backgrounds.

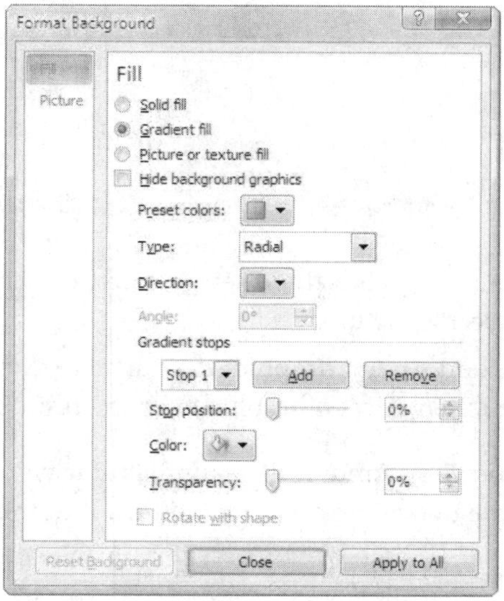

> **tip**
>
> One of the unique formatting operations possible with PowerPoint is the Shadow effect, which you add by clicking the S button on the Ribbon or on the Formatting toolbar. This adds a drop shadow behind the selected text, which can really make the text "pop" off a colored or textured background.

FIGURE 15.3

Use the Format Background dialog box to apply sophisticated slide backgrounds.

Adding Graphics

An all-text presentation is a little boring. To spice up your slides, you need to add some graphics!

Inserting Pictures

You can insert any type of drawing or photograph into a PowerPoint slide. It's easiest to start with a slide layout that anticipates the addition of a picture, however. Follow these steps:

1. From a blank slide, go to the Slides section of the Ribbon and click the Layout button; then select the Title and Content layout. This formats the slide as shown in Figure 15.4, ready to accept different types of content.

2. To add clip art to the slide, click the Clip Art icon; then search for the clip art you want from the Clip Art pane.

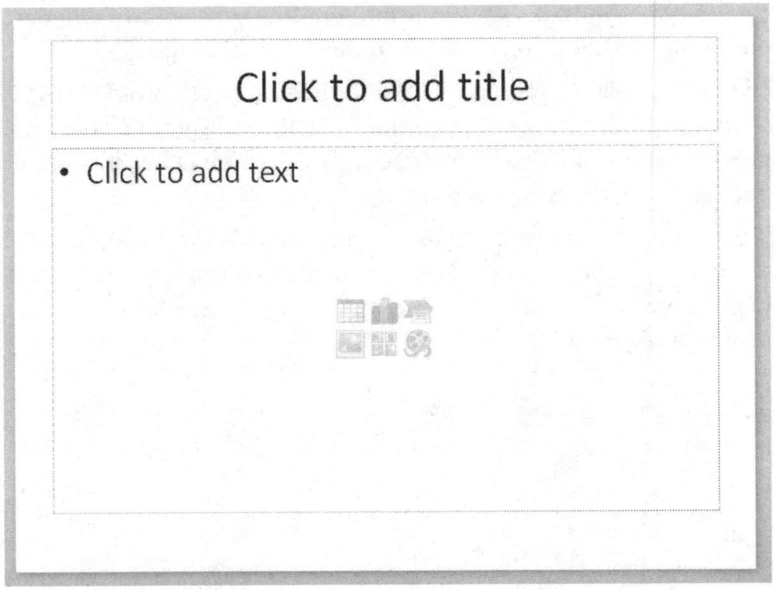

FIGURE 15.4

A slide formatted with the Title and Content layout.

3. To add a picture to your slide, click the Insert Picture from File icon; then navigate to and select a specific picture.

4. To add icons, buttons, and similar graphics to your slide, click the Insert SmallArt Graphic icon; then select a graphic from the resulting dialog box.

After the graphic is added, you can format it in a number of ways. To rotate the graphic, grab the green handle above the graphic and turn it to the left or right. To recolor the graphic, add a border style, insert a drop shadow, or crop the graphic, select the Design Ribbon and use the options there.

Creating Charts

Another way to spice up your presentation is to display numerical data in chart format, as shown in Figure 15.5. The easiest way to create a chart in PowerPoint 2007 is to start with the Title and Content slide layout and then follow these steps:

1. Click the chart icon.

2. When the Insert Chart dialog box appears, choose a chart type.

3. An Excel spreadsheet now opens onscreen. Enter the data for your chart into this spreadsheet and close the spreadsheet when you're finished.

4. Your chart now appears on the slide. Select the Design Ribbon to select a different chart layout or style, or use the Layout Ribbon to format different aspects of the chart.

FIGURE 15.5

Adding a chart to your presentation.

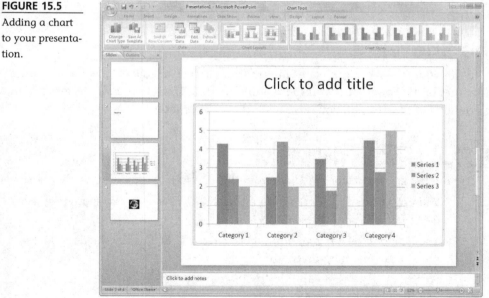

Applying Slide Animations

If you're presenting your slideshow electronically, via a computer attached to a large monitor or projector, you need to do one more thing—add animated transitions between each slide. PowerPoint lets you use a wide variety of slide transitions, all of which are more interesting than just cutting from one slide to the next.

To apply animated transitions in PowerPoint 2007, select the Animations Ribbon, shown in Figure 15.6. Select from the wide variety of transitions in the Transition to This Slide section; make sure that you click the scrollbar to view all the available transitions.

You can also use the Animations Ribbon to apply a sound to the transition or to adjust the transition speed. You can apply this transition to all slides or just to selected slides. Have fun!

tip

You don't have to use the same transitions on every slide. Your presentation will have more visual interest if you use a variety of transitions throughout.

FIGURE 15.6
Choosing transitions from PowerPoint's Animations Ribbon.

Start the Show!

To run your slideshow, complete with transitions, click the Slide Show button at the bottom of the PowerPoint workspace or on the Slide Transition pane. To move from one slide to the next, all you have to do is click your mouse.

THE ABSOLUTE MINIMUM

Here are the key points to remember from this chapter:

- You use Microsoft PowerPoint to create slides, overhead transparencies, and electronic slideshow presentations.

- The look and feel of your entire presentation is defined by the design template or theme that you choose.

- Each slide you insert can have a different layout, depending on its function.

- A slide can include text, bullets, pictures, and charts.

- When you're presenting an electronic slideshow, add animated transitions between each slide.

PART V

USING THE INTERNET

16

CONNECTING TO THE INTERNET AT HOME AND ON THE ROAD

It used to be that most people bought personal computers to do work—word processing, spreadsheets, databases, the sort of programs that still make up the core of Microsoft Works and Microsoft Office. But today, people also buy PCs to access the Internet—to send and receive email, surf the Web, and chat with other users.

Different Types of Connections

The first step in going online is establishing a connection between your computer and the Internet. To do this, you have to sign up with an Internet service provider (ISP), which, as the name implies, provides your home with a connection to the Internet.

Depending on what's available in your area, you can choose from two primary types of connections—dial-up or broadband. Dial-up is both the oldest and the slowest type of connection; quite frankly, a dial-up connection is too slow for many of the things people like to do online today, such as view YouTube videos and listen to streaming music. Broadband connections are much faster and therefore much more popular today. If you have the option, it's worth paying a few extra dollars a month to get the faster broadband connection.

Whichever type of connection you choose, you'll connect your PC to a *modem*, which will then connect to the phone or cable line coming into your house. Most PCs have a built-in dial-up modem; if you choose broadband service, you'll get an external broadband modem from your ISP. Read on to learn more.

Traditional Dial-Up

A dial-up connection provides Internet service over normal phone lines. The fastest dial-up connections transmit data at 56.6Kbps (kilobits per second), which is okay for normal web surfing but isn't fast enough for downloading music or videos. Most ISPs charge $10 to $20 per month for normal dial-up service.

Broadband DSL

DSL is a phone line-based technology that operates at broadband speeds. DSL service piggybacks onto your existing phone line, turning it into a high-speed digital connection. Not only is DSL faster than dial-up (384Kbps to 3Mbps, depending on your ISP), you don't have to surrender your normal phone line when you want to surf; DSL connections are "always on." Most providers offer DSL service for $30–$50 per month. Look for package deals that offer a discount when you subscribe to both Internet and phone services.

Broadband Cable

Another popular type of broadband connection is available from your local cable company. Broadband cable Internet piggybacks on your normal cable television line, providing speeds in the 500Kbps to 30Mbps range, depending on the provider. Most cable companies offer broadband cable Internet for $30–$50 per month, which is about the same as you pay for a similar DSL connection. As with DSL, look for package deals for your cable company, offering some sort of discount on a combination of Internet, cable, and (sometimes) digital phone service.

Broadband Satellite

If you can't get DSL or cable Internet in your area, you have another option—connecting to the Internet via satellite. Any household or business with a clear line of sight to the southern sky can receive digital data signals from a geosynchronous satellite at speeds ranging from 1Mbps to 5Mbps.

The largest provider of satellite Internet access is HughesNet. (Hughes also developed and markets the popular DIRECTV digital satellite system.) The HughesNet system (www.hughesnet.com) enables you to receive Internet signals via a small dish that you mount outside your house or on your roof. Fees range from $60 to $350 per month, with the typical home plan priced under $100.

Before You Connect

When you sign up with an ISP, both you and the ISP have to provide certain information to each other. You provide the ISP your name, address, and credit card number; in return, your ISP provides you a variety of semi-technical information, including

- Your username and password
- Your email address
- Your email account name and password
- The names of the ISP's incoming and outgoing mail servers (which you'll need to set up your email program)
- The phone number to dial into (if you're using a dial-up connection)

You'll need this information when you configure Windows for your new Internet connection—which we'll discuss next.

note

There's a new type of Internet service called Fiber Optic Service (FiOS). As the name implies, this delivers an Internet connection over a fiber optic network. FiOS connection speeds are similar to those of broadband cable; pricing is also similar. In the home, the FiOS line is connected to a modem-like device called an optical network terminal (ONT) that can split the signal to provide a combination of Internet, television, and telephone service; you typically connect the ONT to your router or PC via Ethernet. In the U.S., FiOS Internet service is available through AT&T and Verizon, in limited areas.

tip

For most ISPs, your username, email account name, and the first half of your email address will all be the same. It's also likely that you will be assigned a single password for both your initial login and email access.

Setting Up a New Connection

Naturally, you need to configure your computer to work with your ISP. In Windows 7, this process is a snap.

In fact, if you have a broadband connection, you probably don't need to do anything to access the Internet. Just connect your computer to the broadband modem (or, if you're on a home network, to a network router that's connected to your broadband modem), and Windows does the rest. You'll have access to the Internet the next time you launch your web browser.

On the other hand, if you're connecting to a dial-up connection (or to one of those few broadband connections that requires a username and password), you have a little work to do. Follow these steps:

1. Click the Network button on the Windows taskbar and select Open Network and Sharing Center.

2. From the Network and Sharing Center, select Set Up a New Connection or Network.

3. When the Set Up a Connection or Network window appears, select Connect to the Internet and then click Next.

4. When the next window appears, select how you're connecting—via Wireless, Broadband, or Dial-Up.

5. If you selected Broadband, enter the user name and password supplied by your ISP, enter a name for this connection, then click Connect.

6. If you selected Dial-Up, enter the ISP's dial-up phone number, along with the username and password assigned by the ISP. Then enter a name for this connection and click Connect.

That's it. Windows does a good job of configuring your Internet connection automatically, without a lot of input on your part.

Sharing an Internet Connection

If you have more than one PC in your home, you can connect them to share a single Internet connection. This is particularly useful if you have a high-speed broadband connection.

You share an Internet connection by connecting your broadband modem to your home network. It doesn't matter whether you have a wired or a wireless network; the connection is similar in both instances. All you have to do is run an Ethernet cable from your broadband modem to your network router, and then Windows will do the rest, connecting your modem to the network so that all your computers can access the connection.

To work through all the details of this type of connection, turn to Chapter 7, "Setting Up a Home Network." It's really quite easy!

Connecting to a Public WiFi Hotspot

If you have a notebook PC, you also have the option to connect to the Internet when you're out and about. Many coffeehouses, restaurants, libraries, and hotels offer wireless WiFi Internet service, either free or for an hourly or daily fee. Assuming that your notebook has a built-in WiFi adapter (and it probably does), connecting to a public WiFi hotspot is a snap.

When you're near a WiFi hotspot, your PC should automatically pick up the WiFi signal. Make sure that your PC's WiFi adapter is turned on (some notebooks have a switch for this, either on the front or on the side of the unit), and then click the Network icon in the Windows taskbar notification area. As you can see in Figure 16.1, this displays a list of available wireless networks near you. Select the network you want to connect to; then click the Connect button.

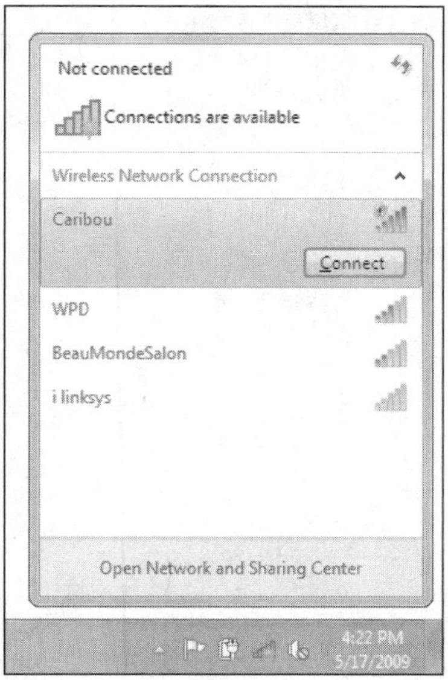

> **note**
>
> A *hotspot* is a public place that offers wireless access to the Internet using WiFi technology. Some hotspots are free for all to access; others require some sort of payment.

FIGURE 16.1

Connecting to a wireless hotspot in Windows 7.

After Windows connects to the selected hotspot, you can log on to the wireless network. This is typically done by opening Internet Explorer or a similar web browser. If the hotspot has free public access, you'll be able to surf normally. If the hotspot requires a password, payment, or other logon procedure, it will intercept the request for your normal home page and instead display its own login page. Enter the appropriate information, and you'll be surfing in no time!

THE ABSOLUTE MINIMUM

When you're configuring your new PC system to connect to the Internet, remember these important points:

- You connect to the Internet through an ISP; you need to set up an account with an ISP before you can connect.

- You can sign up for either dial-up (slower and less expensive) or broadband (faster and more expensive) service.

- There are three common types of broadband service: DSL, cable, and satellite, with the newer FiOS service available in some areas.

- After you have an account with an ISP, you need to configure Windows for your new account.

- If you have more than one computer at home, you can share your Internet connection by connecting your broadband modem to your home network.

- If you have a notebook PC, you can connect to the Internet wirelessly at any public WiFi hotspot, such as those offered by Starbucks, Caribou Coffee, and similar establishments.

17

SURFING THE WEB WITH INTERNET EXPLORER

After you're signed up with an ISP and connected to the Internet, it's time to get surfing. The World Wide Web is a particular part of the Internet with all sorts of cool content and useful services, and you surf the Web with a piece of software called a *web browser*.

The most popular web browser today is Microsoft's Internet Explorer, in no small part because it's included free with Microsoft Windows. This chapter shows you how to use Internet Explorer and then takes you on a quick trip around the Web—just enough to get your online feet wet!

Understanding the Web

Before you can surf the Web, you need to understand a little bit about how it works.

Information on the World Wide Web is presented in *pages*. A web page is similar to a page in a book, made up of text and graphics. A web page differs from a book page, however, in that it can include other elements, such as audio and video and links to other web pages.

It's this linking to other web pages that makes the Web such a dynamic way to present information. A *link* on a web page can point to another web page on the same site or to another site. Most links are included as part of a web page's text and are called *hypertext links*, or just *hyperlinks*. (If a link is part of a graphic, it's called a *graphic link*.) These links are usually in a different color from the rest of the text and often are underlined; when you click a link, you're taken directly to the linked page.

Web pages reside at a *website*. A website is nothing more than a collection of web pages (each in its own computer file) residing on a host computer. The host computer is connected full-time to the Internet so that you can access the site—and its web pages—anytime you access the Internet. The main page at a website is called the *home page*, and it often serves as an opening screen that provides a brief overview and menu of everything you can find at that site. The address of a web page is called a *URL*, which stands for *uniform resource locator*. Most URLs start with http://, add a www., continue with the name of the site, and end with a .com, .org, or .net.

tip

You can normally leave off the **http://** when you enter an address into your web browser. In most cases, you can even leave off the **www.** and just start with the domain part of the address.

Choosing a Web Browser

As noted, you browse the Web with a software program called a *web browser*. The most popular web browser today is Microsoft's Internet Explorer, but it's not the only browser available. Most browsers have similar features, but some users prefer one over another.

Here's an alphabetical list of all the web browsers that you can install on your Windows-based computer system:

- Google Chrome (www.google.com/chrome/)
- Internet Explorer (www.microsoft.com/windows/Internet-explorer/)
- Mozilla Firefox (www.mozilla.com/firefox/)
- Opera (www.opera.com)
- Safari (www.apple.com/safari/)

All of these browsers work in pretty much the same fashion. Some have slightly different advanced features; some (such as Google Chrome) load pages somewhat faster than do others. It's a personal choice as to which browser you use.

Using Internet Explorer 8

The web browser included in Microsoft Windows is Internet Explorer. In Windows 7, the version of IE is Internet Explorer 8. (You'd think they'd get these versions in sync, wouldn't you?)

Internet Explorer 8 (IE8) is easy to use. To launch it, all you have to do is click the Internet Explorer icon on the Windows taskbar.

Figure 17.1 shows the various parts of the IE program, and Table 17.1 tells you what each of the buttons on the toolbar does.

note

You can use any web browser to surf the Web. The instructions here work equally well with other popular browsers such as Mozilla Firefox, Google Chrome, Opera, or Safari. All of these browsers can be downloaded and installed on your computer for free.

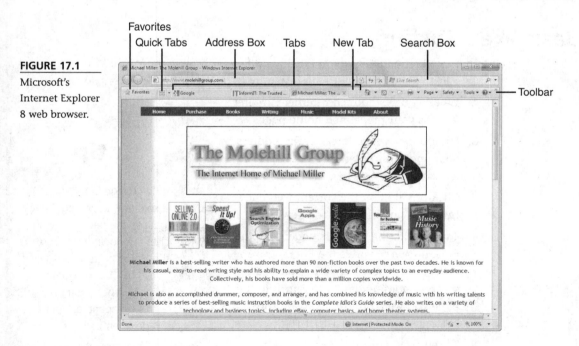

FIGURE 17.1
Microsoft's
Internet Explorer
8 web browser.

TABLE 17.1   Internet Explorer Toolbar Buttons

Button	Operation
Back	Return to the previously viewed page
Forward	View the next page
Stop	Stop loading the current page
Refresh	Reload the current page
Favorites	Go to your favorite web pages
Quick Tabs	View all tabbed pages on a single page
New Tab	Open a new tab to view a new web page
Home	Return to your designated start page
Feeds	View the latest headlines from RSS news feeds
Mail	Open your designated email program
Print	Print the current page
Page	Perform various page-related operations (cut, copy, zoom, send via email, and so on)
Safety	Access security-related settings
Tools	Configure IE's settings

Basic Web Surfing

Internet Explorer enables you to quickly and easily browse the World Wide Web—just by clicking your mouse. Here's a step-by-step tour of IE's basic functions:

1. When you first launch Internet Explorer, it loads your predefined home page.

2. Enter a new web address in the Address box, and press Enter. Internet Explorer loads the new page.

3. Click any link on the current web page. Internet Explorer loads the new page.

4. To return to the previous page, click the Back button (or press the Backspace key on your keyboard). If you've backed up several pages and want to return to the page you were on last, click the Forward button.

5. To return to your start page, click the Home button.

tip

To change Internet Explorer's home page, navigate to the page you want, click the down arrow next to the Home button, and select Add or Change Home Page. When prompted, opt to Use This Webpage as Your Only Home Page; then click OK.

Using Tabbed Browsing

Internet Explorer 8 utilizes a multidocument interface that lets you display multiple web pages on separate tabs within a single browser window. This use of tabs lets you keep multiple web pages open simultaneously—which is great when you want to keep previous pages open for reference or want to run web-based applications in the background.

To open a web page on a new tab, just click the next (empty) tab and enter a URL. You can also choose to open a link within a page in a new tab by right-clicking the link and selecting Open in New Tab.

You switch between tabs by clicking a tab with your mouse or by pressing Ctrl+Tab on your keyboard. You can also reorder your tabs by dragging and dropping them into a new position.

You can view the contents of all open tabs with IE's Quick Tabs feature. When you click the Quick Tab icon or press Ctrl+Q, all open web pages are displayed as thumbnails in a single window, as shown in Figure 17.2. Click any thumbnail to open that tab in the full window.

FIGURE 17.2
Viewing multiple pages via the Quick Tabs feature.

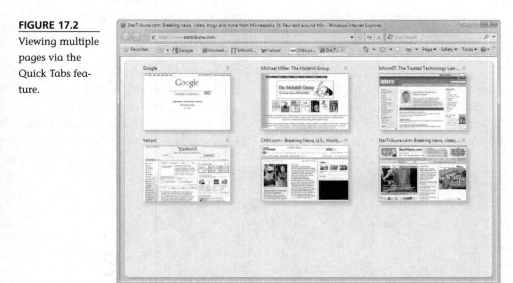

Advanced Operations

Internet Explorer can do much more than simple browsing. Let's take a quick look at some of the more advanced operations in Internet Explorer that can make your online life a lot easier.

Searching from the Browser

If you search the Web a lot, and I know you do, you spend a lot of time going to your favorite search site. Fortunately, Internet Explorer lets you speed up your searches by searching from the browser window itself, via an Instant Search box next to the Address box. This lets you perform web searches without having to first navigate to a separate search site.

note

Learn more about web searching in Chapter 18, "Searching the Web."

To conduct a search from within IE8, just enter your query into the Instant Search box and press the Enter key on your keyboard. Your query is sent via IE over the Internet to the selected search provider. The search site receives the query, searches its own previously compiled index of web pages, and returns a page of search results, which is displayed in the Internet Explorer window. It's that easy.

By default, IE routes your search to Microsoft's Windows Live Search site. If you prefer to use another search engine, such as Google, you can change this default. Just click the down arrow next to the Search box and click Manage Search Providers. When the Manage Add-Ons window appears, select the provider you want from the list and click the Set as Default button.

If the search site you want isn't listed in the Manage Add-Ons window, click the down arrow next to the IE8 Search box and click Find More Providers. When the Search Providers web page appears, as shown in Figure 17.3, click the Add to Internet Explorer button for the search engine you want to use. You can then return to the Manage Add-Ons window to select this new search engine as your default.

FIGURE 17.3

Choosing a new search provider in Internet Explorer 8.

![Screenshot of the Add-ons Gallery: Search Providers page in Internet Explorer 8]

Saving Your Favorite Pages

When you find a web page you like, you can add it to a list of Favorites within Internet Explorer. This way you can easily access any of your favorite sites just by selecting them from the list.

To add a page to your Favorites list, follow these steps:

1. Go to the web page you want to add to your Favorites list.
2. Click the Favorites button to display the Favorites pane, shown in Figure 17.4.
3. Click Add to Favorites.
4. When the Add a Favorite dialog box appears, confirm the page's name and select the folder where you want to place this link.
5. Click OK.

FIGURE 17.4

Click the Favorites button to display the Favorites pane.

To view a page in your Favorites list, follow these steps:

1. Click the Favorites button to display the Favorites pane.
2. Click the Favorites tab in this new pane.
3. Click any folder in the Favorites pane to display the contents of that folder.
4. Click a favorite page, and that page is displayed in the browser window.

Revisiting History

Internet Explorer has three ways of keeping track of web pages you've visited, so you can easily revisit them without having to re-enter the web page address.

To revisit the last page you visited, click the Back button on the toolbar. You can continue clicking Forward to go the last previous page.

To revisit one of the last half-dozen or so pages viewed in your current session, click the down arrow next to the Back button. This drops down a menu containing the last 10 pages you've visited. Highlight any page on this menu to jump directly to that page.

To revisit pages you've viewed in the past several days, you use the History tab in the Favorites pane. Just follow these steps:

1. Click the Favorites button to display the Favorites pane.
2. In the new pane, click the History tab.
3. Click the View By button to select how you want to view your history—by date, site, most visited, or order visited today.
4. Click a specific page to display that page in the right pane.

Printing

Printing a web page is easy—just click the Print button. If you want to see a preview of the page before it prints, click the down arrow next to the Print button and select Print Preview.

Internet Security with IE8

Internet Explorer 8 includes various technologies that help you browse more safely and securely. We'll look at some of these features next.

Protecting Against Phishing Scams

You learned about phishing scams back in Chapter 10, "Protecting Your PC from Viruses, Spam, and Other Online Nuisances." To protect you from phishing scams, IE8 incorporates a SmartScreen Filter. This filter automatically connects to an online service that contains a huge database of suspicious websites and alerts you if you attempt to go to one of these sites.

If you attempt to click a link to a known phishing site, the SmartScreen Filter blocks access to the site, changes the Address Bar to red, navigates to a neutral page, and displays a warning message. In other words, if the site is fraudulent, IE8 won't let you go there.

In addition, the SmartScreen Filter helps protect you from sites that might be fake. If you attempt to click a link to a site that is not on the list of known fraudulent sites but behaves similarly to such sites, the SmartScreen Filter changes the Address Bar to yellow and cautions you of potentially suspicious content. Unless you're sure the site is good, don't click through.

The SmartScreen Filter is enabled by default in IE8. You can also have the Filter manually check any website. Just click the Safety button and select SmartScreen Filter, Check This Website; the Filter will check the site and display its findings in a new dialog box.

Blocking Pop-Up Ads

If you've surfed the Web for any time at all, you've probably noticed those annoying pop-up windows that appear when you visit some websites. Not so with Internet Explorer 8, which incorporates a Pop-Up Blocker. This feature, which is enabled by default, blocks the automatic opening of unwanted pop-up windows.

When a site tries to open a pop-up window that is blocked by Internet Explorer, a notification appears in the Information bar of the browser window. If you click the notification, you can choose to temporarily or permanently allow pop-ups from this site. Otherwise, say bye-bye to unwanted pop-ups!

Managing Cookies

Even though you might do it in private on your personal computer, browsing the Web is not a private affair. Every website you visit is automatically tracked, which makes it easy for anyone with access to your computer to recover your browsing activity. This goes beyond listing a site in the History pane; the record of the sites you've visited is embedded deep in the system files of your computer.

How Cookies Work

One way that your web browsing is tracked is via a small file called a *cookie*. Websites create and store cookie files on your computer's hard disk; these files contain information about you and your Web activities.

For example, a cookie file for a particular site might contain your username, password, credit card information, and the most recent pages you visited on that site. The cookie file created by a site is accessed by that site each time you visit in the future, and the information within the cookie is used appropriately.

Adjust the Privacy Level

If you value your privacy, you can control how cookies are created and stored on your computer. Internet Explorer lets you adjust the browser's privacy level to determine which types of cookies are automatically accepted—or rejected. You do this by clicking the Tools button and selecting Internet Options; when the Internet Options dialog box appears, select the Privacy tab, shown in Figure 17.5. Adjust the slider to the privacy level you want; then click OK.

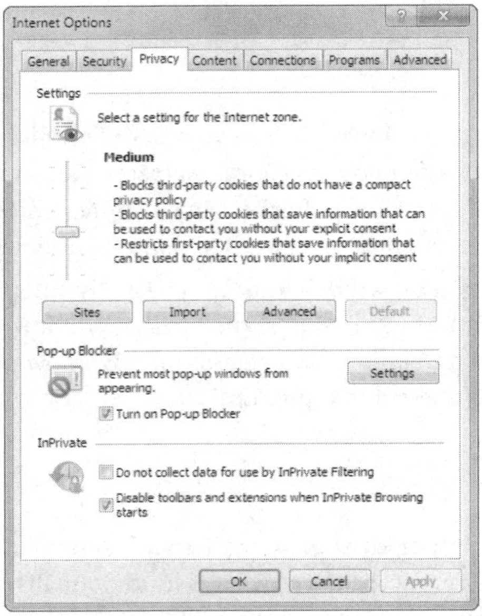

FIGURE 17.5

Configuring cookie and privacy options in Internet Explorer.

Internet Explorer has six levels of cookie management, ranging from accepting all cookies to declining all cookies:

- **Accept All Cookies**—Accepts all first-party and third-party cookies.
- **Low**—Accepts all first-party cookies but blocks third-party cookies from sites that don't have privacy policies. When IE is closed, automatically deletes third-party cookies from sites that use personal information without your implicit consent.
- **Medium**—When IE is closed, automatically deletes first-party cookies from sites that use personal information without your consent. Blocks third-party cookies from sites that don't have privacy policies or from sites that use personal information without your implicit consent.
- **Medium-High**—Blocks first-party cookies from sites that use personal information without your implicit consent. Blocks third-party cookies from sites that don't have privacy policies or from sites that use personal information without your *explicit* consent.

- **High**—Blocks all cookies from sites that don't have privacy policies or from sites that use personal information without your *explicit* consent.

- **Block All Cookies**—Blocks all new cookies. Existing cookies can't be read, even by the sites that created them.

The default setting is Medium, which pretty much blocks all advertising-related cookies and deletes any cookies that contain personal information when you close Internet Explorer. If you'd rather that no website store personal information you haven't explicitly approved, choose the High setting.

Delete All Cookies

Internet Explorer also lets you automatically delete all the cookie files stored on your computer. This is useful if you want to erase all tracks of the websites you've visited; with no cookie files, your employer or spouse won't know about all the different sites you've visited.

To delete all cookie files, click the Safety button and select Delete Browsing History. When the Delete Browsing History dialog box appears, check the Cookies option and click Delete.

InPrivate Browsing

On occasion you might want to visit a website that you don't want others to know you've visited. When you don't want a specific browsing session recorded in IE8's history or cookies, you can use the new InPrivate Browsing feature to browse completely anonymously. With InPrivate Browsing enabled, no record of the pages you visit is kept via any means, cookies or otherwise; no one need know where you've been on the Web.

To enable InPrivate Browsing, click the Safety button and select InPrivate Browsing. This opens a new browser window with the InPrivate logo displayed in the Address bar. When you browse from an InPrivate window, IE stores no data about the web pages you visit; cookies, temporary files, and history are all disabled.

note

A *first-party* cookie originates from the website you are currently viewing and is typically used to store your preferences regarding that site. A *third-party* cookie originates from a website different from the one you are currently viewing and is typically used to feed advertisements from separate ad sites to the current website.

tip

You can also use the Delete Browsing History dialog box to delete your temporary Internet files (cache), browsing history, form data, and any website passwords you've entered.

THE ABSOLUTE MINIMUM

Here are the key things to remember about surfing the Web:

- You surf the Web with a program called a web browser, such as Internet Explorer, Google Chrome, or Mozilla Firefox.

- Internet Explorer 8 is the web browser included as part of Windows 7.

- You can go to a particular web page by entering the page's address in the Address box and then pressing Enter; click a hyperlink on a web page to jump to the linked page.

- IE8 offers tabbed browsing, where new web pages can be opened in additional tabs; click a tab to switch to that web page.

- IE8 lets you search the Web from within the browser, thanks to the Instant Search box at the top of the window.

- IE8 also includes a pop-up window blocker, anti-phishing filter, and anonymous web browsing.

18

SEARCHING THE WEB

Now that you know how to surf the Web, how do you find the precise information you're looking for? Fortunately, there are numerous sites that help you search the Web for the specific information you want. Not surprisingly, these are among the most popular sites on the Internet.

This chapter is all about searching the Web. You'll learn the best places to search and the best ways to search. I'll even help you cheat a little by listing some of the most popular sites for different types of information.

So pull up a chair, launch your web browser, and loosen up those fingers—it's time to start searching!

How to Search the Web

Internet *search engines* are sites that employ special software programs (called *spiders* or *crawlers*) to roam the Web automatically, feeding what they find back to a massive bank of computers. These computers then build giant *indexes* of the Web, billions of pages strong.

When you perform a search at a search engine site, your query is sent to the search engine's index. (You never actually search the Web itself; you only search the index that was created by the spiders crawling the Web.) The search engine then creates a list of pages in its index that match, to one degree or another, the query you entered.

Constructing a Query

Almost every search site on the Web contains two basic components—a *search box* and a *Search button*. You enter your query—one or more *keywords* that describe what you're looking for—into the search box, and then click the Search button (or press the Enter key) to start the search. The search site then returns a list of web pages that match your query; click any link to go directly to the page in question.

How you construct your query determines how relevant the results will be that you receive. It's important to focus on the keywords you use because the search sites look for these words when they process your query. Your keywords are compared to the web pages the search site knows about; the more keywords found on a web page, the better the match.

Choose keywords that best describe the information you're looking for—using as many keywords as you need. Don't be afraid of using too many keywords; in fact, using too *few* keywords is a common fault of many novice searchers. The more words you use, the better idea the search engine has of what you're looking for.

Searching for an Exact Phrase

Normally, a multiple-word query searches for web pages that include all the words in the query, in any order. There is a way, however, to search for an exact phrase. All you have to do is enclose the phrase in quotation marks.

For example, to search for Monty Python, *don't* enter **Monty Python** as your query. Instead, enter **"Monty Python"**—the two keywords surrounded by quotation marks. Putting the phrase between quotation marks returns results about the comedy troupe, while entering the words individually also returns pages about snakes and guys named Monty.

Where to Search

Now that you know *how* to search, *where* should you search? There's one obvious choice and a lot of alternatives.

Google—The Most Popular Search Site on the Web

The most popular search engine today is Google (www.google.com). Google is easy to use, extremely fast, and returns highly relevant results. That's because it indexes more pages than any other site—billions and billions of pages, if you're counting.

Most users search Google several times a week, if not several times a day. The Google home page, shown in Figure 18.1, is a marvel of simplicity and elegant web page design. All you have to do to start a search is to enter one or more keywords into the search box and then click the Google Search button. This returns a list of results ranked in order of relevance, such as the one shown in Figure 18.2. Click a results link to view that page.

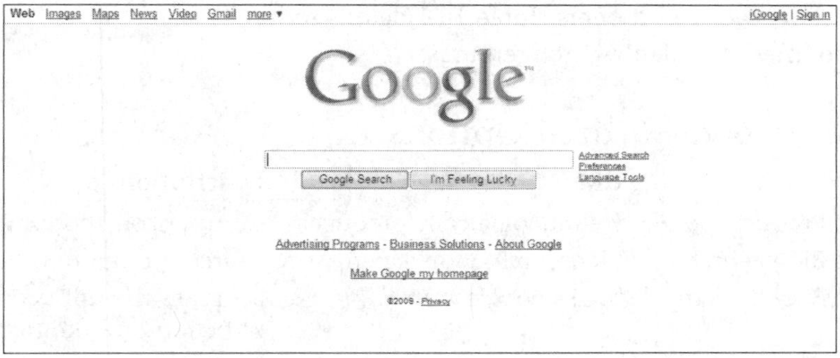

FIGURE 18.1
Searching the Web at Google.

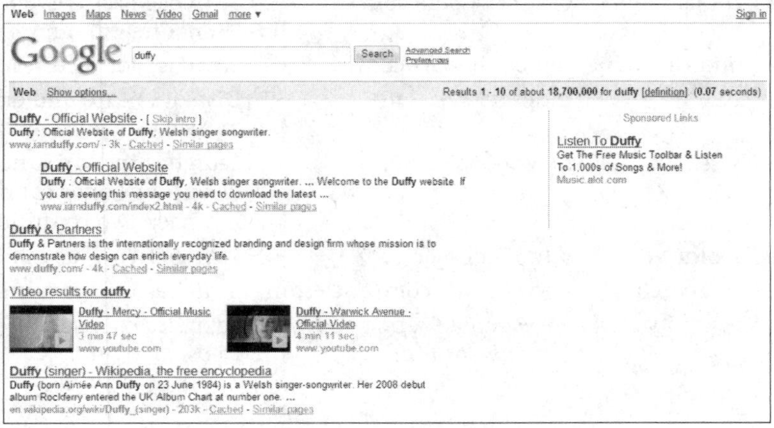

FIGURE 18.2
The results of a Google search.

Google also offers a variety of advanced search options to help you fine-tune your search. Some of these options are displayed in an Options panel that appears when you click the Show Options link. These options let you filter your results by type (Videos, Forums, and Reviews), time (Past 24 Hours, Past Week, and so on), and other factors. It's a nice way to narrow down what you're looking for.

Additional options are found on the Advanced Search page, which you get to by clicking the Advanced Search link on Google's home page. To narrow your search results, all you have to do is make the appropriate selections from the options present.

Another neat thing about Google is all the specialty searches it offers. Table 18.1 details some of these "hidden" search features.

tip

You can also use Google to display stock quotes (enter the stock ticker), answers to mathematical calculations (enter the equation), and measurement conversions (enter what you want to convert). Google can also track USPS, UPS, and FedEx packages (enter the tracking number), as well as the progress of airline flights (enter the airline and flight number).

TABLE 18.1 Google Search Options

Search	URL	Description
Google Product Search	www.google.com/products	Comparison shopping
Google Blog Search	blogsearch.google.com	Searches blogs and blog postings
Google Book Search	books.google.com	Searches the full text of thousands of fiction and nonfiction books
Google Directory	directory.google.com	Editor-selected search results
Google Groups	groups.google.com	Searches user-created groups and Usenet newsgroups
Google Image Search	images.google.com	Searches for pictures
Google Maps	maps.google.com	Displays maps and driving directions—as well as cool satellite photos
Google News	news.google.com	Searches the latest news headlines—as well as historical new archives dating back two centuries
Google Scholar	scholar.google.com	Searches various scholarly papers
Google U.S. Search	www.google.com/unclesam	Searches U.S. government sites
Google University Search	www.google.com/options/universities.html	Searches college and university websites

Google also owns a number of related websites that might be of interest. Of particular interest are Blogger (www.blogger.com), home to tens of thousands of personal weblogs, and YouTube (www.youtube.com), the Web's premiere site for posting and viewing videos.

Other Search Sites

Although Google is far and away the most popular search engine, many other search engines provide excellent (and sometimes different) results. These search engines include

- AltaVista (www.altavista.com)
- Ask.com (www.ask.com)
- Bing by Microsoft (www.bing.com)
- Open Directory (www.dmoz.org)
- Yahoo! (www.yahoo.com)

Searching for People and Businesses

As good as Google and other search sites are for finding specific web pages, they're not always that great for finding people. (Although, to be fair, Google is getting much better at this.) When there's a person (or an address or a phone number) you want to find, you need to use a site that specializes in people searches.

People listings on the Web go by the common name of *white pages directories*, the same as traditional white pages phone books. These directories typically enable you to enter all or part of a person's name and then search for his address and phone number. Many of these sites also let you search for personal email addresses and business addresses and phone numbers.

The best of these directories include

- AnyWho (www.anywho.com)
- InfoSpace (www.infospace.com)
- Switchboard (www.switchboard.com)
- WhitePages.com (www.whitepages.com)

In addition, all of these white pages directories serve as yellow pages directories for looking up businesses. They're one-stop search sites for any individual or business you want to look up!

THE ABSOLUTE MINIMUM

Here are the key points to remember from this chapter:

- When you need to search for specific information on the Internet, you can use one of the Web's many search engine sites.

- The most popular Internet search engine is Google, which indexes billions of individual web pages.

- Other popular search engines and directories include Yahoo!, Windows Live Search, and Ask.com.

- It's better to search for people (and their phone numbers and addresses) at specific people-search sites, such as InfoSpace and Switchboard.

19

RESEARCHING WITH WIKIPEDIA

The Internet is a great place to do research. All sorts of information is out there, if you know where to find it.

While many people use Google or Yahoo! for research, searching the Web for just the right information can sometimes be like looking for a needle in a haystack; the information you get is totally unfiltered and not always accurate. A better way to research is to use Wikipedia—a site that is fast becoming the primary information site on the Web.

How Wikipedia Works

Wikipedia (www.wikipedia.com) is like a giant online encyclopedia—but with a twist. Unlike a traditional encyclopedia, Wikipedia's content is created solely by the site's users, resulting in the world's largest online collaboration.

At present, Wikipedia hosts more than 2.8 million English-language articles, with at least that many articles available in more than 250 different languages. The articles are written and revised by tens of thousands of individual contributors. These users volunteer their time and knowledge at no charge, for the good of the Wikipedia project.

You don't have to be an academic type to contribute to Wikipedia, and you don't have to be a student to use it. Anyone with specialized knowledge can write an article, and regular people like you and me can read them.

Reading Wikipedia Articles

Information on the Wikipedia site is compiled into a series of *articles*. As you can see in Figure 19.1, each article is organized into a summary and subsidiary sections. Longer articles have a table of contents, located beneath the summary. Key information is sometimes presented in a sidebar at the top right of the article.

FIGURE 19.1

A typical Wikipedia article.

One of the things I liked about reading the encyclopedia when I was a kid was jumping around from article to article. This is easier than ever in Wikipedia, as the text of each article contains blue hypertext that links to related articles in the Wikipedia database. Click one of these links to jump to that article.

If you want to know the source for the information in an article, scroll to the bottom of the page, where the sources for key facts within the article are footnoted.

Additional references and information about the topic also appear at the bottom of the page.

And, since Wikipedia articles are continually updated by users, it's often useful to view the history of an article's updates. This way you can see how an article looked before its most recent revisions. To view an article's history, click the History tab; this displays a list of edits and who made those edits. You can also use the History tab to read previous versions of an article.

tip

Some articles feature discussions from users, which can sometimes provide additional insight. Click the Discussion tab to read and participate in ongoing discussions.

Searching Wikipedia

How do you find the articles you want? It's easy; searching for information on Wikipedia is similar to using a traditional search engine.

To find an article on a given topic, enter your query into the search box on Wikipedia's home page and then click the right-arrow button. If an article directly matches your query, Wikipedia displays that article. If a number of articles might match your query, Wikipedia displays the list of articles, organized by type or topic. Click the article name to display the specific article.

For example, if you search Wikipedia for **john adams**, it displays the article on founding father John Adams. If, instead, you search only for **adams**, it displays a disambiguation page with sections for matching people and places bearing the name of "Adams," as shown in Figure 19.2. From there you can find the article on the second president, as well as lots of other articles.

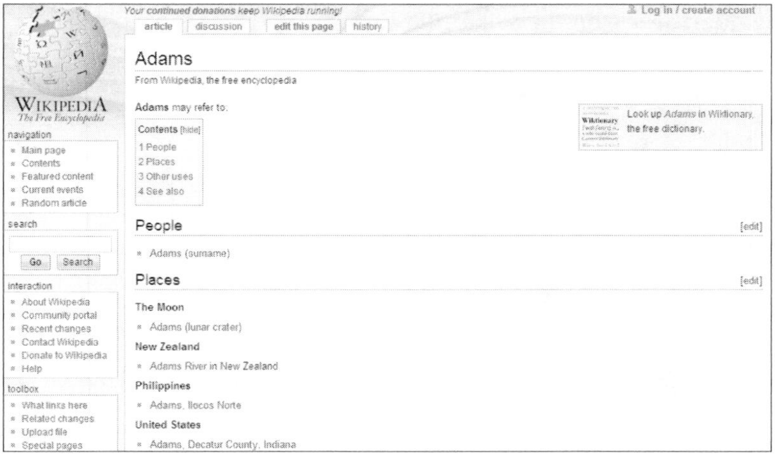

FIGURE 19.2

A disambiguation page—resulting from too wide a search.

Contributing to Wikipedia

Here's the neat thing about Wikipedia—it's a true collaboration. Anyone can contribute original articles or edit articles written by others. You don't have to possess professional qualifications—just an adequate knowledge of the subject chosen.

And if you find an article that you think isn't quite accurate, you can change it. All articles that are submitted to the Wikipedia site can be edited by other users, who can insert additional information or revise the information previously submitted. In this fashion, information in Wikipedia is constantly improved and updated—by its users.

Creating a New Article

As big as Wikipedia is, it isn't big enough yet to include every possible topic imaginable. If you look for a topic that isn't there, you can write an article about that topic yourself and add it to Wikipedia.

The first step in creating a new article is to search for the topic you want to write about. If an article appears, you don't have to create a new one. If no article appears, however, Wikipedia tells you that no article title matches your search.

The next step is to click the Create the Page link; this displays an editing page for the new article, like the one shown in Figure 19.3. Enter your content into the editing box and click the Save Page button when you're done. This places your newly written article on the Wikipedia site.

note

You must have a (free) Wikipedia account and be signed in to create an article. You don't need an account to edit an article.

FIGURE 19.3

Creating a new Wikipedia article.

Editing an Article

Every article on the Wikipedia site is a work in progress. Users are encouraged to correct and expand any and all Wikipedia articles; this group collaboration should result in more accurate and comprehensive information for all.

To edit an existing article, navigate to that article and click the Edit This Page tab. This displays the underlying markup code for the article, as shown in Figure 19.4. You apply your edits directly to the code; then you enter a summary of your edits into the Edit Summary box. When you're finished, click the Save Page button; your changes will be immediately visible.

> **caution**
>
> Don't even think about entering wrong or misleading information into a Wikipedia article. Since other users will quickly read and vet your edits, any incorrect information you enter will either be changed or deleted by the user community.

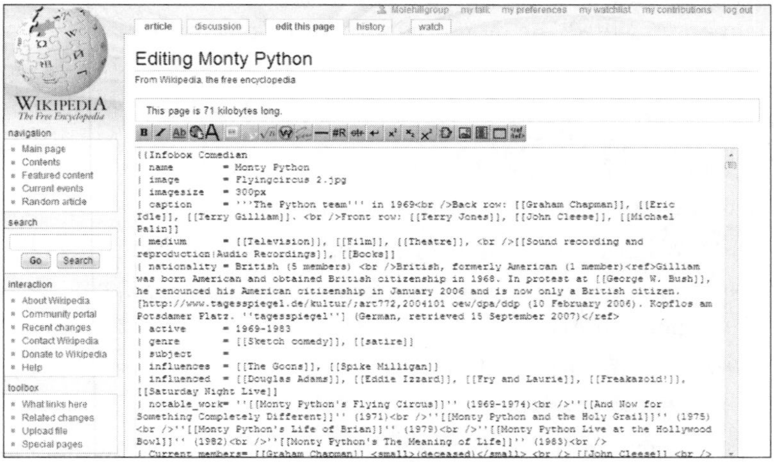

FIGURE 19.4

Editing an existing Wikipedia article.

Is Wikipedia Good for Research?

Not everyone likes Wikipedia. Some educators think that it contributes to student laziness; many researchers question the accuracy of its content. After all, if anyone with Internet access can write or edit an article, how are you to know if the information submitted is correct?

It's certainly possible for Wikipedia articles to be biased, incomplete, or just plain wrong. While the Wikipedia community is self-policing (and the information generally accurate), inaccurate information can seep into the site. Users can intentionally or unintentionally enter misleading or incorrect information, and that information may not quickly (or ever) be discovered by the base of contributing users. Other users have to care enough to read the article in question and know enough to root out the inaccuracies—and that doesn't always happen.

This is why relying on Wikipedia as your sole source of research is dangerous. If a given article contains inaccuracies, your paper or report will be inaccurate, too. It's best to view Wikipedia content as a start, rather than the final word. When you're writing a scholarly or professional paper, you should not use Wikipedia as your sole source, but rather as a guide to additional sources. In addition, it's always a good idea to check the footnotes and other references in a Wikipedia article to confirm the source of information presented; the most accurate articles are well sourced.

> ## caution
>
> Because Wikipedia users suggest the content, it's likely that some popular culture topics are covered in greater depth than topics of a more intellectual bent. This is solely a function of which and how many contributors are interested and expert in a given topic. As such, you can't depend on Wikipedia to always provide *adequate* content on a given topic.

THE ABSOLUTE MINIMUM

Here are the key points to remember from this chapter:

- Wikipedia is an online encyclopedia with articles written by its user base.
- Each article contains links to related articles, as well as footnotes for information sources.
- You can view the history of edits to each article, as well as participate in discussions about the article.
- If you find an article with inaccurate or missing information, you can edit the article to improve it.
- If you feel up to it, you can also write new articles on topics not yet covered on the site.
- Because Wikipedia relies on its user base to correct and improve article content, don't rely on Wikipedia as your sole source when writing papers and reports.

20

SHOPPING ONLINE

Many users have discovered that the Internet is a great place to buy things—all kinds of things. All manner of online merchants make it easy to buy books, CDs, and other merchandise with the click of a mouse.

In spite of the popularity of online retailing, many users are still a little hesitant to do their shopping online. Although there certainly is some amount of online fraud (just as there's plenty of fraud in the real world), in general the Internet is a fairly safe place to shop—if you follow the rules and take a few simple precautions.

Read on, then, to find out the best places to shop online—and how to shop safely.

How to Shop Online

If you've never shopped online before, you're probably wondering just what to expect. Shopping over the Web is actually easy; all you need is your computer and a credit card—and a fast connection to the Internet!

Online shopping is pretty much the same, no matter which retailer you shop at. You proceed through a multiple-step process that goes like this:

1. **Find a product** either by browsing or searching through the retailer's site.
2. **Examine the product** by viewing the photos and information on a product listing page.
3. **Order the product** by clicking a "buy it now" button on the product listing page that puts the item in your online shopping cart.
4. **Check out** by entering your payment and shipping information.
5. **Confirm the order** and wait for the merchant to ship your merchandise.

Let's look at each of these steps separately.

Step 1: Find a Product

The first step in online shopping is the actual shopping. That means finding the site where you want to shop and then either browsing through different product categories or using the site's search feature to find a specific product.

Browsing product categories online is similar to browsing through the departments of a retail store. You typically click a link to access a major product category, and then click further links to view subcategories within the main category. For example, the main category might be Clothing; the subcategories might be Men's, Women's, and Children's clothing. If you click the Men's link, you might see a list of further subcategories: outerwear, shirts, pants, and the like. Just keep clicking until you reach the type of item that you're looking for.

Searching for products is often a faster way to find what you're looking for if you have something specific in mind. For example, if you're looking for a men's silk jacket, you can enter the words **men's silk jacket** into the site's search box and get a list of specific items that match those criteria. The only problem with searching is that you might not know exactly what it is you're looking for; if this describes your situation, you're probably better off browsing. But if you *do* know what you want—and you don't want to deal with lots of irrelevant items—then searching is the faster option.

tip

When searching for items at an online retailer, you can use the same general search guidelines discussed in Chapter 18, "Searching the Web."

Step 2: Examine the Product

Whether you browse or search, you'll probably end up looking at a list of different products on a web page. These listings typically feature one-line descriptions of each item—in most cases, not nearly enough information for you to make an informed purchase.

The thing to do now is to click the link for the item you're particularly interested in. This should display a dedicated product page, complete with a picture and full description of the item. This is where you can read more about the item you selected. Some product pages include different views of the item, pictures of the item in different colors, links to additional information, and maybe even a list of optional accessories that go along with the item.

If you like what you see, you can proceed to the ordering stage. If you want to look at other items, just click your browser's Back button to return to the larger product listing.

Step 3: Order the Product

Somewhere on each product description page should be a button labeled Purchase or Buy Now or something similar. This is how you make the actual purchase: by clicking the Buy Now button. You don't order the product just by looking at the product description; you have to manually click that Purchase button to place your order.

When you click the Purchase or Buy Now button, that particular item is added to your *shopping cart*. That's right, the online retailer provides you with a virtual shopping cart that functions just like a real-world shopping cart. Each item you choose to purchase is added to your virtual shopping cart.

After you've ordered a product and placed it in your shopping cart, you can choose to shop for other products on that site or proceed to the site's checkout. It's important to note that when you place an item in your shopping cart, you haven't actually completed the purchase yet. You can keep shopping (and adding more items to your shopping cart) as long as you want.

You can even decide to abandon your shopping cart and not purchase anything at this time. All you have to do is leave the website, and you won't be charged for anything. It's the equivalent of leaving your shopping cart at a real-world retailer and walking out the front door; you don't actually buy anything until you walk through the checkout line. (Although, with some sites, the items remain in your shopping cart—so they'll be there waiting for you the next time you shop!)

Step 4: Check Out

To finalize your purchase, you have to visit the store's *checkout*. This is like the checkout line at a traditional retail store; you take your virtual shopping cart through the checkout, get your purchases totaled, and then pay for what you're buying.

The checkout at an online retailer typically consists of one or more web pages with forms you have to fill out. If you've visited the retailer before, the site might remember some of your personal information from your previous visit. Otherwise, you'll have to enter your name, address, and phone number, as well as the address you want to ship the merchandise to (if that's different from your billing address). You'll also have to pay for the merchandise, typically by entering a credit card number.

The checkout provides one last opportunity for you to change your order. You can delete items you decide not to buy or change quantities on any item. At some merchants, you can even opt to have your items gift-wrapped and sent to someone as a gift. All these options should be somewhere in the checkout.

You might also have the option of selecting different types of shipping for your order. Many merchants offer both regular and expedited shipping—the latter for an additional charge.

Another option at some retailers is to group all items for reduced shipping cost or ship items individually as they become available. Grouping items is attractive cost-wise, but you can get burned if one of the items is out of stock or not yet available; you could end up waiting weeks or months for those items that could have been shipped immediately.

> **tip**
>
> The better online retailers will tell you either on the product description page or during the checkout process whether or not an item is in stock. Look for this information to help you decide how to group your items for shipment.

Step 5: Confirm the Order

After you've entered all the appropriate information, you're asked to place your order. This typically means clicking a button that says Place Your Order or something similar. (I told you it's easy!) You might even see a second screen asking you whether you *really* want to place your order, just in case you had second thoughts.

After your order has been placed, you'll see a confirmation screen, typically displaying your order number. Write down this number or print out this page; you'll refer to this number in case you ever need to contact customer service. Most online merchants will also send you a confirmation message via email, containing this same information.

And that's all there is to it. You shop, examine the product, place an order, proceed to checkout, and then confirm your purchase. It's that easy!

How to Find the Best Prices Online

Now that you know *how* to shop, *where* should you spend your money online? Just a few short years ago, if you wanted to find the best bargains on the Web, you had to manually visit the sites of dozens of different online retailers—a very time-consuming process. Not so today, as there are numerous sites that exist to automatically do this price comparison for you. Go to a price comparison site, find the product you want, and have the site return a list of merchants offering that product, along with current prices. Choose the merchant that offers what you want, and you're ready to buy!

Price Comparison Sites

The best of these price comparison sites offer more than just pricing information. These full-service sites let you sort and filter their search results in a number of different ways, and they often include customer reviews of both the products and the available merchants. Some even let you perform side-by-side comparisons of multiple products, which is great if you haven't yet made up your mind as to what you want to buy.

The most popular (and useful) of these price comparison sites include

- BizRate (www.bizrate.com)
- Google Product Search (www.google.com/products)
- mySimon (www.mysimon.com)
- NexTag (www.nextag.com)
- PriceGrabber.com (www.pricegrabber.com)
- Shopping.com (www.shopping.com)
- Yahoo! Shopping (shopping.yahoo.com)

Comparing Prices at Shopping.com

All of these comparison shopping sites are good, but my favorite is Shopping.com (shown in Figure 20.1). What I really like about Shopping.com is that it gives you more than just simple price comparisons; you also get customer reviews of both products and merchants, to help you make better purchase decisions.

FIGURE 20.1

Comparing products and prices at Shopping.com.

Like all the other price comparison sites, Shopping.com enables you to either search for specific products or browse through major product categories. Whether you search or browse, you eventually end up at a product listing page like the one shown in Figure 20.2. From here you can filter the results by price, product type, brand, or other product attributes. You can sort the results by best matches (default), price, or product rating. (The product ratings are provided by the customers at Epinions.com, Shopping.com's companion site.) You can also display the products as a grid rather than a list by clicking the View as a Grid link.

FIGURE 20.2

The results of a product search at Shopping.com.

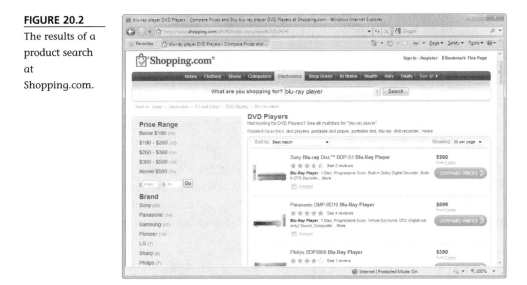

When you're in the process of choosing a particular product, Shopping.com makes it easy to perform side-by-side product comparisons. Just check the Select to Compare box next to the items you're looking at and then click the Compare Selected Items button. The result is a chart with the features of each product displayed in tabular format.

To learn more about a particular product, click the Compare Prices button. This displays a product page where you can read detailed product information (by clicking the See Product Details link) or customer reviews (by clicking the Consumer Reviews link).

Below the product picture is a listing of all stores carrying this product. You can sort this list by store name, store rating (when available, from Epinions.com customers), or price. When you're ready to buy, click the Buy It button to go directly to the merchant's product page.

> **tip**
>
> To see the total price (which includes shipping and taxes), enter your ZIP code into the Enter ZIP box, and then click the Calculate button. Obviously, total price is more important than base price because some merchants like to stick it to you when it comes to shipping and handling charges.

How to Shop Safely

Shopping online is every bit as safe as shopping at a traditional brick and mortar retailer. The big online retailers are just as reputable as traditional retailers, offering safe payment, fast shipping, and responsive service.

How do you know that you're shopping at a reputable online retailer? Simple—look for the following features:

- Payment by major credit card. (Not being able to accept credit cards is the sign of either a very small or fly-by-night merchant.)

- A *secure server* that encrypts your credit card information—and keeps online thieves from stealing your credit card numbers. (You'll know that you're using a secure site when the little lock icon appears in the lower-right corner of your web browser.)

- Good contact information—email address, street address, phone number, fax number, and so on. (You want to be able to physically contact the retailer if something goes wrong.)

- A stated returns policy and satisfaction guarantee. (You want to be assured that you'll be taken care of if you don't like whatever you ordered.)

- A stated privacy policy that protects your personal information. (You don't want the online retailer sharing your email address and purchasing information with other merchants—and potential spammers.)

- Information *before you finalize your order* that tells you whether the item is in stock and how long it will take to ship. (More feedback is better.)

How to Book Travel Reservations Online

One specific type of online shopping deserves special coverage. I'm talking about shopping for travel reservations—plane tickets, hotel rooms, rental cars, and more. Fortunately, many websites are designed to help you book the perfect trip, including the following:

- Expedia (www.expedia.com)
- Hotwire (www.hotwire.com)
- Orbitz (www.orbitz.com)
- Priceline (www.priceline.com)
- TravelNow.com (www.travelnow.com)
- Travelocity (www.travelocity.com)

All these online travel sites offer similar content and services, including the ability to book airline tickets, hotel rooms, and rental cars in one place. Most of these sites (such as Expedia, shown in Figure 20.3) let you search for the lowest rates or for flights and lodging that match your specific requirements.

tip

Credit card purchases are protected by the Fair Credit Billing Act, which gives you the right to dispute certain charges and limits your liability for unauthorized transactions to $50. In addition, some card issuers offer a supplemental guarantee that says you're not responsible for *any* unauthorized charges made online. (Make sure that you read your card's statement of terms to determine the company's exact liability policy.)

tip

When you make reservations online, look for a site that employs real people behind the scenes—and offers a 24/7 toll-free number to contact those people if something goes wrong. Talking to a real person over the phone can be a lifeline if you're stranded somewhere without a reservation.

FIGURE 20.3

Shopping for air-
line and hotel
reservations at
Expedia.

THE ABSOLUTE MINIMUM

Here are the key points to remember from this chapter:

- You can find just about any type of item you want to buy for sale somewhere on the Internet.

- Shopping online is a lot like shopping in a traditional store; you find the product you want, go through the checkout system, and make your payment.

- To find the lowest price online, use a price comparison site, such as Shopping.com or Google Product Search.

- Internet shopping is very safe, especially if you buy from a major merchant that offers a secure server and a good returns policy.

- The Internet is also a great place to make your travel reservations by using an online travel site such as Expedia or Orbitz.

IN THIS CHAPTER

- Who Sells on eBay?
- How Does an eBay Auction Work?
- eBay Bidding, Step-by-Step

21

BUYING AND SELLING ON EBAY

Some of the best bargains on the Web come from other consumers, just like you, selling items via eBay. eBay is one of the Web's largest online marketplaces, facilitating transactions between the people and businesses that have things to sell and the customers who want to buy those things.

Most transactions on eBay are in the form of *online auctions*. An online auction is, quite simply, a Web-based version of a traditional auction. You find an item you'd like to own and then place a bid on the item. Other users also place bids, and at the end of the auction—typically a seven-day period—the highest bidder wins.

Not every transaction on eBay is an auction transaction, however. An increasing number of eBay sales are at a fixed price, no bidding involved, through eBay's Buy It Now feature and through merchants who run their own eBay Stores. With more than 36 million items listed for sale on any given day, you're bound to find something you want to buy; eBay has it all, from rare collectibles and vintage sports memorabilia to trendy clothing and the latest electronics equipment.

Who Sells on eBay?

eBay started out as a pure online auction site. eBay's job was to host the auction listings and facilitate the transactions between buyers and sellers. (Note that eBay doesn't actually sell anything itself, nor does it hold inventory; all the transactions are between individual buyers and sellers, with eBay functioning solely as the middleman.)

In the beginning, eBay sellers were almost exclusively individuals—people like you and me with items they wanted to sell. In this way, eBay functioned like a giant garage sale or yard sale. An individual had something to sell, he listed it on eBay, and another individual decided to buy it. The second individual paid the first individual, who then shipped the item to the buyer. It was pretty simple.

Today, however, eBay is more than just person-to-person transactions. Many of eBay's original sellers have gotten quite big, listing hundreds of auctions every week and turning their eBay sales into real businesses. In addition, many existing businesses have turned to eBay as a way to make additional sales. So when you buy on eBay today, you may be buying from an individual selling just a few items, an individual running a small business out of her home, or a large business selling eBay items on the side.

Whomever you buy from, the process for the buyer is the same—as are the protections. The eBay marketplace is a level one, where all buyers and sellers follow the same rules and regulations. And the process for bidding and buying is the same no matter who you're buying from; just remember, you're buying from an independent seller, not from eBay itself.

note

There is no cost to register with eBay, although if you want to sell items, you'll have to provide your credit card and checking account numbers. (eBay uses this information to help weed out potential scammers and to provide a billing option for the seller's eBay fees.)

How Does an eBay Auction Work?

If you've never used eBay before, you might be a little anxious about what might be involved. Never fear; participating in an online auction is a piece of cake—something hundreds of millions of other users have done before you. That means you don't have to reinvent any wheels; the procedures you follow are well-established and well-documented.

An eBay auction is an Internet-based version of a traditional auction—you know, the type where a fast-talking auctioneer stands in the front of the room, trying to coax potential buyers into bidding *just a little bit more* for the piece of merchandise up for bid. The only difference is that there's no fast-talking auctioneer online (the bidding process is executed by special auction software on the auction site), and your fellow bidders aren't in the same room with you—in fact, they might be located anywhere in the world. Anyone can be a bidder, as long as he or she has Internet access.

Here's how the auction process works, in general terms:

1. You begin (as either a buyer or a seller) by registering with eBay. You can do this by clicking the Register link on eBay's home page, shown in Figure 21.1.

FIGURE 21.1

Where all the auction action starts—eBay's home page.

2. The seller creates an ad for an item and lists the item on the auction site. (eBay charges anywhere from $0.10 to $4.00 to list an item.) In the item listing, the seller specifies the length of the auction (1, 3, 5, 7, or 10 days) and the minimum bid he or she will accept for that item.

3. A potential buyer searching for a particular type of item (or just browsing through all the merchandise listed in a specific category) reads the item listing and decides to make a bid. The bidder specifies the maximum amount he or she will pay; this amount has to be equal to or greater than the seller's minimum bid, or higher than any other existing bids.

4. eBay's built-in bidding software automatically places a bid for the bidder that bests the current bid by a specified amount—but doesn't reveal the bidder's maximum bid. For example, the current bid on an item might be $25. A bidder is willing to pay up to $40 for the item, and enters a maximum bid of $40. eBay's "proxy" software places a bid for the new bidder in the amount of $26—higher than the current bid but less than the specified maximum

bid. If there are no other bids, this bidder wins the auction with a $26 bid. Other potential buyers, however, can place additional bids; unless their maximum bids are more than the current bidder's $40 maximum, they are informed (by email) that they have been outbid—and the first bidder's current bid is automatically raised to match the new bids (up to the specified maximum bid price).

5. At the conclusion of an auction, eBay informs the high bidder of his or her winning bid. The seller is responsible for contacting the high bidder and arranging payment. When the seller receives the buyer's payment (typically via PayPal), the seller then ships the merchandise directly to the buyer.

6. Concurrent with the close of the auction, eBay bills the seller for a small percentage (starting at 8.75%) of the final bid price. This selling fee is directly billed to the seller's credit card.

> **note**
>
> Learn even more about eBay auctions in my companion book, *Absolute Beginner's Guide to eBay*, 5th Edition (Que, 2008), available where you purchased this title.

eBay Bidding, Step-by-Step

Bidding in an online auction is kind of like shopping at an online retailer—except that you don't flat-out make a purchase. Instead, you make a bid—and you only get to purchase the item at the end of the auction if your bid was the highest bid made.

Here's how it works:

1. You look for items using eBay's search function (via the Search box on eBay's home page) or by browsing through the product categories.

2. When you find an item you're interested in, take a moment to examine all the details. A typical item listing (like the one shown in Figure 21.2) includes a photo of the item, a brief product description, shipping and payment information, and instructions on how to place a bid.

> **note**
>
> Some auctions have a *reserve price*. The high bid must be above this price (which is hidden) to actually win the auction. If bids don't reach the reserve, the seller is not obligated to sell the item.

FIGURE 21.2

An eBay item
listing—ready to
bid?

3. Now it's time to place your bid, which you do by clicking the Place Bid button. Remember, you're not buying the item at this point; you're just telling eBay how much you're willing to pay. Your bid must be at or above the current bid amount. My recommendation is to determine the maximum amount you'd be willing to pay for that item, and bid that amount—regardless of what the current bid level is.

4. eBay uses automatic proxy bidding software to automatically handle the bidding process from here. You bid the maximum amount you're willing to pay, and eBay's proxy software enters the minimum bid necessary—without revealing your maximum bid amount. Your bid will be automatically raised (to no more than your maximum amount) when other users bid.

5. The auction proceeds. Most auctions run for seven days, although sellers have the option of running 1-, 3-, 5-, 7-, and 10-day auctions.

6. If you're the high bidder at the end of the auction, eBay informs you (via email) that you're the winner.

note

If an item is listed at a fixed price, you'll see a Buy It Now button instead of or in addition to the Place Bid button. Click the Buy It Now button to purchase the item for that fixed price, as described in the "Buy It Quick with Buy It Now" section later in this chapter.

7. You can pay immediately (via the PayPal service) by clicking the Pay Now button in this end-of-auction notice. Your payment should include both the cost of the item (the winning bid amount) and a reasonable shipping/handling charge, as determined by the seller.

8. The seller ships the item to you.

It's important to note that even though you've been using the services of the eBay site, the ultimate transaction is between you and the individual seller. You don't pay eBay; eBay is just the middleman.

Buy It Quick with Buy It Now

Tired of waiting around for the end of an auction, only to find out you didn't have the winning bid? Well, there's a way to actually *buy* some items you see for auction without going through the bidding process. All you have to do is look for those auctions that have a Buy It Now (BIN) option.

Buy It Now is an option that some (but not all) sellers add to their auctions. With Buy It Now, the item is sold (and the auction ended) if the first bidder places a bid for a specified price. (For this reason, some refer to Buy It Now auctions as "fixed-price" auctions—even though they're slightly different from eBay's *real* fixed-priced listings.)

Buying an item with Buy It Now is really simple. If you see an item identified with a Buy It Now price (as shown in Figure 21.3), just enter a bid at that price. You'll immediately be notified that you've won the auction (and instructed to pay—typically via PayPal), and the auction will be officially closed.

note

PayPal is a service (owned by eBay) that lets sellers accept credit card payments in their auctions. PayPal functions as a middleman; the buyer pays PayPal (via credit card), and then PayPal deposits the funds in the seller's bank account. Because the majority of buyers prefer to pay by credit card, using PayPal to accept credit card payments is a necessity for sellers!

tip

To increase your chances of winning an auction, use a technique called *sniping*. When you snipe, you hold your bid until the very last seconds of the auction. If you bid high enough and late enough, other bidders won't have time to respond to your bid—and your high bid will win!

FIGURE 21.3

An item for sale at a fixed price via Buy It Now.

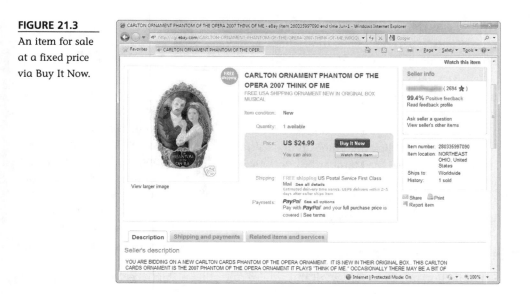

Other eBay sellers choose to skip the auction process entirely and sell their items at a fixed price. These listings also display the Buy It Now button but without a bidding option. Fixed-priced listings are common in eBay Stores, where larger sellers offer a constant supply of fixed-priced merchandise for sale all year round.

Protecting Yourself Against Fraudulent Sellers

When you're bidding for and buying items on eBay, you're pretty much in "buyer beware" territory. You agree to buy an item, almost sight unseen, from someone whom you know practically nothing about. You send that person a check and hope and pray that you get something shipped back in return—and that the thing that's shipped is the thing you thought you were buying, in good condition. If you don't like what you got—or if you received nothing at all—the seller has your money. And what recourse do you have?

> **tip**
>
> Even if a seller offers the Buy It Now option, you don't have to bid at the Buy It Now price. You can bid at a lower price and hope that you win the auction, which then proceeds normally. (The Buy It Now option disappears when the first bid is made—or, in a reserve price auction, when the reserve price is met.)

Checking Feedback

The first line of defense against frauds and cheats is to intelligently choose the people you deal with. On eBay, the best way to do this is via the Feedback system.

Next to every seller's name is a number and percentage, which represents that seller's Feedback rating. You should always check a seller's Feedback rating before you bid. If the number is high with an overwhelmingly positive percentage, you can feel safer than if the seller has a lot of negative feedback. For even better protection, click the seller's name in the item listing to view his Member Profile, where you can read individual feedback comments. Be smart and avoid those sellers who have a history of delivering less than what was promised.

> **tip**
>
> If you're new to eBay, you can build up your feedback fast by purchasing a few low-cost items—preferably using the Buy It Now feature, so you get the transaction over quickly. It's good to have a Feedback rating of 20 or better before you start selling!

Getting Help After a Bad Transaction

What do you do if you follow all this advice and still end up receiving unacceptable merchandise—or no merchandise at all? Fortunately, PayPal offers a Buyer Protection plan for any auction transaction gone bad.

To qualify for PayPal Buyer Protection, your transaction must meet all of these requirements:

- You used PayPal to pay for the item.
- You paid in a single payment. (Items purchased with PayPal's multiple-payment plan are not eligible for protection.)
- You open a dispute within 45 days of the date you sent the payment.
- The item itself is eligible for the Buyer Protection plan; look for the PayPal Buyer Protection logo in the item listing.

To open a PayPal Buyer Protection case, click the Resolution Center link at the bottom of any eBay page and follow the instructions from there. Again, you have to dispute a transaction within 45 days from your PayPal payment. At that point, the seller has seven days to respond. If no satisfactory action has been taken by the eighth day, you can return to the Resolution Center and escalate your dispute to a full-fledged claim.

If PayPal finds in your favor, you should be reimbursed for your claim. In the United States, PayPal protects you for the full price of the merchandise; this coverage is capped in some other countries. See the PayPal site for more details.

eBay Selling, Step-by-Step

Have some old stuff in your garage or attic that you want to get rid of? Consider selling it on eBay. Selling on eBay is a little more involved than bidding but can generate big bucks if you do it right. Here's how it works:

1. If you haven't registered for an eBay seller account yet, do so now. You'll need to provide eBay with your credit card and checking account number for verification and billing purposes.

2. Before you list your first item, you need to do a little homework. That means determining what you're going to sell and for how much, as well as how you're going to describe the item. You'll need to prepare the information you need to write a full item description, as well as take a few digital photos of the item to include with the listing.

3. Homework out of the way, it's time to create the auction listing. Start by clicking the Sell button on eBay's home page. As you can see in Figure 21.4, eBay displays a series of forms for you to complete; the information you enter into these forms is used to create your item listing. You'll need to select a category for your item; enter a title and description; determine how long you want your auction to run and what kind of payments you'll accept; insert a photo of the item, if you have one; and enter the amount of the desired minimum (starting) bid.

> **note**
>
> eBay makes its money by charging sellers two types of fees. (Buyers don't pay fees to eBay.) *Insertion fees* are based on the minimum bid or reserve price of the item listed. *Final value fees* are charged when you sell an item, based on the item's final selling price. Fees are typically charged directly to the seller's credit card account.

FIGURE 21.4

Creating a new eBay item listing.

4. After you enter all the information, eBay creates and displays a preliminary version of your auction listing. If you like what you see, click OK to start the auction.

5. Sit back and wait for the auction to progress.

6. When the auction is over, eBay notifies you (via email) of the high bid and provides the email address of the winning bidder.

tip

You can monitor the progress of all your current auctions with the My eBay page. Just click the My eBay link at the top of eBay's home page.

7. Many winning bidders pay via credit card (using the PayPal service) as soon as the auction is over by clicking the Pay Now link in the end-of-auction notice they receive. If the high bidder doesn't pay immediately, email him an invoice containing the final bid price and the shipping/handling charges.

8. After you've been paid, pack the item and ship it out.

That's it—you've just completed a successful eBay auction!

THE ABSOLUTE MINIMUM

Here are the key points to remember from this chapter:

- An eBay auction is a lot like a real-world auction; a seller lists an item for sale, interested people bid increasing amounts on the item, and the highest bid wins.

- To bid on an item, enter the highest price you're willing to pay and let eBay's proxy bidding software do the rest.

- Many items feature the Buy It Now option, which lets you purchase the item immediately for a fixed price, without waiting for the entire auction process to end.

- To protect against fraudulent sellers, check the seller's feedback rating before you bid; if a transaction goes bad, eBay has processes in place to protect you.

- To sell an item, make sure you have all the information you need to write a detailed item description—as well as a few digital photos of the item.

22

BUYING AND SELLING ON CRAIGSLIST

eBay isn't the only place to buy and sell items on the Web. When you want to buy or sell something locally, craigslist is the place.

Craigslist is a network of local online classifieds sites. On craigslist you pick your local site and then create a classified ad for what you're selling; potential buyers browse the ads, contact the seller, and pay for and pick up the items locally.

Understanding Online Classifieds

Like eBay, craigslist is just a middleman, facilitating sales between individual buyers and sellers. Unlike eBay's online auctions, however, items on craigslist are typically listed at a fixed cost; there is no bidding process. As with traditional print-based classified ads, some sellers might accept lower prices than listed if you make an offer or might list an item at a fixed price "or best offer." All negotiations are between the seller and the buyer. Most sales are paid for with cash.

Another big difference between eBay and craigslist is that eBay is a fairly full-featured marketplace; it offers a number of tools for both buyers and sellers that help to automate and take the guesswork out of the process. Not so with craigslist, which resembles what eBay was like about 10 years ago, before it became more sophisticated. Creating an ad is pretty much filling in a blank text box, with little help from craigslist on how to do it. Craigslist doesn't even get involved in the selling process; buyers pay sellers directly, often in cash. There's no PayPal to deal with, and no way to pay via credit card.

For that matter, craigslist doesn't offer the buyer and seller protection plans that you find on eBay—which makes buying via classified ad that much more risky. If a buyer pays with a bad check, there's not much the seller can do about it; if a seller gets an item home and finds out it doesn't work as promised, *caveat emptor.*

> **note**
>
> Learn more about eBay in Chapter 21, "Buying and Selling on eBay."

> **tip**
>
> Since craigslist is a collection of local sites, it's important to know that not all of these local sites have a large number of listings. In most big cities, such as New York and San Francisco, craigslist is a vibrant marketplace. If you're in some smaller cities and towns, however, you may find fewer listings—and, if you're selling, far fewer potential buyers.

Browsing the Listings

As I said in the introduction to this chapter, craigslist is actually a network of individual local sites. In fact, the craigslist home page, shown in Figure 22.1, is nothing more than a listing of these local sites. So to use craigslist, you first have to navigate to your specific local site; you do this by going to the national craigslist home page and then clicking your city or state from the list.

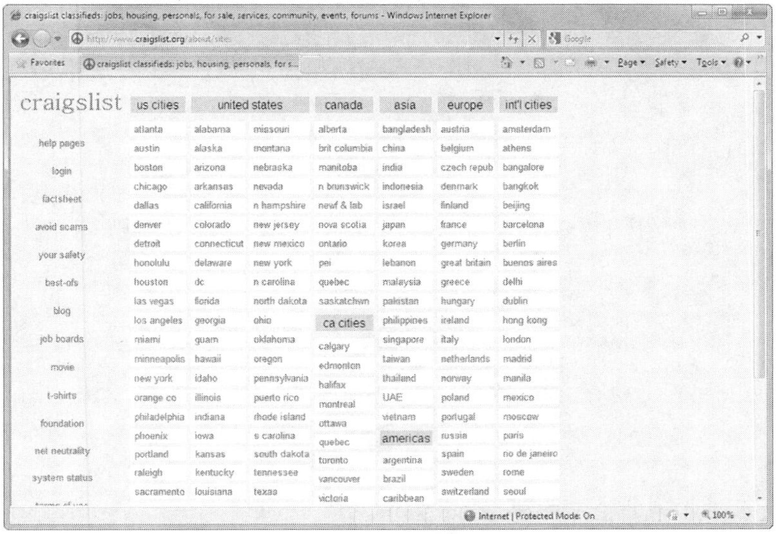

FIGURE 22.1

The global craigslist site.

Once you're on your local craigslist site, you see links to all the product and service categories offered by craigslist in your area. As you can see in Figure 22.2, the categories available mirror those in a typical newspaper classifieds section. You'll find the following major categories:

- Community (musicians wanted, lost and found, local news, and so on)
- Housing
- Jobs
- For Sale
- Services
- Gigs
- Resumes
- Personals
- Discussion forums

If you're looking for an item for sale, it's probably going to be in the For Sale category. If you're looking for something else, however, then the other categories might hold interest. It might surprise you to know that in many cities craigslist is the largest marketplace for job wanted ads; it's also a big site for home and apartment listings. For that matter, craigslist has a thriving personals section, in case that's what you're looking for.

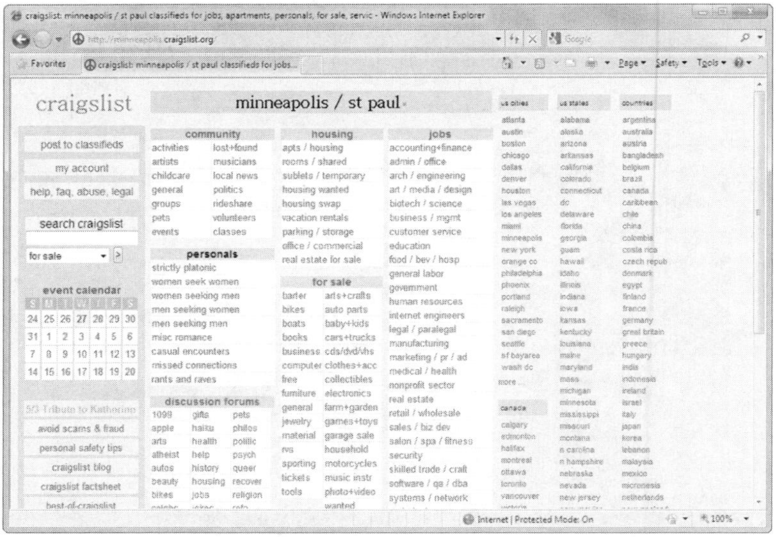

FIGURE 22.2

Category listings on craigslist.

Buying on Craigslist

If you want to buy a specific type of item, you need to browse craigslist's For Sale listings. Within this major category you'll find additional subcategories, such as Computers, Furniture, Musical Instruments, Electronics, Tools, and the like. Click through to a subcategory to view the ads within that category.

As you can see in Figure 22.3, a typical craigslist ad includes a title, a description of the item being sold, and one or more pictures of the item. Unlike with eBay, craigslist offers no direct mechanism for contacting the seller or for purchasing directly from the listing page. While some ads include the seller's phone number, most don't. Instead, you contact the seller by clicking the email link included in the ad.

So if you're interested in the item, contact the seller via email and express your interest. You can then arrange a time to view the item; if you like what you see, you can pay for it then and take it with you.

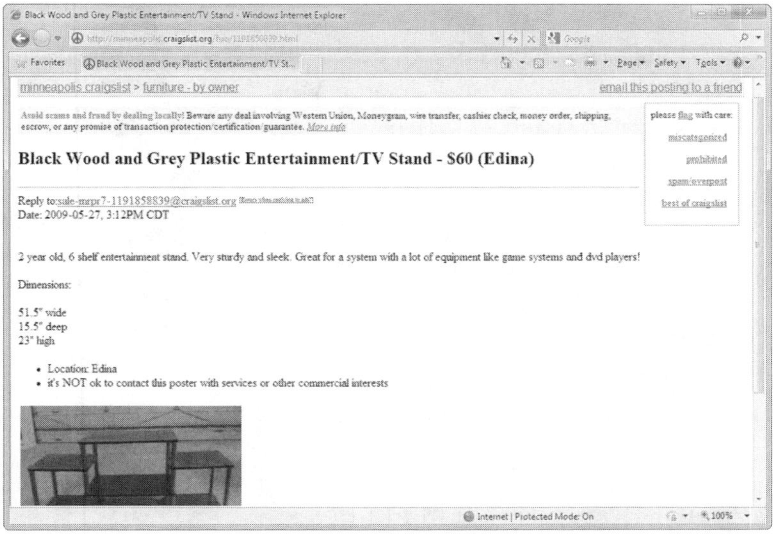

FIGURE 22.3

A typical craigslist For Sale ad.

Listing an Item for Sale

If you're a seller, the big difference between eBay and craigslist is that craigslist is absolutely free. The site charges nothing to list an item, and it charges no final value or commission fees. This makes craigslist quite attractive to sellers; you can list anything you want and don't have to pay if it doesn't sell.

Listing an item for sale on craigslist is similar to listing a fixed-price item on eBay. The differences are more in what you *don't* have to do; there are fewer "blanks" to fill in—and fewer options for your listing.

To list an item for sale on the craigslist site, follow these steps:

> **note**
>
> While the vast majority of craigslist ads are free, not all are. In particular, craigslist charges for job listings in some major cities, brokered apartment listings in New York City, and all listings in the adult services category.

1. Navigate to the home page for your local craigslist community; then click the Post to Classifieds link on the left side of the page.

2. When the next page appears, click the category in which you want to list— probably the For Sale category.

3. You're now prompted to select an appropriate subcategory. Do so.

4. You now see the listing creation page, as shown in Figure 22.4. Here you enter information into the appropriate fields: Price, Specific Location, Posting Title, Posting Description, Your Email Address, and Reply To (to have craigslist "anonymize" your email address).

tip

Selling on craigslist is better than eBay when you have a big or bulky item that might be difficult to ship long distances. Local buyers will pick up the items they purchase.

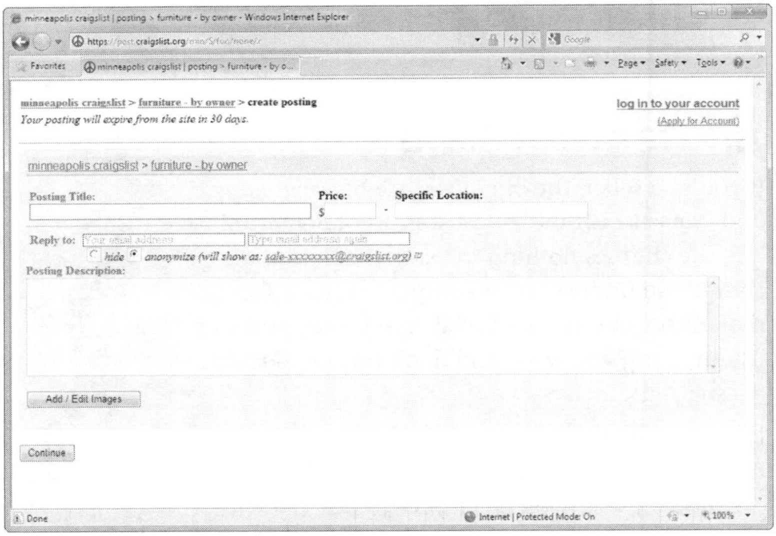

5. If you want to include digital photos of your item in the listing, click the Add/Edit Images button and select the files you want to upload.

FIGURE 22.4

Creating a new craigslist classified listing.

6. After you've entered all the necessary information, click the Continue button.

7. Craigslist now displays a preview of your listing; if you like what you see, click Continue. (If you don't like what you see, click the Edit button and make some changes.) Your listing will appear on the Craigslist site within the next 15 minutes or so.

For your protection, craigslist displays an anonymized email address in your item listing. Buyers email this anonymous address, and the emails are forwarded to your real email address. That way you won't get email stalkers from your craigslist ads—in fact, no one will know exactly who is doing the posting!

Making the Sale

When someone replies to your listing, craigslist forwards you that message via email. You can then reply to the potential buyer directly; in most instances, that means arranging a time for that person to come to your house to either view or purchase the item of interest.

caution

If you're not comfortable with strangers visiting your house and you're selling something portable, arrange to meet at a neutral location. If you're selling a larger item, make sure another family member or friend is home when the buyer is supposed to visit.

Unlike eBay, where you have to ship the item to the buyer, craigslist buyers more often than not pick up the items they purchase. That means you have to be at home for the buyer to visit, and you have to be comfortable with strangers visiting. You also have to be prepared to help the buyer load up whatever it is you're selling into his or her vehicle for the trip home—which can be a major issue if you're selling big stuff and you're a small person.

As to payment, the vast majority of craigslist purchases are made with cash. You might want to keep some spare cash on hand to make change, in case the buyer pays with larger bills.

For higher priced items, you might want to accept payment via cashier's check or money order. Just be sure that the check or money order is made out for the exact amount of the purchase; you don't want to give back cash as change for a money order purchase.

caution

Under no circumstances should you accept payment via personal check. It's far too easy for a shady buyer to write you a check and take off with the merchandise, only for you to discover a few days later that the check bounced. If you *must* accept a personal check, hold onto the merchandise for a full 10 working days to make sure the check clears; it's probably easier for all involved for the buyer to just get the cash.

The Absolute Minimum

Here are the key points to remember from this chapter:

- Craigslist is a network of local sites for online classified ads.
- Buyers purchase directly from craigslist sellers, typically paying cash and picking up the items themselves.
- Unlike eBay, craigslist offers few buyer or seller tools—or protections.
- Also unlike eBay, selling on eBay is completely free—no charges for anyone.

23

BANKING AND PAYING BILLS ONLINE

Tired of standing in line at your local bank? Well, if you have a personal computer and an Internet connection, you can do all your normal banking tasks online. No more standing in line; now you can transfer funds, find out account balances, and pay your bills from the convenience of your own home. It's online banking, either over the Web or with a personal finance program such as Quicken.

Online Banking: How It Works

There are two basic approaches to online banking. With *web-based banking* you use your web browser to access your bank's website from any PC. Or you can use a program such as Quicken to do *software-based banking.* Each approach has its pros and cons.

Web-based banking is the easiest type of online banking, and almost all banks offer it. No expensive software is necessary, and many banks offer web-based access free or at a low monthly cost. Best of all, you can do it from any computer; just open your web browser, go to your bank's website, enter your username and password, and you're in. (Initial registration might take a little longer, of course.)

Software-based banking costs more money but also offers more functionality. You have to pay for the software itself, of course. Many banks also charge more for Quicken access than they do for web-based banking. In addition, not all banks offer Quicken access, preferring their own web-based interfaces. But when you go the software route, you get all the money-management features built into the software, which typically let you manage not just your bank accounts but also credit cards, loans, IRA/401K accounts, stocks and bonds, and the like.

Which is the best approach for you? Well, if you're just getting started and want the easiest possible approach, go with web-based banking. If you're comfortable with more advanced financial management, however—and if your bank interfaces with Quicken—you may prefer the cross-account management capabilities of a financial management program.

> **tip**
>
> Some banks charge either a monthly or per-transaction fee to access their online banking features. Other banks offer web-based banking (and sometimes software-based banking) free. If you anticipate doing a lot of online banking, it pays to shop around for the best deal.

Web-Based Banking

Most banks today have their own websites and thus offer some form of web-based banking. You probably have to sign up to use your bank's web-based services; make sure you have all your account numbers (and possibly your ATM PIN) handy when you're signing up. You're then assigned a username and password, and you're ready for future sessions.

Why use web-based banking? First, it's great to be able to access and manage your checking and savings accounts from home or on the road; you don't have to be physically present to check your account balances or transfer funds between accounts. Second, when compared to software-based banking, anyone can go the

Web route; you don't need to purchase and learn any particular software program to do your banking. Then there's the fact that you can access a bank's web page from any PC connected to the Internet, so that you can do your banking when you're on the road and away from home. The same can't be said for software programs that are installed on specific machines. In addition, setting up your account at a web-based bank is relatively easy, compared to all the information-entering you have to do with Quicken. On a website, once you enter your account number and password, your account should be ready to access. Finally, with web-based banking, all your financial information is stored on the bank's website, so if your computer crashes, your data won't be lost. It's useful, easy, and reliable—what's not to like?

Ask your local banker about what online services the bank offers—and to find out the bank's website address.

Accessing a bank's website is simple. After you've signed up for your bank's online service, you access your bank's website by entering your assigned username and password. From there, you can typically click to view details about any and all accounts you have at that bank, as shown in Figure 23.1. You can view your latest statement online, view your most recent transactions, and perform specific operations—such as transferring funds from one account to another. Even better, many banks offer online bill payment services, so you can use your bank's website to electronically pay all your bills. That's convenient.

FIGURE 23.1
A typical online banking site.

Software-Based Banking

The other approach to online banking is to use a software program, such as Quicken. There are several benefits to going this route, including the fact that you can do a lot of your work offline, without hogging your Internet connection; you need only log on to upload your instructions and download your recent transactions. Second, you can use your financial management program to handle *all* your personal finances from multiple accounts and multiple banks. With web-based banking, you have to access different websites for each of your

note

Learn more about Quicken at quicken.intuit.com.

bank and credit card accounts. Finally, Quicken offers a raft of account management and financial analysis tools, so you can track your budget, see how your investments are performing, and such. There's lots of functionality, even if you have to pay for it.

If you're using Quicken (shown in Figure 23.2), you first have to configure it to work with your bank. To see if your bank interfaces with Quicken (not all do), click Online, Participating Financial Institutions. When the next window appears, select your bank from the list and then click the Apply Now button and follow the onscreen instructions. Once set up, all you have to do to update your account information over the Internet is to click the One Step Update button on the Quicken toolbar; this downloads all your latest transactions from your bank to the Quicken program.

FIGURE 23.2

Tracking bank accounts and more with Quicken.

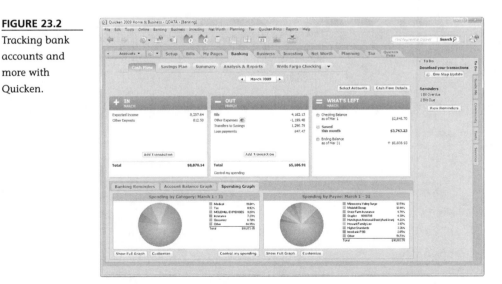

As noted, Quicken lets you track more than just your bank accounts. You can set up either program to automatically record a regular paycheck, track expenses by category, and track credit card and investment accounts. All your accounts show up on the program's home page; click an account to view more details.

Paying Your Bills Online

One of the primary reasons to participate in online banking is to pay your bills online. Both web-based and software-based banking solutions offer online bill-paying functionality.

How It Works

How you pay your bills online depends on how you do your online banking.

If you're using a web-based banking service, online bill paying is handled at your bank's website by your bank. You need to sign up for your bank's bill-paying service and then enter information about each bill—the payee's mailing address, your account number, the payment amount, that sort of thing. From there it's a simple matter of clicking the appropriate link or button at your bank's website to pay a given bill when it's due. This bill-paying service might be offered free by your bank, although it's more common for a monthly charge to be assessed.

> **tip**
>
> Some payees also let you make payments (via credit card) at their websites. Check with the billing company to see if online payment of this sort is offered.

If you're using Quicken, online bill paying is handled by the software program (*not* your bank). You enter information about each payee and bill into the program; then you click the appropriate button to initiate payments. You might have to pay for this service, too.

Whichever approach you take, you can typically set up a recurring payee list so that paying a monthly bill is as simple as clicking your mouse. (One-time-only payees will have to be set up as they arise.) You can even instruct your bill payment service to automatically pay selected bills each month, such as your mortgage or car payment. Payment is typically sent electronically from your bank to each payee.

> **note**
>
> In those instances where a payee is not set up to accept electronic payments, your bank or bill-paying service writes a physical check to the payee.

Bill Payment Services

There are also several dedicated companies that offer online bill payment services, for a fee. These companies let you pay all your bills electronically for those accounts that accept electronic funds transfers. If an account still requires a physical check, the online bill payment firm will cut and mail a check at your electronic command.

The most popular online bill-payment services include the following:

- MyCheckFree (www.mycheckfree.com)
- MyEZBills (www.myezbills.com)
- Paytrust (www.paytrust.com)
- Xpress Bill Pay (www.xpressbillpay.com)

THE ABSOLUTE MINIMUM

Here are the key points to remember from this chapter:

- Online banking lets you check account balances, transfer funds between accounts, and even pay your bills from your own PC.
- With web-based banking, you use any web browser to connect to your bank's website and perform all your banking tasks from there.
- Quicken lets you manage all your financial accounts from a single program, which then connects to the Internet to download transactions from your bank.
- Both web-based and software-based banking solutions offer online bill-payment services, which let you pay all your bills from your home computer.

24

WATCHING VIDEOS ON THE WEB

Want to rewatch last night's episode of *The Daily Show*? Or maybe a classic music video from your favorite band? How about the most recent network newscast? Or that latest "viral video" you've been hearing about?

Here's the latest hot thing on the Web—watching your favorite television programs, films, and videos via your web browser. Assuming you have a fast enough Internet connection, you can find tens of thousands of free and paid videos to watch at dozens of different websites. And, if you have an Apple Video iPod or Sony PlayStation Portable, you can transfer the videos you find to your portable device to watch while you're on the go.

Read on to learn more.

Looking for Videos on the Web

The first trick to viewing videos on your PC is to find some videos you want to watch. This isn't difficult; many sites specialize in online videos, and many regular websites offer videos as part of their regular content.

Videos on Regular Websites

For example, the CBS News site (www.cbsnews.com) features all sorts of videos on its home page. As you can see in Figure 24.1, you can watch the most recent broadcasts of *60 Minutes*, *Face the Nation*, and the *CBS Evening News*, along with individual segments from each program and special web-only newscasts. All you have to do is select the video you want to watch and then click the Play button on the embedded video player; there's no separate software to launch.

> **note**
>
> Many sites offer their web-based videos free. Others charge a fee to view or download their videos. At this point in time, there's no standard as to what's free and what's not, so browse around before you enter your credit card number.

Similarly, you can go to the NBC website (www.nbc.com) to view full episodes of its top prime-time shows. Missed this week's episode of *Heroes* or *The Office*? They're available online, for free—as you can see in Figure 24.2.

FIGURE 24.1

Watch news broadcasts for free at the CBS News website.

FIGURE 24.2

Prime-time shows online at NBC's website.

Most network TV sites have similar free video offerings. Check out ABC.com (abc.go.com), CBS.com (www.cbs.com), Fox on Demand (www.fox.com), and Comedy Central (www.comedycentral.com). For your favorite music videos, both current and classic, you can't beat MTV.com (www.mtv.com) and VH1.com (www.vh1.com). And to get your daily sports fix, check out the Motion Video link at the ESPN website (espn.go.com).

Video-Only Websites

Then there are the websites that specialize in web-based videos. These sites offer videos, videos, and nothing but videos—often for free.

The most popular of these online video sites include

- **AOL Video** (video.aol.com)
- **Hulu** (www.hulu.com)
- **Joost** (www.joost.com)
- **Metacafe** (www.metacafe.com)
- **Veoh** (www.veoh.com)
- **Yahoo! Video** (video.yahoo.com)
- **YouTube** (www.youtube.com)

These sites offer a mix of commercial and homemade videos. For example, Hulu (shown in Figure 24.3) offers episodes from major-network TV shows, as well as new and classic feature films. YouTube, on the other hand, offers millions of free videos uploaded by its users.

FIGURE 24.3

TV shows and movies for online viewing at Hulu.

Whichever service you use, you typically watch the videos in your web browser, using a technique called *streaming video*. This means that there's no downloading necessary (except, perhaps, for an initial plug-in to enable video streaming); the video streams from the website to your computer in real time. Just click the Play button and settle back to watch the show.

Viewing Videos on YouTube

Unquestionably, the biggest video site on the Web is YouTube (www.youtube.com), shown in Figure 24.4. What's cool about YouTube is that all the videos are uploaded by other users, so you get a real mix of professional-quality and amateur clips.

Searching for Videos

Looking for an early performance clip of the Beatles? Or a classic toy commercial from the 1970s? Or maybe a homemade mashup of news clips with a hip hop soundtrack? Or something to do with dancing monkeys? What you're looking for is probably somewhere on YouTube; all you have to do is search for it, using the top-of-page search box.

note

Sites that offer videos for sale, such as the iTunes Store, let you download the videos to your PC. Once they're downloaded, you can watch any video at your leisure and (in some instances) copy the video to your iPod for portable viewing. Learn more in the "Downloading Videos from the iTunes Store" section later in this chapter.

FIGURE 24.4

View user-
uploaded videos
at YouTube.

FIGURE 24.4

View user-
uploaded videos
at YouTube.

The results of your search are shown on a separate page, such as the one shown in Figure 24.5. Each matching video is listed with a representative thumbnail image, the length of the video, a short description (and descriptive tags), the name of the user who uploaded the video, and a viewer rating (from zero to five stars).

caution

While YouTube has strict content policies and a self-policing community, there are no parental controls on the site—so it's viewer beware!

FIGURE 24.5

Searching for
YouTube videos.

Viewing Videos

When you find a video you like, click the image or title, and a new page appears. As you can see in Figure 24.6, this page includes an embedded video player, which starts playing the video automatically. Use the Pause and Play controls as necessary.

FIGURE 24.6

FIGURE 24.6

Watching a
video on
YouTube.

Sharing Videos

Videos become viral when they're shared between hundreds and thousands of users—and the easiest way to share a YouTube video is via email. YouTube lets you send an email containing a link to the video you like to your friends. When a friend receives this email, he or she can click the link in the message to go to YouTube and play the video.

When you want to share a video, go to that video's page and click the Share tab underneath the YouTube video player. When the Share tab expands, scroll to the Send This Video from YouTube section and enter the email addresses of the intended recipients into the To box. (Separate multiple addresses with commas.) Enter a personal message if you want, and then click the Send button. In a few minutes your recipients will receive the message, complete with a link to the selected video.

> **tip**
>
> Most YouTube videos can also be watched full-screen; just click the full-screen button beneath the video. If a video is available in high-definition, click the HD button to view it in all its high-resolution, widescreen glory. (If there's no HD button, the video wasn't uploaded in high definition.)

To view the video, all a recipient has to do is click the video thumbnail in the message. This opens a web browser, accesses the YouTube site, and starts playing the video you shared.

Uploading Your Own Videos to YouTube

Anyone can upload a movie or video to the YouTube site. Once it's uploaded, users can view the video—and if you're lucky, the video will go viral!

Video Requirements

You can shoot YouTube videos with any computer webcam or consumer camcorder. Just make sure the videos you shoot conform to these YouTube specifications:

- MPEG-4 format video with either the DivX or XviD codecs
- MP3 or AAC format audio
- 320×240 pixel minimum resolution; 640×480 resolution for high quality playback; 720×480 pixel resolution for widescreen playback; 1280×720 pixel resolution for high definition playback
- Frame rate of 24 frames per second (FPS) or higher (30 FPS is best)
- Length of 10 minutes or less
- File size of 2GB or less

Making the Upload

Assuming your video is in the right format, follow these steps to upload it to the YouTube site:

1. Click the Upload button at the top of any YouTube page; then select Upload Video File.
2. When the Video File Upload page appears, click the Upload Video button.
3. When the next dialog box appears, navigate to and select the file to upload; then click the Open button.
4. While the video uploads, you're prompted to enter information about the video, including title, description, tags, category, and privacy level, as shown in Figure 24.7. Do so, and then click the Save Changes button.

That's it. After the video uploads, YouTube converts it to the proper viewing format and creates a viewing page for the video. To view your video, click the My Videos link on any YouTube page, and then click the thumbnail for your new video.

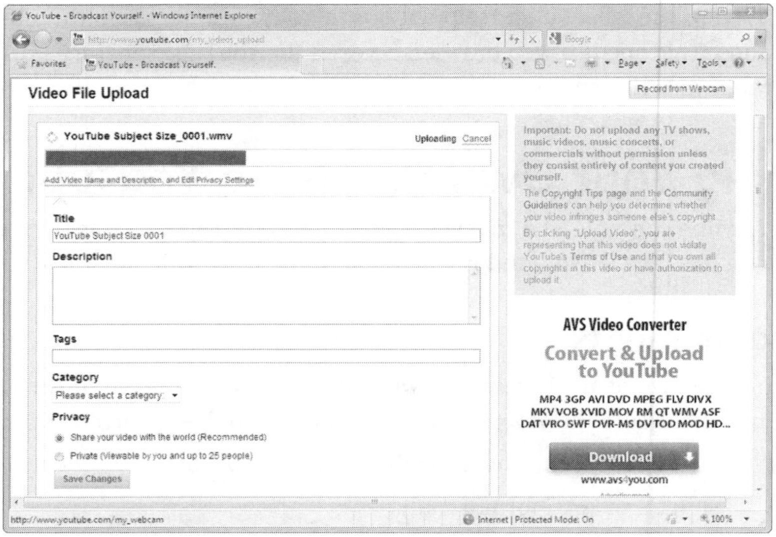

FIGURE 24.7

Entering infor-
mation about an
uploaded video.

Downloading Videos from the iTunes Store

If you're the proud owner of an Apple iPod with video playback features (or just an
iPod-less schmuck who wants to watch videos on his PC), you can find a lot of
videos to download from Apple's iTunes Store. Just open the iTunes player and click
the iTunes Store link in the Source pane. When the store's home page appears, click
the Movies, TV Shows, or Music Videos link, depending on what type of video you
want.

Purchasing Videos

iTunes offers a variety of material for purchase and download. Most TV shows go for
$1.99 per episode, although you can also buy a "season pass" to view all episodes in
a season for a discounted price. (Figure 24.8 shows some of the TV shows available
for purchase.) Music videos typically go for $1.99 also; movies are priced from $9.99
to $14.99, depending on age and studio.

Purchasing a video is as simple as clicking the Buy button. Your credit card is
charged, and the video is automatically downloaded to your computer. After the
download is complete, it appears in your iTunes library in either the Movies or TV
Shows section. You can then view the item from within the iTunes player; just select
the item in your library and click the Play button.

FIGURE 24.8
TV shows for download from the iTunes Store.

Transferring Videos to Your iPod

If you have an iPod or iPhone with video capability, you can transfer your down-loaded videos and movies to your portable device via the iTunes software. Just check the items to transfer in the library window, connect your iPod, and let the transfer happen automatically. Remember, though, that video files are much larger than music files; you'll fill up your iPod's disk drive pretty quick if you load up a lot of long videos and movies!

THE ABSOLUTE MINIMUM

Here are the key points to remember from this chapter:

- Numerous websites offer videos for online viewing or downloading.

- Most major TV networks offer episodes of their top series for online viewing.

- The most popular video download site today is YouTube—which also lets you upload your own videos for others to view.

- Apple's iTunes Store sells many TV shows, music videos, and movies to down-load and transfer to your video iPod.

25

USING WEB-BASED APPLICATIONS

Did you know you can write memos and balance your budget online without the trouble or expense of installing a software program such as Microsoft Word or Excel? So-called *web-based applications* offer most of the functionality of traditional software programs but run over the Internet, so you can access your documents from any PC at any time. It's a great way to get your work done—at home, in the office, or on the road!

Understanding Web-Based Applications

Web-based applications are just like software-based applications except they run over the Internet. You access the application by pointing your web browser to the application's website; from there, you run the application and create or open any documents you want to work with.

With traditional software applications, you have to install a copy of the application on each computer you own; the more computers you use, the more expensive that gets. Web-based applications, on the other hand, are typically free to use. I don't know about you, but free is pretty attractive these days.

Then there's the issue of your documents. With traditional software applications, the documents you create are stored on the computer on which they were created. If you want to edit a work document at home, you have to transfer that document from one computer to another—and then manage all the different "versions" you create.

Document management is different with a web-based application. That's because your documents aren't stored on your computer; instead, they're stored on the Internet, just like the applications are. You can access your web-based documents from any computer, wherever you might be. So it's a lot easier to edit that work document at home or access your home budget while on the road.

> **tip**
>
> Web-based applications are also great for group collaboration. Multiple users from different locations can access the same document over the Internet in real time.

> **note**
>
> Web-based computing is sometimes called *cloud computing* because everything is stored on a "cloud" of Internet-based servers. Learn more in my companion book, *Cloud Computing: Web-Based Applications That Change the Way You Work and Collaborate Online* (Que, 2008).

Web-Based Calendars

To my mind, a web-based calendar just makes sense. It's one thing to keep a private schedule on a single PC, but most of us have schedules that include a lot of public or shared events. Let's face it, if you keep a personal calendar on your home PC, you can't reference it from work or when you're traveling. That limits the calendar program's usefulness.

That's why, instead of using a calendar that's wedded to a single computer, many users are moving to web-based calendars. A web-based calendar service stores your calendars on the Internet, where they can be accessed from any computer that has an Internet connection. This lets you check your schedule when you're on the road, even if your assistant in the office or your spouse at home has added new appointments since you left. Web-based calendars are also extremely easy to share with other users in any location, which makes them great for collaborative projects.

Most web-based calendars are free and offer similar online sharing and collaboration features. The most popular of these calendars include

- 30Boxes (www.30boxes.com)
- AOL Calendar (calendar.aol.com)
- Apple MobileMe Calendar (www.apple.com/mobileme/)
- CalendarHub (www.calendarhub.com)
- Famundo (www.famundo.com)
- Google Calendar (calendar.google.com), shown in Figure 25.1
- Hunt Calendars (www.huntcal.com)
- Windows Live Calendar (mail.live.com/mail/calendar.aspx)
- Yahoo! Calendar (calendar.yahoo.com)

FIGURE 25.1

Google Calendar—one of the most popular web-based calendars.

Web-Based Task Management

Just as you can track your appointments with a web-based calendar, you can track your to-do lists with web-based task management applications. These applications let you manage everything from simple to-do lists to complex group tasks, all over the Internet and collaboratively with other users.

The most popular of these web-based task management applications include the following:

- Bla-Bla List (www.blablalist.com)
- HiTask (www.hitask.com)
- Hiveminder (www.hiveminder.com)
- iPrioritize (www.iprioritize.com)
- Remember the Milk (www.rememberthemilk.com)
- Ta-da List (www.tadalist.com)
- TaskTHIS (taskthis.elucidate-apps.com)
- Trackslife (www.trackslife.com)
- Tudu List (www.tudulist.com)
- Vitalist (www.vitalist.com)
- Voo2Do (www.voo2do.com)
- Zoho Planner (planner.zoho.com)

Web-Based Office Suites

Microsoft Office is the most-used application today. It's actually a suite of applications. To that end, several companies are offering web-based office suites to compete with Microsoft Office. Most of these suites offer word processing, spreadsheet, and presentation components.

The most popular of these web-based office suites include the following:

- Glide Business (www.glidedigital.com)
- Google Docs (docs.google.com)
- Peepel Online Office (www.peepel.com)
- ThinkFree Office (www.thinkfree.com)
- WebEx Web Office (www.weboffice.com)
- Zoho Office (office.zoho.com)

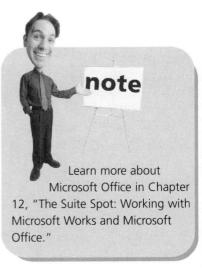

note

Learn more about Microsoft Office in Chapter 12, "The Suite Spot: Working with Microsoft Works and Microsoft Office."

Of these suites, I'm a big fan of both Google Docs and Zoho Office. Both offer similar functionality with the major applications, although Zoho Office has more pieces and parts available.

Web-Based Word Processing

The most popular component of the office suite is the word processor. You use a word processor, such as Microsoft Word, to write memos, letters, thank-you notes, fax coversheets, reports, and newsletters. It's an essential part of our computing lives.

That said, there are a number of web-based replacements for Microsoft's venerable Word program. All of these programs let you write your letters and memos and reports from any computer, no installed software necessary, as long as that computer has a connection to the Internet. And every document you create is housed on the Web,

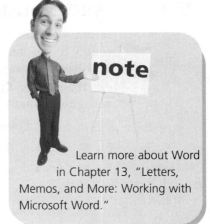

note

Learn more about Word in Chapter 13, "Letters, Memos, and More: Working with Microsoft Word."

so you don't have to worry about taking your work with you. It's cloud computing at its most useful, and it's here today.

The most popular web-based word processors include the following:

- Adobe Buzzword (buzzword.acrobat.com), shown in Figure 25.2
- Glide Write (www.glidedigital.com)
- Google Docs (docs.google.com)
- iNetWord (www.inetword.com)
- KBdocs (www.kbdocs.com)
- Peepel WebWriter (www.peepel.com)
- ThinkFree Write (www.thinkfree.com)
- Zoho Writer (writer.zoho.com)

FIGURE 25.2

The Adobe Buzzword web-based word processor.

Web-Based Spreadsheets

Several web-based spreadsheet applications are worthy competitors to Microsoft Excel. If you're at all interested in moving your number crunching and financial analysis into the cloud, these web-based applications are worth checking out:

- EditGrid (www.editgrid.com)
- eXpresso (www.expressocorp.com)
- Glide Crunch (www.glidedigital.com)
- Google Spreadsheets (docs.google.com)
- Num Sum (www.numsum.com)
- Peepel WebSheet (www.peepel.com)
- ThinkFree Calc (www.thinkfree.com)
- Zoho Sheet (sheet.zoho.com), shown in Figure 25.3

note

Learn more about Excel in Chapter 14, "Crunching Numbers: Working with Microsoft Excel."

FIGURE 25.3

The Zoho Sheet web-based spreadsheet.

Web-Based Presentations

Web-based presentation programs enable you to create, collaborate, and give presentations over the Internet. While none of these programs have the full functionality of Microsoft PowerPoint, some do offer compelling experiences for groups who need to collaborate on presentations.

The best of these web-based presentation applications include the following:

- BrinkPad (www.brinkpad.com)
- Empressr (www.empressr.com)
- Google Presentations (docs.google.com), shown in Figure 25.4
- Preezo (www.preezo.com)
- Presentation Engine (www.presentationengine.com)
- PreZentit (www.prezentit.com)
- SlideRocket (www.sliderocket.com)
- ThinkFree Show (www.thinkfree.com)
- Zoho Show (show.zoho.com)

note

Learn more about PowerPoint in Chapter 15, "Presenting Yourself: Working with Microsoft PowerPoint."

FIGURE 25.4

Google Presentations— for web-based presentations.

THE ABSOLUTE MINIMUM

Here are the key points to remember from this chapter:

- Web-based applications let you write memos, crunch numbers, and manage your appointments from any computer connected to the Internet.

- Web-based applications run in your web browser; your documents are stored on the Internet, not on your own computer.

- You can find web-based versions of all popular applications, including calendars, to-do lists, word processors, spreadsheets, and presentation applications.

26

CREATING YOUR OWN WEB PAGE

Browsing sites on the Web is fine, but what if you want to create a web page or website of your own? Fortunately, anyone can create her own page or site on the Web. All you need is a web page editing program (to create your pages) and a web hosting community (to host your pages). And to no surprise, many hosting sites offer both these features.

Read on to learn how to create your own pages on the Web.

Building a Web Page at a Home Page Community

If you want a one-stop solution to creating and hosting your own web pages, turn to one of the major *home page communities* on the Web. These sites not only help you create your own web pages, they even host your pages on the Web. And, in many cases, this basic hosting service is free!

tip

Many of these sites also offer tools for building and hosting your own personal blog. Learn more about blogs in Chapter 31, "Exploring Blogs and Podcasts."

Visiting the Communities

The most popular of these home page communities include

- Angelfire (angelfire.lycos.com)
- Bravenet (www.bravenet.com)
- FortuneCity (www.fortunecity.com)
- Freeservers (www.freeservers.com)
- Google Sites (sites.google.com)
- Homestead (www.homestead.com)
- Microsoft Office Live (office.microsoft.com/en-us/officelive/)
- Rediff (homepages.rediff.com)
- Tripod (www.tripod.lycos.com)
- Webs (www.webs.com)

When you join a home page community, you're provided with a specified amount of space on its servers, anywhere from 15MB to a full 1GB—which should be more than enough to host your personal pages. You can then use the tools on the site to create your web pages or upload previously created pages to the site.

All the major home page communities work in a similar fashion. Those that don't charge fees try to make their money by posting ads on your pages; they collect the advertising revenues, not you. Even those that purport to be free sometimes offer a variety of additional (not free) services and will be glad to charge you for additional storage space, domain name registration, e-commerce tools, and the like.

tip

Many Internet service providers also offer free personal home pages to their subscribers; check with your ISP to see what services are available.

Building a Home Page with Tripod

Tripod (tripod.lycos.com) is one of the largest and most established home page communities, and we'll use it as an example for how to create your own simple web pages. Like all home page communities, Tripod is essentially a collection of personal web pages.

Tripod offers both free and paid hosting plans. The free plan provides hosting for an unlimited number of web pages, 20MB of storage, 1GB of monthly bandwidth for site visitors, and easy-to-use page creation tools—including predesigned page templates. The paid plans offer more storage, bandwidth, and features.

caution

Tripod subsidizes its free plan by placing advertisements on all the web pages you create. If you want to avoid ads on your pages, you'll have to sign up for one of Tripod's paid plans.

To sign up for free hosting, go to Tripod's home page and click the Start Now button. When the next page appears, click the Sign Up button for the Tripod Free plan. You then have to create the customary username and password as well as provide other pertinent information.

Once you've created your free account, Tripod displays your account management page. To start building your new site, follow these steps:

1. From the home page or account management page, click the Site Builder button.

2. On the next page, click the Start with a Multi-Page Template link.

3. Tripod lists several categories of page templates. Click a category to see the available templates, as shown in Figure 26.1; then click the Choose link next to the template you want to use.

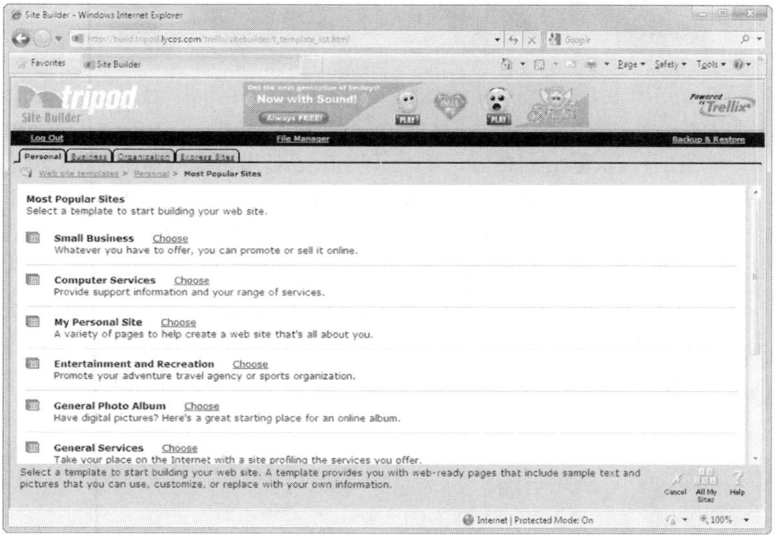

FIGURE 26.1

Choosing a Tripod web page template.

4. Tripod now displays a form page for you to fill out. Enter the required information about the site you want to create and then click Continue.

5. You now see a suggested visual design for your page. If you like this design, click the Use the Suggested Design button. To view more designs, click the Choose from All Designs button; click any design to view a preview, and then click the Use This Design button to select a design.

6. Tripod now displays the first page of your site with placeholder text and graphics, as shown in Figure 26.2. To enter your own text, click the Edit Text button next to each text block. When the text editing page appears, enter your text. Use the formatting controls to change font, font size, font color, and formatting.

FIGURE 26.2

Building the content for your web page.

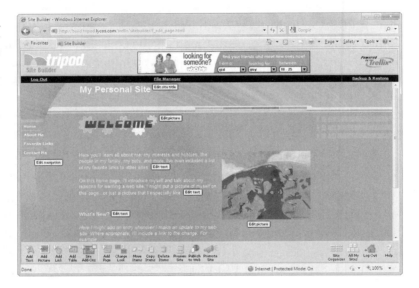

7. To insert your own picture, click the Edit Picture button next to a placeholder image. When the next page appears, click Choose a Different Picture and then click the Upload Picture button. Browse your hard disk for the picture you want to upload, and then click the Done button. When the Picture Gallery page appears, click the Choose link next to the photo you want to insert; when the Edit the Picture Settings page appears, click the Done button.

8. To add any other features to the page, scroll down and click the Edit Site Add-On button. This lets you add a variety of content modules, including search boxes, page counters, an interactive guestbook, and more.

9. When you're done editing your page, click the Publish to Web icon at the bottom of the window.

Your new web page is now saved and published to the web. The congratulations page you see includes the URL for your website, in the form of *username*.tripod.com, with your username in the place of the italics. To view your web page, click the link on this page or enter the URL into your web browser. (Figure 26.3 shows a typical Tripod web page.)

tip

To add more pages to your site, go to the Site Organizer page and click the Add Page icon. To delete a page from your site, go to the Site Organizer page and click the Delete link next to the unwanted page.

FIGURE 26.3
A basic Tripod web page; ads appear above and below this content.

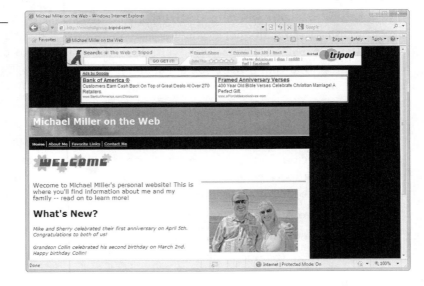

Using Page-Building Software

The web page you create at a web hosting community is a relatively simple one. If you want to create more sophisticated pages—or multiple pages in a complete website—you need a more powerful tool. Fortunately, there are numerous software programs available you can use to build really fancy web pages.

The two most popular web page editing programs are Adobe Dreamweaver (www.adobe.com/products/dreamweaver/) and Microsoft Expression Web Designer (www.microsoft.com/ expression/). Both of these programs let you design everything from simple personal pages to sophisticated e-commerce websites; you can construct pages using a WYSIWYG (what you see is what you get) interface, or enter raw HTML code.

Uploading Your Pages to a Web Host

If you build your own web pages with a program such as Dreamweaver or Expressions Web Designer, you still have to find a site on the Web to host your pages. Most home page communities offer separate page hosting services (usually for a fee), geared toward personal web pages. If you need a host for a complete website (or for small business purposes), you should probably examine a service that specializes in more sophisticated website hosting.

A website hosting service will manage all aspects of your website. For a monthly fee, you'll receive a fixed amount of space on their servers, your own website address (and your own personal domain, if you want to pay for it), and a variety of site management tools. Pricing for these services typically starts at $10 or so a month, and it goes up from there.

> **note**
>
> All web pages are based on a special programming code, called *Hypertext Markup Language* (HTML). Fortunately, most web page editing programs and services enable you to create web pages without hand-coding the pages in HTML—although you can still edit the raw HTML code if you want.

The best way to look for a website host is to access a directory of hosting services. Most of these directories let you search for hosts by various parameters, including monthly cost, disk space provided, programming and platforms supported, and extra features offered. Among the best of these host search sites are the following:

- HostIndex.com (www.hostindex.com)
- HostSearch (www.hostsearch.com)
- TopHosts.com (www.tophosts.com)

THE ABSOLUTE MINIMUM

Here are the key points to remember from this chapter:

- Web pages are built using the HTML programming language—although you don't have to know how to program to create a simple web page.
- To create a personal web page, check out one of the large page building communities, such as Tripod or Angelfire.
- To create a more sophisticated web page or website, use a dedicated page-building program, such as Adobe Dreamweaver or Microsoft Expression Web Designer.

27

EXPLORING OTHER COOL AND USEFUL WEBSITES

Throughout this section of the book we've looked at many different kinds of websites—search engines, online auctions, price comparison sites, even sites where you can watch videos online. But there's even more on the Web than that—much more.

That's where this chapter comes in. Without further ado, this chapter presents some of the most popular sites on the Web—and some of my personal favorites.

News, Sports, and Weather

The Internet is a great place to find both news headlines and in-depth analysis. Most news-related websites are updated in real time, so you're always getting the latest news—on your computer screen, when you want it.

News Sites

Some of the biggest, most popular news sites on the Web are run by the major broadcast and cable news networks or by the major national newspapers. You can turn to these sites to get the latest headlines and—in many cases—live audio and video feeds.

The major news sites on the Web include

- **ABC News** (abcnews.go.com)
- **BBC News** (news.bbc.co.uk)
- **CBS News** (www.cbsnews.com)
- **CNN** (www.cnn.com)
- **Fox News** (www.foxnews.com)
- **MSNBC** (www.msnbc.com)
- **New York Times** (www.nytimes.com)
- **USA Today** (www.usatoday.com)

tip

If all you want is a quick overview of the latest headlines, check out Google News (news.google.com). This site offers the top headlines from a variety of news sources; click any headline to read the complete story.

Sports Sites

The Web is also a great resource for sports fans of all shapes and sizes. Whether you're a fan or a participant, at least one site somewhere on the Web focuses on your particular sport.

The best sports sites resemble the best news sites—they're actually portals to all sorts of content and services, including up-to-the-minute scores, post-game recaps, in-depth reporting, and much more. If you're looking for sports information online, one of these portals is the place to start:

- **CBS Sports** (www.cbssports.com)
- **ESPN.com** (espn.go.com)
- **FOX Sports** (msn.foxsports.com)
- **NBC Sports** (nbcsports.msnbc.com)
- **SI.com—Sports Illustrated** (sportsillustrated.cnn.com)
- **SportingNews.com** (www.sportingnews.com)

tip

If you follow a particular sports team, check out that team's local newspaper on the Web. Chances are you'll find a lot of in-depth coverage there that you won't find at these other sites.

Weather Sites

Then there's the issue of weather. Although you can't do much about the weather, you can find a lot of weather-related information on the Web.

First, know that most of the major news portals and local websites offer some variety of weather-related services. The Web also offers many dedicated weather sites, all of which provide local and national forecasts, weather radar, satellite maps, and more.

Here are the most popular weather sites on the Web:

- **AccuWeather.com** (www.accuweather.com)
- **Intellicast.com** (www.intellicast.com)
- **Weather Underground** (www.wunderground.com)
- **Weather.com** (www.weather.com)

Financial Information

The Internet is a great place to find up-to-the-minute information about stocks and other securities. Several sites and services specialize in providing real-time (or slightly delayed) stock quotes—free!

Here's a short list of the best financial sites on the Web—both free and for a fee:

- **CNN/Money** (money.cnn.com)
- **Google Finance** (www.google.com/finance)
- **Marketwatch** (www.marketwatch.com)
- **Motley Fool** (www.fool.com)
- **MSN Money** (moneycentral.msn.com)
- **Yahoo! Finance** (http://finance.yahoo.com)

Medical Information

When you're looking for useful health-related information, you don't have to wait for your next doctor's appointment. A number of websites offer detailed information about illnesses, diseases, and medicines. Many of these sites focus on preventive medicine and wellness, and almost all help you match symptoms with likely illnesses and treatments. Indeed, some of these sites provide access to the same medical databases used by most physicians—without requiring you to wait for an appointment!

caution

As useful as these health sites are, they should not and cannot serve as substitutes for a trained medical opinion.

The top medical sites on the Web include

- **HealthCentral.com** (www.healthcentral.com)
- **KidsHealth** (www.kidshealth.org)
- **MedicineNet** (www.medicinenet.com)
- **National Library of Medicine** (www.nlm.nih.gov)
- **WebMD** (www.webmd.com)

tip

You can also use the Web to search for a new or specialist physician in your area. Two of the best physician search sites are AMA DoctorFinder (http://webapps. ama-assn.org/doctorfinder/) and DoctorDirectory.com (www.doctordirectory.com).

Photos, Clip Art, and Other Images

Next up, let's look at some sites where you can view and download photos, graphics, clip art, and other artwork. Some of these sites let you view for free; others charge to download their image files.

- **Classroom Clipart** (www.classroomclipart.com)
- **Clip Art Center** (www.clip-art-center.com)
- **Clipart.com** (www.clipart.com)
- **Corbis** (pro.corbis.com)
- **Freefoto.com** (www.freefoto.com)
- **Getty Images** (www.gettyimages.com)
- **Google Image Search** (images.google.com)
- **MediaBuilder** (www.mediabuilder.com)
- **Photos.com** (www.photos.com)
- **Smithsonian Photographic Services** (photo2.si.edu)

Maps and Travel Guides

If you're going on a trip, the Web is a great source of travel information. From maps and driving directions to full-fledged travel guides, these sites will help you find your way:

- **AAA Travel Services** (www.aaa.com)
- **AOL CityGuide** (cityguide.aol.com)
- **Concierge.com** (www.concierge.com)
- **Fodors** (www.fodors.com)
- **Frommer's Travel Guides** (www.frommers.com)

- **Google Maps** (maps.google.com)
- **GORP.com Adventure Travel and Outdoor Recreation** (gorp.away.com)
- **Lonely Planet** (www.lonelyplanet.com)
- **MapQuest** (www.mapquest.com)
- **Rand McNally** (www.randmcnally.com)
- **Rough Guides** (www.roughguides.com)
- **TripAdvisor** (www.tripadvisor.com)
- **VirtualTourist.com** (www.virtualtourist.com)
- **Windows Live Maps** (www.bing.com/maps/)
- **Yahoo! Maps** (maps.yahoo.com)

Job Hunting

Looking to change jobs? Then check out these jobs and careers sites. Most let you post your resume online and search for open positions locally or nationwide.

- **Career.com** (www.career.com)
- **CareerBuilder** (www.careerbuilder.com)
- **EmploymentGuide.com** (www.employmentguide.com)
- **Indeed** (www.indeed.com)
- **JobWeb** (www.jobweb.com)
- **Monster** (www.monster.com)
- **NationJob** (www.nationjob.com)
- **snagajob.com** (www.snagajob.com)
- **Yahoo! Hot Jobs** (hotjobs.yahoo.com)

tip

Craigslist is also a great marketplace for help wanted ads. Learn more in Chapter 22, "Buying and Selling on Craigslist."

Religion

The Web is a treasure trove of information about all the world's major religions. You can find everything from searchable Bible databases to full-featured spiritual portals. Try these websites:

- **Bible Search** (www.biblesearch.com)
- **BibleGateway.com** (www.biblegateway.com)
- **BuddhaNet** (www.buddhanet.net)

- **Crosswalk.com** (www.crosswalk.com)
- **eSpirituality.com** (www.espirituality.com)
- **Hindu Universe** (www.hindunet.org)
- **Islam 101** (www.islam101.com)
- **IslamWorld** (www.islamworld.net)
- **Net Ministries** (www.netministries.org)
- **Religious Tolerance** (www.religioustolerance.org)
- **World of Religions** (www.religionworld.org)

Entertainment

The Web is a fount of information about all things entertainment-related, from the latest movie reviews to the inside scoop on upcoming films and TV shows. Here's just a sampling of the entertainment sites online:

- **Ain't It Cool News** (www.aintitcool.com)
- **All-Movie Guide** (www.allmovie.com)
- **All-Music Guide** (www.allmusic.com)
- **Dark Horizons** (www.darkhorizons.com)
- **E! Online** (www.eonline.com)
- **Entertainment Weekly** (www.ew.com)
- **Film.com** (www.film.com)
- **Internet Movie Database** (www.imdb.com)
- **Rotten Tomatoes** (www.rottentomatoes.com)
- **TV Guide Online** (www.tvguide.com)

Education and Reference

Whether you need to look up a relevant fact or get some help with homework, the Web is the place to look. The following are a few education and reference sites:

- **Awesome Library** (www.awesomelibrary.org)
- **Discovery Education Classroom Resources** (school.discoveryeducation.com)
- **Fact Monster** (www.factmonster.com)
- **Homework Center** (www.factmonster.com/homework/)
- **HomeworkSpot** (www.homeworkspot.com)
- **Internet Public Library** (www.ipl.org)

- **Kid Info Homework Resource** (www.kidinfo.com)
- **KidsClick** (www.kidsclick.org)
- **Library of Congress** (www.loc.gov)
- **MadSci Network** (www.madsci.org)
- **Refdesk.com** (www.refdesk.com)
- **Word Central** (www.wordcentral.com)

Games

All work and no play would make for a boring Internet. So when your kids are finished doing their homework, turn to one of these game sites to have a little fun:

- **All Game Guide** (www.allgame.com)
- **All Games Free** (www.allgamesfree.com)
- **ArcadeTown** (www.arcadetown.com)
- **Boxerjam** (www.boxerjam.com)
- **Games Kids Play** (www.gameskidsplay.net)
- **Games.com** (www.games.com)
- **GameSpot** (www.gamespot.com)
- **GameSpy** (www.gamespy.com)
- **Gamesville** (www.gamesville.lycos.com)
- **GameZone** (www.gamezone.com)
- **Internet Chess Club** (www.chessclub.com)
- **Internet Park Word Games** (www.internet-park.com)
- **iWin.com** (www.iwin.com)
- **MSN Games** (zone.msn.com)
- **Play Later** (www.playlater.com)
- **Pogo.com** (www.pogo.com)

Sites For and About Kids

If you're a parent looking for fun and safe sites for your kids to visit, look no further—here's a quick list of some of the most popular kids sites on the Web:

- **ChildFun Family Website** (www.childfun.com)
- **FamilyFun.com** (familyfun.go.com)
- **Funology.com** (www.funology.com)

- **Grossology** (www.grossology.org)
- **Kaboose** (www.kaboose.com)
- **Kids' Space** (www.kids-space.org)
- **KidsCom** (www.kidscom.com)
- **MaMaMedia** (www.mamamedia.com)
- **Yahoo! Kids** (kids.yahoo.com)

Sites for Seniors

Just as the Web has plenty of sites for younger surfers, it also has sites for those on the other end of the age spectrum. Here are just a few of the online sites dedicated to seniors:

- **AARP** (www.aarp.org)
- **Senior Women Web** (www.seniorwomen.com)
- **SeniorJournal.com** (www.seniorjournal.com)
- **SeniorNet** (www.seniornet.com)
- **SeniorSite.com** (www.seniorsite.com)
- **Seniors Site** (www.seniors-site.com)
- **ThirdAge** (www.thirdage.com)

THE ABSOLUTE MINIMUM

Here are the key points to remember from this chapter:

- The latest news, sports, and weather information can be found at numerous news-related websites.
- Both financial and medical information is in abundance online.
- The Web is home to tons of free (and not-so-free) images and clip art you can download to your PC.
- If you're planning a vacation, go online for maps, driving directions, and travel guides.
- The Web is also a good resource if you're looking to change jobs.
- You can also find numerous websites that specialize in other types of information about religion, entertainment, and so on.
- Kids can find all sorts of useful information to help them with their homework—or relax with a fun online game.

PART Vi

COMMUNICATING VIA THE INTERNET

28

SENDING AND RECEIVING EMAIL

Email is a modern way to communicate with friends, family, and colleagues. An email message is like a regular letter, except that it's composed electronically and delivered almost immediately via the Internet.

You can use a dedicated email program, such as Microsoft Outlook or Windows Live Mail, to send and receive email from your personal computer. Or you can use a web mail service such as Gmail or Hotmail to manage all your email from any web browser on any computer. Either approach is good and lets you create, send, and read email messages from all your friends, family, and colleagues.

How Email Works

Email—short for "electronic mail"—is like traditional postal mail, except that messages are composed electronically and delivered via the Internet. When you send an email message to another Internet user, that message travels from your PC to your recipient's PC through a series of Internet connections and servers, almost instantaneously. Email messages can be of any length and can include file attachments of various types.

To make sure your message goes to the right recipient, you have to use your recipient's *email address.* Every Internet user has a unique email address, composed of three parts:

- The user's name
- The @ sign
- The user's domain name (usually the name of the Internet service provider)

As an example, if you use Comcast as your Internet provider (with the domain name **comcast.net**) and your login name is **jimbo**, your email address is **jimbo@comcast.net**.

POP Email Versus Web Mail

There are actually two different ways to send and receive email via the Internet.

The traditional way to send and receive email uses a protocol called the Post Office Protocol (POP). POP email requires the use of a dedicated email software program and—at the ISP level—separate email servers to send and receive messages.

The other way to send and receive email is via Web-based email services, also known as *web mail.* Unlike POP email, web mail can be accessed from any computer, using any web browser; no special software is required.

POP Email

POP email is the standard type of email account you receive when you sign up with an Internet service provider. You're assigned an email account, given an email address, and provided with the necessary information to configure your email program to access this account.

To use POP email, you have to use a special POP email program, such as Microsoft Outlook or Windows Live Mail. That email program has to be configured to send email to your ISP's outgoing mail server (called an *SMTP server*) and to receive email from your ISP's incoming mail server (called a *POP3* or *IMAP server*). If you want to access your email account from another computer, you'll have to use a similar email program and go through the entire configuration process all over again on the second computer.

The most popular POP email programs today include

- Microsoft Outlook (included with the Microsoft Office suite)
- Microsoft Outlook Express (included with Windows XP and previous versions of Windows)
- Windows Mail (included with Windows Vista)
- Windows Live Mail (not included as part of Windows 7, but downloadable for free from download.live.com)
- Mozilla Thunderbird (downloadable for free from www.mozillamessaging.com)

Web Mail

You're not limited to using the "hard-wired" POP email offered by your ISP; you can also send and receive email from web mail services, such as Google's Gmail and Microsoft's Windows Live Hotmail. These web mail services enable you to access your email from any computer, using any web browser.

If you use a PC in multiple locations—in the office, at home, or on the road—this is a convenient way to check your email at any time of day, no matter where you are. You don't have to go through the same sort of complicated configuration routine that you use with POP email. All you have to do is go to the email service's website, enter your user ID and password, and you're ready to send and receive messages.

tip

Your ISP may offer Web-based access to its traditional POP email, which is convenient when you're away from home and need to check your email.

Most web mail services are completely free to use. Some services offer both free versions and paid versions, with paid subscriptions offering additional message storage and functionality.

The largest web mail services include the following:

- AOL Mail (webmail.aol.com)
- Gmail (mail.google.com)
- Lycos Mail (mail.lycos.com)
- Mail.com (www.mail.com)
- Windows Live Hotmail (www.hotmail.com)
- Yahoo! Mail (mail.yahoo.com)

Using Gmail

One of the largest web mail services today is Google's Gmail. It's the web mail service I use, and one I definitely recommend.

Navigating Gmail

You access the Gmail home page at mail.google.com. If you don't yet have a Google account, you'll be prompted to sign up for one. Do so now; signing up is free.

After you activate your Gmail account, you're assigned an email address (in the form of *name*@gmail.com), and you get access to the Gmail Inbox page.

The default view of the Gmail page is the Inbox, shown in Figure 28.1, which contains all your received messages. You can switch to other views by clicking the appropriate links on the left side, top, or bottom of the page. For example, to view all your sent mail, simply click the Sent Mail link on the left; to view only unread messages, click the Unread link at the top or bottom.

FIGURE 28.1

The Gmail Inbox.

Each message is listed with the message's sender, the message's subject, a snippet from the message, and the date or time the message was sent. (The snippet typically is the first line of the message text.) Unread messages are listed in bold; after a message has been read, it's displayed in normal, nonbold text with a shaded background. And if you've assigned a label to a message, the label appears before the message subject.

To perform an action on a message or group of messages, put a check mark by the message(s) and then click one of the buttons at the top or bottom of the list. Alternatively, you can pull down the More Actions list and select another action to perform.

Reading Messages

To read a message, all you have to do is click the message title in the Inbox. This displays the full text of the message on a new page.

If you want to display this message in a new window, click the New Window link. To print the message, click the Print All link. To return to the Inbox, click the Back to Inbox link.

Viewing Conversations

One of the unique things about Gmail is that all related email messages are grouped in what Google calls *conversations*. A conversation might be an initial message and all its replies (and replies to replies). A conversation might also be all the daily emails from a single source with a common subject, such as messages you receive from subscribed-to mailing lists.

A conversation is noted in the Inbox list by a number in parentheses after the sender name(s). If a conversation has replies from more than one person, more than one name is listed.

To view a conversation, simply click the message title; this displays the most recent message in full. To view the text of any individual message in a conversation, click that message's subject. To expand *all* the messages in a conversation, click the Expand All link. All the messages in the conversation are stacked on top of each other, with the text of the newest message fully displayed.

Replying to a Message

Whether you're reading a single message or a conversation, it's easy enough to send a reply. In the original message, click the Reply button; this expands the message to include a reply box. Or if a conversation has multiple participants, you can reply to all of them by clicking the down arrow next to the Reply button and then selecting Reply to All.

The text of the original message is already quoted in the reply. Add your new text above the original text. Since the original sender's address is automatically added to the To line, all you have to do to send the message is click the Send button.

Composing a New Message

To compose and send a new message, follow these steps:

1. Click the Compose Mail link at the top of any Gmail page.

2. When the Compose Mail page appears, as shown in Figure 28.2, enter the recipient's email address in the To box. Separate multiple recipients with commas.

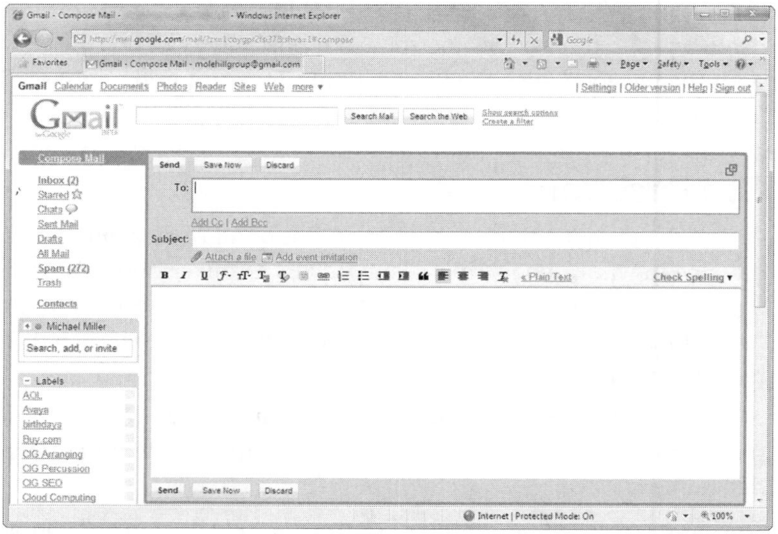

FIGURE 28.2

Composing a new Gmail message.

3. Enter a subject for the message into the Subject box.

4. Enter the text of your message in the large text box. Use the formatting controls (bold, italic, font, and so forth) to enhance your message as desired.

5. When you're done composing your message, click the Send button.

tip

You can also carbon copy and blind carbon copy additional recipients by clicking the Add Cc and Add Bcc links. This expands the message to include Cc or Bcc boxes, into which you enter the recipients' addresses.

Adding New Contacts

You can store frequently emailed addresses in Gmail's Contacts list. Once they're added, it's easy to send messages to your contacts.

To add a new contact, follow these steps:

1. Click the Contacts link on any Gmail page.

2. Click the New Contact button.

3. When the window expands, enter the name, email address, and other information for this contact.

4. Click Save.

Once a contact has been added, you can email that contact by opening a new message and typing the person's name in the To box. All matching contacts will appear; choose the one you want to email.

Sending Files via Gmail

When you need to send a digital photo or other file to a friend or colleague, you can do so via email. To send a file via email, you attach that file to a standard email message. When the message is sent, the *file attachment* travels along with it; when the message is received, the file is right there, waiting to be opened.

Dangers of File Attachments

It's an unfortunate fact that email file attachments are the biggest sources of computer virus and spyware infection. Malicious users attach viruses and spyware to email messages, oftentimes disguised as legitimate files; when a user clicks to open the file, his computer is infected with the virus or spyware.

This doesn't mean that all file attachments are dangerous, simply that opening file attachments—especially those you weren't expecting—is risky. As such, you should avoid opening any file sent to you from a user you don't know. You should also avoid opening files that you weren't expecting from friends and colleagues.

Learn more about computer viruses and spyware in Chapter 10, "Protecting Your PC from Viruses, Spam, and Other Online Nuisances."

The only relatively safe file attachments are those that come from people you know who previously told you they were being sent. So if your boss previously emailed you to tell you he'd be sending you an important Excel file, and you later get an email from him containing an .XLS-format file, that file is probably safe to open. On the other hand, if you receive an email from a complete stranger with an unknown file attached, that's almost definitely a malicious file that you shouldn't open.

What should you do when you receive an unexpected or unwanted file attachment? Fortunately, just receiving an email attachment doesn't activate it; you have to open the file to launch the virus or spyware. What you should do, then, is delete the entire message. Don't open the file attachment; just delete the whole thing— message and attachment together. What's deleted can't harm you or your computer.

Attaching a File in Gmail

It's easy to send file attachments in Gmail. Just follow these steps:

1. Compose a new message and then click the Attach a File link.

2. When the Choose File to Upload dialog box appears, navigate to and select the file you want to attach, and then click the Open button.

3. The file you selected now appears under the Subject box on the new message page. Continue to compose, and then send your message as normal.

> **caution**
>
> Gmail blocks the transmittal of all executable program files (with an .EXE extension), including those in .ZIP files, in an attempt to prevent potential computer viruses.

Opening an Attachment in Gmail

When you receive a Gmail message with an attachment, you see a paper clip icon next to the message subject/snippet. To view or save an attachment, click the message to open it, and then scroll to the bottom of the message.

If you can view the attachment in Gmail, you'll see a View As link (this might be a View as HTML link), like the one shown in Figure 28.3. Click this link to view the file in your web browser. To save the file to your hard disk, click the Download link. When the File Download dialog box appears, click the Save button, select a location for the file, and then click the second Save button.

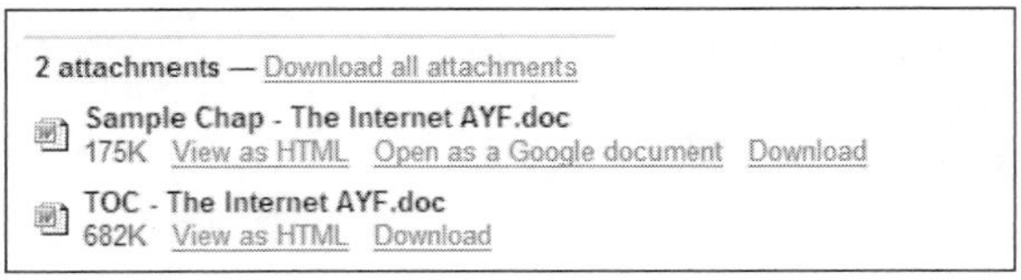

FIGURE 28.3

Viewing and downloading attachments to an email message.

2 attachments — Download all attachments

Sample Chap - The Internet AYF.doc
175K   View as HTML   Open as a Google document   Download

TOC - The Internet AYF.doc
682K   View as HTML   Download

THE ABSOLUTE MINIMUM

Here are the key points to remember from this chapter:

- Email is a fast and easy way to send electronic letters over the Internet.

- There are two types of email: POP email, which requires a separate email program, and web mail, which can be sent and received from any web browser.

- The most popular web mail services include Google's Gmail, Microsoft's Windows Live Hotmail, and Yahoo! Mail.

- Sending a new message in Gmail is as easy as clicking the Compose Mail link; reading a message is as easy as selecting it in the Message list.

- Don't open unexpected files attached to incoming email messages; they might contain computer viruses!

29

SENDING AND RECEIVING INSTANT MESSAGES

People like to talk—even when they're online.

When you want to hold a private one-on-one talk, you use an application called *instant messaging*. When you instant message, or IM, someone, you send a short text-based message directly to that person. It's a way of keeping in touch when you're online—and everybody's doing it!

Understanding Instant Messaging

Instant messaging lets you communicate one on one, in real time, with your friends, family, and colleagues. It's faster than email and less chaotic than chat rooms. It's just you and another user—and your instant messaging software.

There are several big players in the instant messaging market today, including

- AOL Instant Messenger (www.aim.com)
- Google Talk (www.google.com/talk/)
- ICQ (www.icq.com)
- Windows Live Messenger (messenger.live.com)
- Yahoo! Messenger (messenger.yahoo.com)

> **caution**
>
> Instant messaging only works if both parties are online at the same time; you can't send an instant message to someone who isn't available. That said, some IM programs save your messages until the recipient returns online, and then sends them.

Unfortunately, many of these products don't work well (or at all) with each other; if you're using Yahoo! Messenger, for example, you won't be able to communicate with someone running AOL Instant Messenger. That means you'll want to use the IM program that all your friends are using—so find that out before you download any software.

That said, some instant messaging networks are taking steps to work with other networks. For example, the Windows Live Messenger and Yahoo! Messenger networks do talk to each other, as do Google Talk and AOL Instant Messenger. But that's about it for interoperability for now.

Using AOL Instant Messenger

The most popular instant messaging program today is AOL Instant Messenger, or AIM, with Yahoo! Messenger a close second. AIM is especially popular among the teen and preteen crowd, although people of all ages can and do use it. We'll use AIM for the examples in this chapter, but know that all instant messaging programs work in pretty much the same fashion.

Downloading the AIM Software

To use AIM, you first have to download the AIM client software. AIM is free to both download and use on a daily basis.

Go to the AIM website (www.aim.com) and click the Downloads menu. Several versions of AIM are available; the most current version, as of this writing, is AIM 6.9. (Be on the lookout for newer versions, however.) Click the Download button to begin the download; follow the onscreen instructions from there to complete the installation.

Launching AIM and Signing In

After you have AIM installed, you launch the program by either clicking the AIM icon that the program installs on your desktop or selecting Start, All Programs, AIM, AIM. The program opens with the main window displayed, as shown in Figure 29.1.

FIGURE 29.1

The main AIM window, complete with online and offline buddies.

After you have your screen name and password, you have to sign into the AIM service before you can start messaging. When you launch the AIM software, enter your screen name and password, and then click the Sign In button. This connects you to the service and notifies any of your friends that you're online and ready to chat.

tip

If you're a new user, you'll need to choose a screen name before you can start using the program. You do this by clicking the Get a Screen Name link in the AIM window. Follow the onscreen instructions to choose a screen name and password for your account.

Adding New Buddies

The people you chat with via AIM are called your *buddies*. To send an instant message to another user, that person has to be on your Buddy List.

When you first launch AIM, you're prompted to import buddies from your existing Hotmail, Outlook, Outlook Express, and Yahoo! contacts. Do this if you have friends and contacts who you know use the AIM service.

After this initial import, you can manually add users to your AIM Buddy List. To add a new buddy, click the Buddy List Setup button at the bottom of the AIM window and select Add Buddy. When the New Buddy window appears, as shown in Figure 29.2, enter the person's screen name and then click the Save button. This person is now added to your Buddy List.

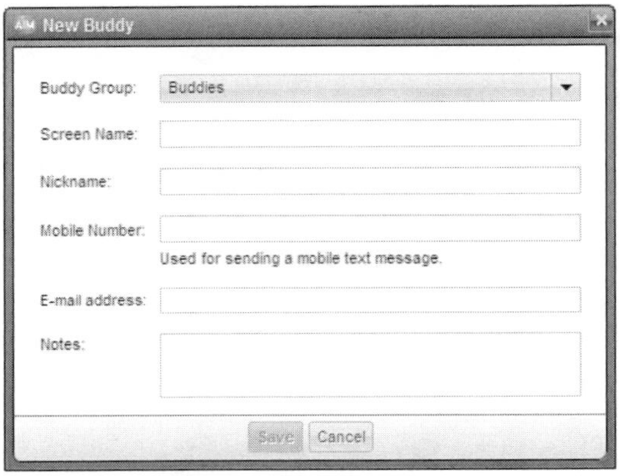

FIGURE 29.2

Adding a new buddy to your Buddy List.

After you've added people to your Buddy List, they show up in the main AIM window. Buddies who are online and ready to chat are displayed on the top of the list; Buddies who aren't currently online appear at the bottom of the list in the Offline section.

Sending a Message

To send an instant message to one of your buddies, double-click that person's name in your Buddy List. This opens a separate IM window, like the one shown in Figure 29.3. Enter your message in the lower part of the window and then click the Send button (or press Enter).

Your message appears in the top part of the window, as does the reply from your buddy. Continue talking like this, one message after another. Your entire conversation is displayed in the top part of the window, and you can scroll up to reread earlier messages.

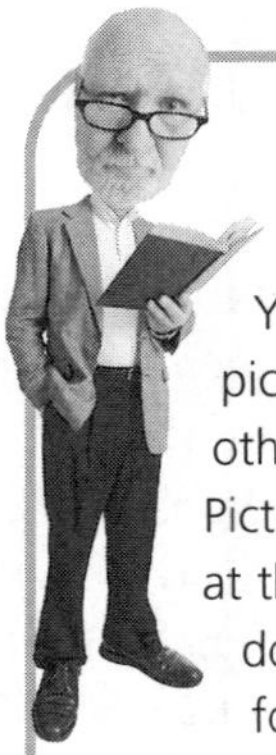

tip

You can use AIM to send pictures and other files to other users; just click the Pictures or Send Files buttons at the bottom of any IM window. AIM can also be used for voice and video messaging, if you have a microphone or webcam connected to your PC. Click the Talk or Video buttons in any AIM window to initiate a voice or video chat.

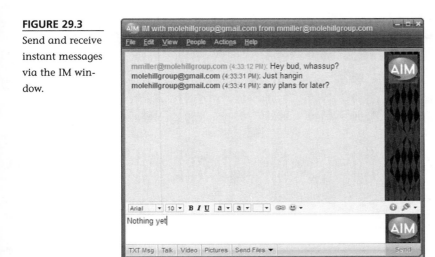

FIGURE 29.3
Send and receive instant messages via the IM window.

Receiving a Message

When you're logged onto the AIM service and someone else sends you an instant message, AIM lets out a little bleeping sound and then displays an alert in the lower-right corner of your screen. To reply to the message, click the alert; this opens a new IM window for your chat.

THE ABSOLUTE MINIMUM

Here are the key points to remember from this chapter:

- Whereas email is great for longer, more formal messages, instant messaging is better for short one-on-one conversations.

- There are many different instant messaging networks, including AOL Instant Messenger (AIM), Google Talk, ICQ, Windows Live Messenger, and Yahoo! Messenger.

- To message another user, you both must be online at the same time, using the same instant messaging software.

- The people you message with become part of your friends or Buddy List; double-click a name on this list to start a live chat session.

30

SOCIAL NETWORKING WITH FACEBOOK, MYSPACE, AND TWITTER

Want to find out what your friends, family, and colleagues are up to? Want to let them know what you're doing today? Then you need to hop onboard the social networking trend, via websites such as Facebook and MySpace.

Social networking enables people to share experiences and opinions with each other via community-based websites. These websites collect millions of individual web pages from active users that combine to create an interactive social network. It's how savvy online users are connecting today.

How Social Networks Work

In practice, a social network isn't a network at all; it's just a large website that aims to create a community of users. Each user of the community posts his or her own personal profile on the site, in the form of a *profile page*. There's enough personal information in each profile to enable other users with similar interests to connect as "friends"; one's growing collection of friends helps to build a succession of personal communities.

Most profile pages include some form of blog, discussion forum, or chat space so that friends can communicate with the person profiled. In many instances, individual users also post a running list of their current activities so that their friends always know what they're up to.

Connecting via Social Networks

Social networks are all about hanging out—virtually. Most users spend a fair amount of time cruising through the profiles, finding out what their friends are doing today. They play music and watch videos posted on other profile pages. They see who's online, and they send instant messages, bulletins (short messages), and emails to each other.

In addition, users spend time updating their own profile pages—their face to the online world. They post short updates that let others know what they're doing or thinking, as well as upload pictures of themselves and their friends. A profile page is your own little home on the Web, ideal for telling other people about yourself.

Finding Friends

Social networks are all about connecting to new and existing friends. The process of finding new friends is called *friending*, and some specific rules are involved.

First, it's important to be connected to all your real-world friends and acquaintances. Second, you want to be connected to people whom you might not personally know, but whom you've heard of and respect. Third, although it's important to have a lot of friends, the coolness of your friends matters more than the number of them. In other words, it's better to have 10 good friends than 100 nobodies.

Know, however, that when you add someone as friend, that doesn't imply they're a friend in the traditional use of the word. It doesn't even mean that you know that person or want to know that person—only that you've added him or her to your friends list.

After a time, linking from one friend to a friend of that friend to a friend of a friend of a friend leads to a kind of "six degrees of separation" thing. It's fun to see how many friends it takes to connect you to various people. And you get to find new friends by seeing who your friends are friends with.

Using Facebook

The leading social network today is Facebook (www.facebook.com). This site attracts an older audience than MySpace, including many adult users.

Friending on Facebook

Finding people on Facebook is a matter of using the search function. Just enter the user's real name or username into the search box at the top of any Facebook page, and then press Enter. The search results page will display all matching users; click the Add as Friend link to send that person a friend invite. If he or she accepts your invitation, you'll be added to each other's friends list.

Once someone is on your friends list, all of that person's activities are displayed on your Facebook home page, shown in Figure 30.1. Just go to the home page and click the News Feed button; all friend activity is displayed there. Alternatively, you can click the Status Updates button to view updates to your friends' status, or the Photos tab to see your friends' latest pictures.

FIGURE 30.1

Catching up on friends and family from the Facebook home page.

Viewing Profiles

A Facebook profile page is a person's home page on the community. As shown in Figure 30.2, each profile includes three main tabs:

- The Wall tab displays your recent activity and notes from friends.
- The Info tab displays your personal information.
- The Photos tab displays any photos you've uploaded.

FIGURE 30.2

A typical
Facebook profile.

Additional tabs can be created and accessed by clicking the + tab. In addition, key information and your friends list is displayed in a left-hand sidebar.

Creating Your Own Profile

You create your profile when you first sign up for the Facebook service. You can also edit your profile at any time by going to your profile page and clicking the Edit My Profile link.

The Profile Info page displays all the information you need to supply for your Facebook profile:

■ Basic information includes your gender, birthday, hometown, and such.

■ Personal information includes your activities, interests, favorite movies and TV shows, and the like.

■ Contact information includes your email address, IM screen names, and so on.

■ Education and work information lets you tell people where you've gone to school and worked.

You can also add a personal photo to your profile. Just click the profile picture area (or your current picture, if you've already added one but want to change it). When the next page appears, click Change Profile Picture. When prompted, select which photo you want to upload, and then upload it.

Writing on the Wall

Want to tell your friends what you're doing at this moment? It's easy to do. Just go to your home page or profile page and enter a few words into the What's On Your Mind box. Click the Share button, and your updated activity is displayed on your Wall and on the home pages of all your friends.

If you want to write a comment directly on a friend's Wall, go to that person's profile page and select the Wall tab. Enter your message into the Write Something box at the top of the page, click the Share button, and your comments will immediately appear on your friend's Wall.

Uploading Photos

Facebook lets you upload personal photos to the site and create themed photo albums. Your photos appear on the Photos tab on your Profile page.

To upload a photo, go to your Profile page, select the Photos tab, and then click the Create a Photo Album button. When the next page appears, give the album a name, enter your location (or the location where you shot the photos), and write a description of what's included. If you want your photos to be public for all to see, make sure Everyone is selected from the Privacy list; you can also opt for your photos to be seen by Only Friends or Friends of Friends. Click Create Album to proceed.

If this is the first time you're adding photos, Facebook installs its photo uploading software within your Web browser. When the next page appears, select the Add Photos tab and navigate to where the photos are stored on your computer's hard drive. Select the photos you want to upload, and then click the Upload button.

You can change the order of the photos in your album by opening the album and selecting Organize Photos. To "tag" individuals within a photo (that is, to identify your Facebook friends in your photos), select Edit Photos. To add more photos to the album, click Add More Photos.

Emailing Other Users

Writing on someone's wall is one way to "talk" with them online, but it's a public conversation—all of that person's friends can read what you wrote. If you prefer a more private conversation, Facebook offers email functionality that lets you send messages directly to other users.

To send an email via Facebook, select Inbox, Compose New Message from the toolbar. When the new message page appears, enter the recipient's username or email address into the To box, the subject of the message into the Subject box, and the text of your message into the Message box. Click the Send button to send the message to your friend's Facebook Inbox.

To view messages in your own Inbox, select Inbox, View Message Inbox. This displays all recent messages; click a message header to view the text of a specific message. You can then reply to that message by entering your text into the Message box at the bottom of the message page. Click the Send button to send your reply on its way.

Managing your Facebook Inbox is easy. To delete older or unwanted messages, just check those messages and then click Delete. You can also mark unread messages as read, and vice versa.

Using MySpace

The number-two social network in the United States is MySpace (www.myspace.com). Like Facebook, MySpace is free to use, although you do need to sign up for an account to access many of the site's features. Users of MySpace tend to be a little younger than Facebook users; it's the preferred site for junior high and many high school students. In addition, MySpace is a big site for musicians and other artists, who use the site to promote their latest works.

Friending on MySpace

You can find new friends on MySpace by either browsing or searching. You browse for friends by selecting Friends, Browse People from the MySpace menu bar. This displays the Browse Users page, where you set your browse criteria. The Basic tab on this page lets you filter your browsing by gender, age range, location, and other criteria.

For more sophisticated browsing, click the Advanced tab on this page. This adds more browsing options, including ethnicity, body type, height, and lifestyle (smoker, drinker, sexual orientation, education, religion, income, children). You can choose to sort results by recently updated, last login, new to MySpace, or physical distance from your location.

If you know who you're looking for, you can search the MySpace profiles for a specific user. All you have to do is click the Web link inside the search box at the top of the page and select People; enter the user's actual name or profile name into the search box and then click the Search button. MySpace returns a list of matching profiles; make sure you click the Next button if the profile you want doesn't show up in the first page of results.

After you find the person you want to make your friend, click the Add to Friends icon next to that person's name. You're now prompted to confirm your friend request; when you do so, that person is sent a message asking if she wants to be your friend. If she says yes, you're friends. If she doesn't know you or doesn't want to be your friend, that's that.

You can follow your friends' activities and comments from the MySpace home page. The activities are displayed at the top middle of your home page, so you'll always know what your friends are up to.

Viewing a Profile

Figure 30.3 shows a typical MySpace profile. Because users can personalize their profile pages, few MySpace profiles look the same. Still, most MySpace profiles have common elements, including

- **Blurbs**—Tells visitors a little about the user. This section contains two parts: About Me and Who I'd Like to Meet.

- **Interests**—Lists favorite music, movies, television shows, books, and so on.

- **Details**—Gives more information about the person, including marital status, location, astrological sign, and so on.

- **Contact Info**—Contains links to send email and instant messages and to add this person to your friends list.

- **Blog**—That's right, MySpace functions as a blog hosting site. Users can create their own personal blogs and link to blog postings from their profile pages.

- **Images**—Lets users post pictures—lots of them, if they want—on their profile pages. One default image is shown on the main page; additional photos are accessed via the Pics link.

- **Videos**—Lets users upload videos to their profile pages. Click the Videos link to view.

- **Calendar**—For users who post their schedules online.

- **Friend Space**—Lists all friends. This section includes a list of the user's total friends, a list of the user's top eight friends (as determined by the user), and a link to view all the user's friends.

- **Comments**—Displays comments made by the user's friends for the user and all other visitors to read.

As mentioned previously, MySpace profile pages are fully customizable. In fact, if the user is conversant with HTML, CSS, and JavaScript, some fancy customization is possible. Otherwise, users can choose their own themes, backgrounds, colors, and content modules. This is why no two MySpace pages look the same!

FIGURE 30.3

A typical Myspace profile.

Commenting

If a friend has a Comments module on his or her MySpace page, you can leave your comments for that friend (and all their friends) to read. Simply scroll down to the Comments module and click the Add Comment link. When the next page appears, enter your message in the box provided, and then click the Post a Comment button. (You can also add a photo to your comment, if you wish.) Your comment now appears at the top of your friend's public comments.

Creating Your Own MySpace Profile

To create your own MySpace profile, you first have to sign up to MySpace. You do this from the MySpace home page by clicking the Sign Up button.

Signing up is simple (and free). All you have to provide is your desired password, name, date of birth, and gender.

After you've signed up, you're prompted to upload a photo of yourself. The photo can be in JPG or GIF format, must be smaller than 5MB, and shouldn't contain nudity.

Next, you're encouraged to invite your friends to view your MySpace page. Enter their email addresses, if you want, and then click the Invite button.

note

Every new MySpace user starts with one friend—MySpace founder Tom Anderson.

MySpace now dumps you into your own personal account page. This is your home page on the MySpace site because it lists any email or bulletins you've received as well as all your friends. It also includes the URLs for your profile and blog pages.

To personalize your profile, start by clicking the Pick Your MySpace Name/URL link. This lets you choose your MySpace display name—the name that others will know you by. Choose this name carefully; once it's chosen, you can't change it. Ever.

Next, return to your home page and select Profile, Edit Profile. This takes you to the Profile Edit page, shown in Figure 30.4, which is where you start constructing your profile page. Fill in the blanks as appropriate; then click the Save All Changes button. Click through the links at the top of the pages to tab to additional content pages—Interests & Personality, Name, Basic Info, Background & Lifestyle, Schools, Companies, Networking, and Song & Video on Profile.

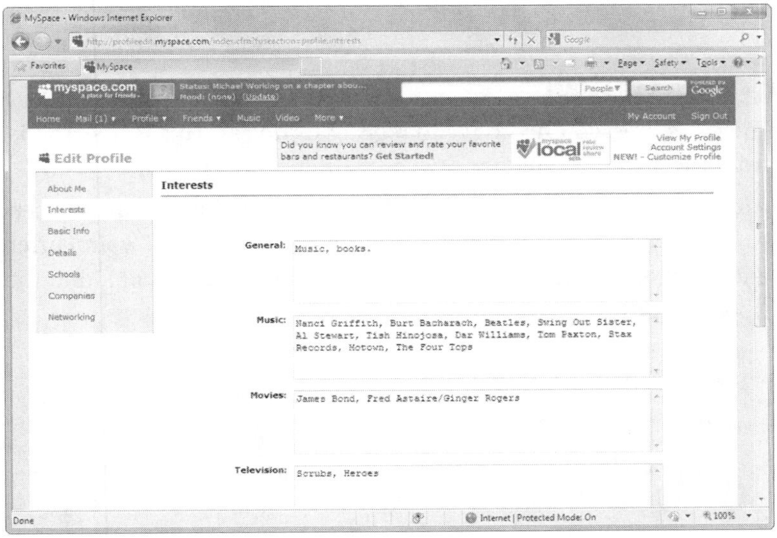

FIGURE 30.4

Adding content to your MySpace profile.

This adds content to your profile page. To change the look of your profile, return to your home page and select Profile, Customize Profile. From here you can select which page elements to display (and where), as well as choose a predesigned theme for your page. To more fully customize your page, select either the Advanced Edit option or—if you want to use HTML code—the CSS option. Click the Publish button when you're done making changes.

Adding Photos

To add photos to your MySpace profile page, select Profile, My Photos from the toolbar. When the My Photos page appears, click the Upload Photos link.

The first time you upload photos, MySpace installs the necessary MySpace Image Loader software in your browser. You can then navigate to and select the photos on your hard drive that you want to upload. Click the Upload button to upload the photos.

A Photos link now appears at the top of your profile page. Your friends can view your photos by clicking this link.

Using Twitter

Social networking isn't the only way to let your friends and family know what you're up to. Twitter is a kind of micro-blogging service that lets you create short (up to 140 characters in length) text posts with ease. Anyone subscribing to your posts receives updates via the Twitter site, RSS feed, or SMS text messages on their mobile phones.

Tweeting with Twitter

To use Twitter, you first have to register as a user. This is free and is accomplished from the Twitter home page (www.twittter.com).

After you've registered and signed in, the top Twitter home page changes to a What Are You Doing box, as shown in Figure 30.5. To "tweet" your current activity, just enter a short description of what you're doing into this box and then click the Update button.

FIGURE 30.5

Micro-blogging with Twitter.

Your most recent "tweets" are now displayed on your home page beneath this box—and broadcast to anyone subscribing to your feed. In addition, tweets from people you're following are displayed on the home page, so you know what they're up to.

Following Other Users

If friends or family members are on Twitter, you can follow their activities by subscribing to their "tweets." This is called *following* users. (Although some might call it stalking...)

To find people to follow, go the Twitter home page and click the Find People link at the top of the page. When the next page appears, click the Find on Twitter tab to search for that person on the Twitter network. You can also find people on other networks or invite your friends to join Twitter; just click the appropriate tab.

> **caution**
>
> Some users protect their profiles so that strangers can't follow them without their permission. When you click the Follow link for these users, they have to register their approval before you can follow them.

To follow a Twitter user, go to that person's profile page and click the Follow link under the profile picture. All "tweets" from this user will now appear on your Twitter home page.

To stop following a user, click the Following link on the home page to display the list of people you're following. Click the Actions button next to that user and then select Unfollow the resulting menu.

Following via Mobile Phone

You can also follow fellow Twitterers from your mobile phone. You'll need to know their usernames in advance, but then it's a simple matter of sending a text message to twitter with the message **follow *username***. To send a text message to Twitter in the United States, dial 40404 from your mobile phone. In Canada, dial 21212. In most other countries, dial +44 762 4801423.

> **caution**
>
> If you receive "tweets" via text messaging on your phone, normal text messaging charges will accrue.

Once you've sent the text message, you'll receive a text message whenever that user makes a "tweet."

Blocking Followers

If you don't want to be publically followed on Twitter, you can protect your profile. Click the Settings link at the top of the Twitter home page; then select the Account tab. Scroll to the bottom of this page and check the Protect My Updates option; then click Save. This requires you to approve a follower before he or she can receive your updates.

You can also block individual users from following you, which is a great way to evade cyberstalkers. Go to that person's profile page and click the Block link in the Actions section of the right-hand sidebar. This will block that user from receiving "tweets" you make.

tip

To customize the profile that other Twitter users see, click the Settings link at the top of the Twitter home page. Select the Account tab to edit your name, location, and bio; click the Picture tab to upload a personal picture; and click the Design tab to select a theme for your profile page.

Protecting Your Children on Social Networks

Given that MySpace and Facebook are so popular among teenagers and preteens, many parents worry about their children being cyberstalked on these sites. That worry is not ill-founded, especially given the amount of personal information that most users post on their social networking profiles.

Self-Policing Policies

It's important to note that both MySpace and Facebook try to police themselves. For example, on MySpace users with ages set to 14 or 15 years automatically have private profiles—that is, they're not browsable by the mass MySpace public. Users who are 16 or older have the option to restrict profile access to people on their friends list, although most teens don't exercise this option. (Of course, MySpace doesn't actually verify ages, so a younger child can claim to be older to get more access.)

In addition, both MySpace and Facebook work to keep known sex offenders off their sites. Both sites constantly monitor lists of known sex offenders and cull those users from their sites.

Parental Supervision

The best way to protect your children on social networking sites, however, is to monitor what they do on those sites. As such, it's important that you become "friends" with your children on MySpace and Facebook and visit their profile pages on a regular basis. You might be surprised what you find there.

It's an unfortunate fact that not all teens and preteens are wise about what they put online. It's not unusual to find provocative pictures posted on their social networking profiles; you probably don't want your children exposing themselves in this fashion.

You also need to warn your kids that not everyone on MySpace or Facebook is truly a "friend." They should be circumspect about the information they make public and about whom they communicate with. It's also worth noting that kids shouldn't arrange to meet in person strangers who they're "friends" with online; it's not unheard of for unsavory adults to use social networks as a stalking ground.

In other words, teach your kids to be careful. Hanging out on MySpace or Facebook is normally no more dangerous than hanging out at the mall, but even malls aren't completely safe. Caution and common sense are always called for.

Protect Yourself

The advice you give to your children regarding social networks also applies to yourself. Think twice before posting personal information or incriminating photographs, and don't broadcast your every move on your profile page. Also, don't automatically accept friend requests from people you don't know.

Most important, don't view MySpace or Facebook as online dating services. Yes, you might meet new friends on these social networks, but use caution about transferring online friendships into the physical world. If you decide to meet an online friend offline, do so in a public place and perhaps with another friend along. Don't put yourself at risk when meeting strangers—and remember that until you get to know them in person, anyone you correspond with online remains a stranger.

THE ABSOLUTE MINIMUM

Here are the key points to remember from this chapter:

- Social networking sites let you keep in touch with what your friends and family are doing.

- The largest social networking site today is Facebook; number-two MySpace caters to a slightly younger crowd.

- Both Facebook and MySpace let users create their own profile pages, complete with personal info, photos, lists of friends, blog entries, and so forth.

- Another way to let friends know what you're up to is to send short "tweets" via Twitter, a micro-blogging site.

31

EXPLORING BLOGS AND PODCASTS

If you've been on the Internet for any length of time, you've probably heard something about blogs. A blog (short for "web log") is a kind of online journal that its author updates frequently with new musings and information.

Hundreds of thousands of blogs are on the Internet, from the intensely personal to the most gregariously public; some blogs are so influential that they actually make the news from time to time. What you might not know is that anyone can create a blog. It's easy and can be fun.

Whether you want to create your own blog or read someone else's, blogs are an essential part of the Internet today. Read on to learn more!

Welcome to the Blogosphere

When it comes to blogs, you have to get used to a whole new vocabulary. A *blog*, of course, is a journal that's hosted on the Web and visible to other web users. *Blogging* is the activity of updating a blog; someone who keeps a blog is a *blogger*; and the entire universe of blogs is called the *blogosphere*. Got that?

Some people view their blogs as a kind of personal-yet-public scrapbook—an online diary to record their thoughts for posterity. Even if no one else ever looks at it, it's still valuable to the author as a repository of thoughts and information he can turn to later.

Other bloggers are more focused. Some blogs are devoted to hobbies, sports teams, local events, particular industries, and so on. Some people blog for a cause, political or otherwise. (In fact, many people get their first exposure to the blogosphere via the network of left-wing and right-wing political blogs—especially during an election year!)

In a way, the most serious bloggers are like columnists in the traditional media. They write with a passion, a point of view, and a personal sensibility that makes their blogs interesting to read. Even bloggers who don't inject personal comments into their posts still offer a viewpoint based on what they choose to include and link to in their blogs. The blogosphere is an interesting world, and it's revolutionizing journalism (and journals) for the new online reality.

Of course, a blog can be more—or less—than personal comments and observations. A big part of blogging is about interlinking to other blogs and to news and information on the Web. Look at any blog, and you're likely to see a list of related blogs (sometimes titled "friends of …"). Bloggers like to link to other blogs that they enjoy—as well as to news stories, photos, audio files, you name it.

In fact, many blogs are nothing more than links to interesting blog entries—there isn't always a lot of original content in these types of blogs. The blogger finds something interesting and then uses his blog to draw attention to that other posting. In this way, bloggers are a lot like radio disc jockeys, "spinning" links and snippets just as a DJ spins songs.

note

For what it's worth, I contribute to several blogs—all of which are hosted by Blogger. I have blogs for many of my books: *Googlepedia: The Blog* (googlepedia.blogspot.com), *iPodpedia: The Blog* (ipodpediatheblog.blogspot.com), *YouTube 4 You: The Blog* (youtube4u.blogspot.com), and *Video Blogging for Business* (businessvideoblog.com). In addition, *The Curmudgeon Speaks* (curmudgeonspeaks.blogspot.com) is my personal "ranting and raving" blog, and I have all manner of family photos on *Mike and Sherry's Family Pictures* (mikeandsherrypictures.blogspot.com). That's a lot of blogs to keep up-to-date!

That said, serious bloggers not only sort through the blogosphere to find the most interesting articles, they provide some background and organization to these postings, and in many cases they add their own commentary. The best blogs have a definite point of view, no matter what content they're linking to.

Reading—and Commenting on—Blogs

What does a blog look like? As you can see in Figure 31.1, a typical blog is a collection of individual *posts*, or articles. The posts are arranged in reverse chronological order, with the newest posts at the top. Older posts are relegated to the blog archives, which are generally accessible via a link in the sidebar column.

note

A blog's sidebar column is also where you'll find links to other items of interest, as determined by the blog's host. You might find links to the blogger's favorite books or videos, or to related websites, for example.

At the end of each post is generally a link to comments on that post. Depending on the blog, readers might be able to post their own personal comments about any given post. Click the comments link to read all the comments to date or to post your own comment.

FIGURE 31.1

A typical blog.

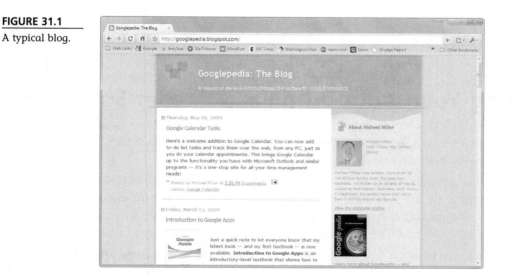

Most blogs are all text, but blogs can also display photos, audio files, and even videos. It's all up to the blogger and how involved he wants his blog to be. (Some blogs even have multiple hosts, with posts coming from a number of different authors.)

Searching for Blogs

The Web has literally hundreds of thousands of blogs, covering just about any topic you can think of. How do you find blogs of interest to you?

To find a particular blog, check out the following blog directories:

- BlogCatalog (www.blogcatalog.com)
- Blog Hints (www.bloghints.com)
- Blog Search Engine (www.blogsearchengine.com)
- Blogging Fusion (www.bloggingfusion.com)
- Bloghub.com (www.bloghub.com)
- Globe of Blogs (www.globeofblogs.com)
- Google Blog Search (blogsearch.google.com)
- Weblogs.com (www.weblogs.com)

Tracking Your Blogs with Feed Reader Software

Many blogs let you subscribe to a *feed* of their posts. This is an updated list of all new posts; a feed subscription uses Real Simple Syndication (RSS) technology to notify you of all new posts made to that blog.

You typically subscribe to a blog's RSS feed directly from the blog. Look for a "subscribe" or "feed" or "RSS" button. (An alternative form of syndication, Atom feeds, is sometimes offered; it works the same way as RSS.) Click the button to display the feed page, and then copy this page's URL into your feed reader program.

Ah, but what's a feed reader? That's a software program that monitors and displays all the RSS feeds you've subscribed to. Some of the more popular feed readers include FeedDemon (www.feeddemon.com) and Feedreader (www.feedreader.com). You can also monitor your RSS subscriptions with a web-based feed aggregator site, such as Bloglines (www.bloglines.com), Google Reader (reader.google.com), or NewsGator (www.newsgator.com).

Even better, you can use Internet Explorer 8 to monitor all your RSS subscriptions. IE8 includes an integrated feed reader; when you go to a blog's RSS page, the browser displays a boxed message at the top of the page. Click the Subscribe to This Feed link, and IE8 will track all new posts made to this blog. You can view all your blog feeds by opening IE8's Favorites pane and clicking the Feeds tab.

Creating Your Own Blog

Bloggers typically update their blogs on a regular basis—weekly, daily, or even hourly, depending on the blogger. The process of updating a blog is facilitated by the blogging software used. Hosting a blog requires little or no technical expertise on the part of the blogger; all the heavy lifting is handled by the blogging software or the site that hosts the blog.

If you want to create your own personal blog, look for a blog hosting community. These websites offer easy-to-use software tools to build and maintain your blog, and they do all the hosting for you—often for free.

Some of the most popular blog hosting communities include

- BlogEasy (www.blogeasy.com)
- Blogger (www.blogger.com)
- Blogsome (www.blogsome.com)
- eBloggy (www.ebloggy.com)
- tBlog (www.tblog.com)
- TypePad (www.typepad.com)
- WordPress (www.wordpress.com)

Of these communities, Blogger (which is owned by Google) and TypePad are probably the biggest. As you can see in Figure 31.2, these sites make it easy to create your own blog—it's really a matter of clicking a few buttons and filling out a few forms. And after your blog is created, you can update it as frequently as you want, again by clicking a link or two. (Figure 31.3 shows how easy it is to create a new blog entry with Blogger.) After you get started blogging your daily thoughts, you'll never want to stop!

note

Twitter (www.twitter.com) is a kind of micro-blogging service that lets you post only short (140-character) posts. Learn more in Chapter 30, "Social Networking with Facebook, MySpace, and Twitter."

tip

Both MySpace and Facebook offer blogging features, as you learned in Chapter 30. In addition, many traditional website hosting communities offer blogging features. Learn more in Chapter 26, "Creating Your Own Web Page."

FIGURE 31.2
Use Blogger to create and host your personal blog.

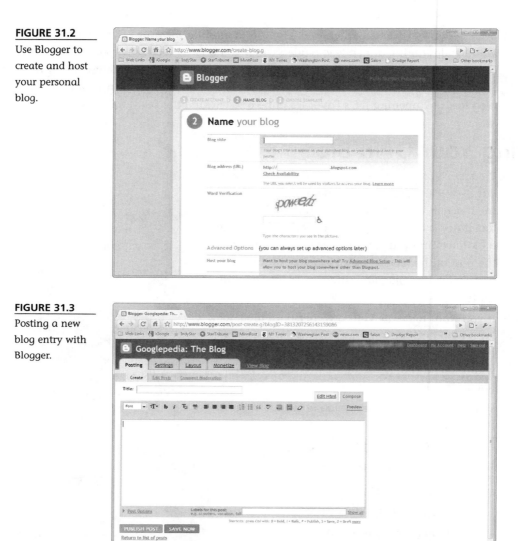

FIGURE 31.3
Posting a new blog entry with Blogger.

Blogs on the Radio: Listening to Podcasts

A text-based blog isn't the only way to express yourself online. If you have an iPod or other portable MP3 player, you can listen to audio blogs called *podcasts*. A podcast is essentially a homegrown radio program, distributed over the Internet, that you can listen to on your PC or download and play on any portable audio player—iPods included.

How Podcasts Work

Anyone with a microphone and a computer can create her own podcasts. That's because a podcast is nothing more than an MP3 file posted to the Internet. Most podcasters deliver their content via an RSS feed, which enables users to easily find future podcasts by subscribing to the podcaster's feed. The podcasts are then downloaded to the listener's portable audio player and played at the listener's convenience.

What kinds of podcasts are out there? It's an interesting world, full of all sorts of basement and garage productions. Probably the most common form of podcast is the amateur radio show, where the podcaster assembles a mixture of personally selected music and commentary. But there are also professional podcasts by real radio stations and broadcasters, interviews and exposés, and true audio blogs that consist of running commentary and ravings. The variety is staggering, and the quality level ranges from embarrassingly amateurish to surprisingly professional.

Finding Podcasts

Want to jump into the wild, wonderful world of podcasts? Then you need to browse through a podcast directory and see what's there for the listening. Some of the most popular podcast directories include

- Digital Podcast (www.digitalpodcast.com)
- Podcast Alley (www.podcastalley.com)
- Podcast Bunker (www.podcastbunker.com)
- Podcast Directory (www.podcastdirectory.com)
- Podcast.com (www.podcast.com)
- Podcasting Station (www.podcasting-station.com)
- Podcast Pickle (www.podcastpickle.com)
- PodCastZoom (www.podcastzoom.com)
- Podfeed.net (www.podfeed.net)

Podcasts on the iPod

If you're an iPod owner, you've probably noticed the Podcasts item on your iPod's menu. This lets you dial up all your stored podcasts and then play them back in any order.

You download podcasts to your iPod via the iTunes Podcast Directory. Just click iTunes Store in the Source pane of the iTunes software and then click the Podcasts link. As you can see in Figure 31.4, you can browse or search through the available podcasts, download the ones you like, and subscribe to the ones you want to hear again. Most of the podcasts here are relatively professional, including programs from several major news and sports outlets. Best of all, most of the podcasts from iTunes are free.

FIGURE 31.4

Browsing for podcasts in the iTunes Podcast Directory.

When you subscribe to a podcast, iTunes automatically checks for updates and downloads new episodes to your computer. Your downloaded podcasts are accessible by clicking the Podcasts link in the iTunes Source pane. Naturally, the new podcasts are transferred to your iPod when it's next connected and synced. It's a quick and easy way to check out the whole podcast phenomenon—as long as you're an iPod owner, that is.

Creating Your Own Podcasts

If you think podcasts are cool, why not create your own? It's surprisingly easy to do. Here's what you need:

- A microphone (any type will do)
- A PC (no special technical requirements)
- Audio recording software, such as Audacity (audacity.sourceforge.net), ePodcast Creator (www.industrialaudiosoftware.com), or Propaganda (www.makepropaganda.com). Alternatively, many podcast-hosting communities supply their own podcast recording software.
- Headphones (optional, but nice)

■ An Internet connection so you can post your podcasts to the Web

■ A podcast hosting service or RSS syndicator

Making a podcast recording doesn't have to be any more complex than setting the volume levels, clicking the Record button in the recording software, and then talking into the microphone. Naturally, you can stop and restart the recording as necessary; you can even go back and rerecord any section that you don't like. Most recording programs also let you edit your recordings by snipping out unwanted sections and moving sections around as necessary.

Your original recording should be saved in high-quality WAV format, and you should stay in the WAV format throughout the editing process. After your podcast is in its final form, you then export the file into MP3 format. If the podcast is voice-only, a relatively low bit rate (32 or 64kbps) is fine. If the podcast has a lot of music, consider a higher bit rate, up to 128kbps. Make sure you add the appropriate metatags for all the podcast info, and it's ready for distribution.

After you save your podcast in MP3 format, you have to upload the MP3 file to a server. If you have your own personal website, you can use that server to store your podcasts. You'll need a fair amount of storage space; audio files can get large, depending on the recording quality and length. For example, a 30-minute podcast saved at 64kbps in mono will be about 8MB in size. Use a higher bit rate, and the file size goes up accordingly.

If you don't have your own server, consider using an audio blog hosting service, such as Hipcast (www.hipcast.com), Podbean.com (www.podbean.com), Podbus.com (www.podbus.com), or any of the podcast directories discussed previously. You'll pay $5–$10 per month for file storage, and most of these sites will help you with the RSS syndication of your podcasts.

The final step of the process is the RSS syndication. This is best accomplished via an audio blog hosting service, or via blogging software. Most blogging software and services can generate an RSS feed, or you can use FeedBurner (www.feedburner.com) to do the work for you (for free). If you use FeedBurner, you'll have to create a link on your website to the FeedBurner file so that people can find the feed.

And that's that. All you have to do now is wait for users to find your podcasts and subscribe to your feed!

THE ABSOLUTE MINIMUM

Here are the key points to remember from this chapter:

- A blog is a private or public journal on the Internet, consisting of numerous individual posts.
- Most blogs let readers comment on the blog posts.
- You can use a blog-hosting community, such as Blogger, to create and host your own blog.
- A blog in audio format is called a podcast.
- One of the best ways to find and download podcasts is via the iTunes Podcast Directory.

PART **VII**

EXPLORING THE DIGITAL LIFESTYLE

32

ORGANIZING AND EDITING YOUR DIGITAL PHOTOS

Chances are, you've already traded in your old film camera for a new digital camera. Good for you! Now you can use your PC to not only store your digital photos, but also edit them—to touch up bad spots and red eye, crop the edges, and apply all sorts of special effects.

And, after you've touched up all your photos, you can choose to create digital photo albums, use them in all manner of picture-related projects and documents, or print them out—either on your own four-color printer or at a traditional photo processor. The combination of digital photography and personal computing is definitely the way to go—and it's a lot more versatile than traditional film-based photography!

Transferring Pictures from Your Camera to Your PC

If you want to edit or print your digital photos, you'll need to connect that digital camera to your PC—which is relatively easy to do. You can transfer digital photos directly from your camera's memory card, download pictures from your camera via a USB connection, or even scan existing photo prints.

Transferring Pictures via USB

Connecting a digital camera or scanner to your PC is easy. Most digital cameras today come with a USB connector, so you can connect your camera directly to your PC using a USB cable. With this type of setup, Windows recognizes your camera or scanner as soon as you plug it in and installs the appropriate drivers automatically.

When you connect a USB cable between your camera and your PC, one of several things is likely to happen:

- If you're using Windows 7 or Windows Vista, it should recognize when your camera is connected and automatically download the pictures in your camera, while displaying a dialog box that notifies you of what it's doing.
- If you've installed a proprietary picture management program that comes with your digital camera, it may launch and ask to download the pictures from your camera. Follow the onscreen instructions to proceed.
- If you've installed a third-party photo-editing program, such as Adobe Photoshop Elements, it may launch and ask to download the pictures from your camera. Follow the onscreen instructions to proceed.
- If nothing happens when you connect your camera, click the Start menu and select Computer. When Computer Explorer opens, there should be a new icon for your digital camera. Double-click this icon to view the current contents of your camera and to copy files from your camera to a location on your PC's hard drive.

Transferring Pictures from a Memory Card

Copying digital pictures via USB cable is nice—if your camera supports this method. For many users, an easier approach is to use a memory card reader. Some PCs have memory card readers built in; if yours doesn't, you can always add a low-cost external memory reader via USB. You then insert the memory card from your digital camera into the memory card reader, and your PC recognizes the card as if it were another hard disk.

You can then use Computer Explorer to copy files from the memory card to your computer. Just open the Explorer and click the drive icon for the memory card. This displays the card's contents, typically in a subfolder labeled DCIM. You can then move, copy, and delete the photos stored on the card, as you would with any other type of file in Windows.

Scanning a Picture

If your photos are of the old-fashioned print variety, you can still turn them into digital files, using a flatbed scanner. The scanning starts automatically when you press the Scan button on your scanner. Your print photo is now saved as a digital file for future use.

Note that some third-party software programs, such as Adobe Photoshop Elements, also let you scan photos from the program. In most instances, scanning via one of these programs offers more options than scanning via Windows; you can change the resolution (in dots per inch) of the scanned image, crop the image, even adjust brightness and contrast if you want. If you're scanning a lot of old, washed-out prints, this approach may produce better results.

tip

Many color photo printers include memory card slots that let you print directly from your camera's memory card, bypassing your computer entirely.

Storing Your Photos in Windows

Where are all your photos stored after they've been scanned or downloaded from your digital camera? By default, Windows stores all your pictures in the Pictures library, shown in Figure 32.1. This folder includes a number of features specific to the management of picture files, including

- **Preview** in a photo-editing program
- **Share with** other users in your network HomeGroup
- View as a **Slide Show**
- **Print** your photos at various sizes
- **E-mail** selected photos
- **Burn** selected photos to CD

From here you can also perform all the normal file-related tasks, such as copying, moving, or even deleting your photos. If you want to edit your photos, however, you have to use a different program—which we discuss next.

FIGURE 32.1

Use the Pictures library to store and organize your digital pictures.

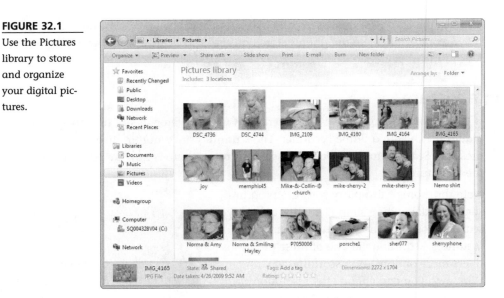

Choosing a Photo-Editing Program

To manage and edit your photos, you need a full-featured photo organization and editing program. This type of program lets you organize and catalog all the digital photos on your system, edit your photos (to remove red eye, crop out unwanted elements, adjust color and brightness, and so forth), and create full-sized prints or multiple-photo contact sheets on your PC's printer.

When it comes to picking a photo-editing program, you have a lot of choices. You can choose a low-priced, consumer-oriented program or a high-priced program targeted at professional photographers. For most users, the low-priced programs do everything you need. The most popular of these include the following:

- Adobe Photoshop Elements (www.adobe.com), $99.99
- Paint Shop Pro Photo (www.corel.com), $99.99
- Picasa (www.picasa.com), free
- Ulead PhotoImpact (www.ulead.com), $69.99

note

Don't confuse the affordable Adobe Photoshop Elements with the much higher-priced (and more sophisticated) Adobe Photoshop CS4, used by most professional photographers.

In addition, Microsoft offers the Windows Live Photo Gallery program free for all Windows 7 users. You can download Photo Gallery from download.live.com. It's a good alternative, especially if you're on a budget.

These programs perform many of the same functions. You'll be able to organize your photos; tag your photos with useful data; resize your photos larger or smaller; adjust your photos' brightness, contrast, color, and tint; crop your photos to focus on the main part of the picture; make your photos sharper or softer; and, in some cases, add various types of special effects.

note

Windows Photo Gallery was included free with Windows Vista, but it was "unbundled" from Windows 7 and made available as a free download.

Editing Your Photos with Windows Live Photo Gallery

Not all the pictures you take are perfect. Sometimes an image is a little out of focus or off center, or maybe your subject caught the glare of a flash for a "red eye" effect. The nice thing about digital pictures is that you can easily edit them to correct for these and other flaws.

One of the easiest photo-editing programs to use is Windows Live Photo Gallery, available free from Microsoft. You can use Photo Gallery to edit your photos and to organize them on your hard disk.

Organizing Your Photos

As you can see in Figure 32.2, the Photo Gallery window is initially divided into two panes. The left pane is used for navigation—selecting which folders and photos to view. The right pane displays thumbnails of all the photos in the currently selected folder.

The navigation pane is especially useful because it lets you find your photos in a number of different ways:

- To view all your photos, organized by folder, click My Pictures under All Photos and Videos.

- To view photos of a particular person, click that person's name in the People Tags section.

- To view photos by a particular characteristic, click a tag in the Descriptive Tags section. (Of course, you first have to assign tags to your photos...)

FIGURE 32.2

Organizing photos in Windows Live Photo Gallery.

- To view pictures taken in a given year, click the year in the Date Taken section.
- To view photos in a particular folder, click the folder (and subfolder) in the All Photos and Videos section.

To view a photo full size, all you have to do is double-click the photo. This shows the photo full frame, without the other thumbnails or the navigation pane. (Information about the photo still appears in the right-hand pane.) You can move to the next or previous photo by using the navigation controls at the bottom of the Photo Gallery window. Return to your other photos by clicking the Back To Gallery button at the top left of the window.

Editing a Photo

Windows Live Photo Gallery is more than just a photo manager or viewer. It also lets you touch up your digital photos, with easy-to-use photo-editing controls.

To fix a photo, all you have to do is select it in the Photo Gallery and then click the Fix button. This displays the photo in the full window, with a series of editing controls in the right-hand pane, as shown in Figure 32.3. Here's what you can do:

tip

You can also search for a particular folder by using the Search box at the top of the window.

tip

To add descriptive tags to a photo, select the photo in the Photo Gallery window and then click Add Tags in the Information pane. (You may have to click the Info button on the toolbar to display the Information pane.) You can then enter words and phrases to describe the photo; you can later sort by or search for these tags.

▪ To do a quick touch-up of brightness and color, click Auto Adjust.

▪ To increase or decrease brightness and contrast, click Adjust Exposure. This displays Brightness and Contrast sliders; move the sliders to adjust these parameters.

FIGURE 32.3

Touching up a photo in Windows Live Photo Gallery.

▪ To adjust the color levels, click Adjust Color. This displays three color sliders—Color Temperature (slide left to make the picture cooler, or more blue; slide right to make the picture warmer, or more red), Tint, and Saturation.

▪ To crop out unwanted areas at the edges of the picture, click Crop Picture. This displays a rectangular area within your picture, as shown in Figure 32.4; use your mouse to drag the edges of this rectangle to reframe your picture; then click Apply.

▪ To remove the red eye effect, click Fix Red Eye; then click and drag the cursor to draw a rectangle around each eye you want to fix.

> **tip**
>
> You can crop to exact print dimensions by clicking the Proportion button and then choosing a print size.

After you've made a fix, click the check mark in that editing control section. If you want to reject a fix, click the Undo button at the bottom of the pane and select which fix you want to undo; you can undo any or all fixes you've made to a particular photo.

FIGURE 32.4

Cropping a photo.

Emailing a Resized Photo

Here's something else neat about Windows Live Photo Gallery. You can email photos from within the Gallery and have the application automatically resize your photos for smoother emailing.

All you have to do is select one or more photos from within Windows Photo Gallery. Then click the E-mail button at the top of the window. Photo Gallery displays an Attach Files dialog box, as shown in Figure 32.5. Click the Picture Size button and select the desired size—Smaller, Small, Medium, Large, or Original Size. The file size, in kilobytes, is shown beneath this button; you probably want to keep the files you send to less than 250KB apiece.

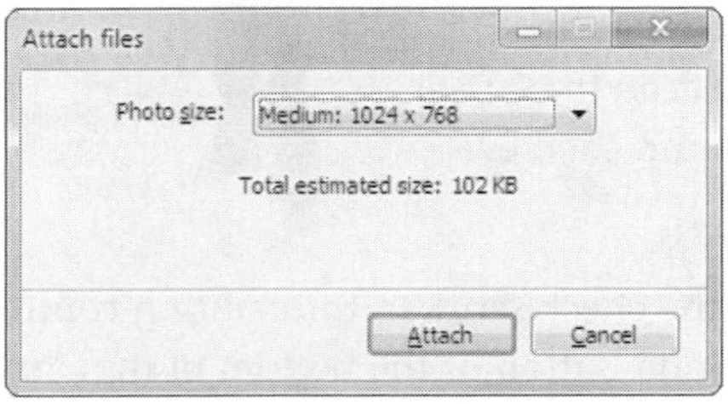

> **tip**
>
> To select multiple photos, hold down the Ctrl key as you click the different photos.

FIGURE 32.5

Resizing a photo for email.

After you've selected a size, click the Attach button. This opens a new email message, with the selected photo(s) already attached. Enter the recipient's email address(es), add some text of your own, and then click the Send button. The message will be sent, along with the photos you selected.

Printing Your Photos

After you've touched up (or otherwise manipulated) your photos, it's time to print them—a task that's really easy in Windows.

Choosing the Right Printer and Paper

If you have a color printer, you can make good-quality prints of your image files. Even a low-priced color inkjet can make surprisingly good prints, although the better your printer, the better the results.

Some manufacturers sell printers specifically designed for photographic prints. These printers use special photo print paper and output prints that are almost indistinguishable from those you get from a professional photo processor. If you take a lot of digital photos, one of these printers might be a good investment.

The quality of your prints is also affected by the type of paper you use. Printing on standard laser or inkjet paper is okay for making proofs, but you'll want to use a thicker, waxier paper for those prints you want to keep. Check with your printer's manufacturer to see what type of paper it recommends for the best quality photo prints.

tip

In Windows Live Photo Gallery, you have the additional option of sending your photos to an online photo service for printing. Just click the Print button and select Order Prints.

Making the Print

Any photo-editing program lets you print your pictures from within the program. You can also print directly from Windows or from the Windows Live Photo Gallery program.

You can start the print process from the Pictures Explorer or from the Windows Live Photo Gallery application; what happens next is the same, no matter how you start.

Begin by selecting the photo(s) to print and then click the Print button at the top of the window. This displays the Print Pictures window, shown in Figure 32.6. Here's where the fun begins.

Start by using the buttons at the top of the window to select which printer to use, as well as the printer's paper size, print quality, and paper type. Then use the selections on the right side of the window to select how many pictures per page to print. The options here depend on the size of your original photo and the size paper you're using. In most instances, you can choose from a full-page photo, two 4- by 6-inch photos, two 5- by 7-inch photos, one 8- by 10-inch photo, four 3.5- by 5-inch photos, nine wallet-sized photos, or 35 photos on a contact sheet. (This last option is useful if you selected more than one photo to print.)

FIGURE 32.6

Printing a photo
in Windows.

Finally, select how many copies you want to print and then click the Print button. Your photos are sent to your printer, and the printing begins.

Printing Photos Professionally

If you don't have your own photo-quality printer, you can use a professional photo-processing service to print your photos. You can create prints from your digital photos in two primary ways:

- Copy your image files to CD or memory card and deliver the CD or card by hand to your local photo finisher.

- Go to the website of an online photo-finishing service and transfer your image files over the Internet.

The first option is convenient for many people, especially because numerous drug stores, supermarkets, and discount stores (including Target and Wal-Mart) offer onsite photo printing

tip

Some photo services, particularly those associated with retail chains, offer the option of picking up your prints at a local store—often with same-day service!

services. Often the printing service is via a self-serve kiosk; just insert your CD or memory card, follow the onscreen instructions, and come back a half-hour later for your finished prints.

The second option is also convenient, if you don't mind waiting a few days for your prints to arrive. You never have to leave your house; you upload your photo files from your computer over the Internet and then receive your prints in your postal mailbox. These web-based services are often lower priced than local print services, too—although don't forget to factor in the mailing costs.

note

Learn more about using online photo sites in Chapter 33, "Sharing Your Digital Photos Online."

THE ABSOLUTE MINIMUM

Here are the key points to remember from this chapter:

- You can connect a digital camera to your PC via USB or use a memory card reader to transfer files from the camera's media card.

- When you scan a photo print, your photo is converted to a digital file that is saved on your hard disk.

- To touch up or edit your photos, use a photo-editing program, such as Adobe Photoshop Elements or Windows Live Photo Gallery.

- Some of the most popular "touch-ups" include removing red eye, adjusting brightness and contrast, changing color and tint, and cropping the edges of the photo.

- You can print your photos to any four-color printer or send them (via the Internet) to an online photo processor for printing.

33

SHARING YOUR DIGITAL PHOTOS ONLINE

In the old days, if you wanted to share your photos with friends and family, you had to have extra prints made and then hand them out or mail them off, as appropriate. This approach is not only time-consuming, it's costly; you have to pay money for each extra print you make.

In today's age of digital photography, you can still make photo prints. (In fact, you can make the prints on your own PC, as you learned in Chapter 32, "Organizing and Editing Your Digital Photos.") But now you also can share your photos digitally, online, with anyone who has an Internet connection. Let's look at how you can do this.

Emailing Digital Photos

Perhaps the easiest way to share your digital photos is to email them. No special software or service is involved; all you have to do is attach your photos to an email message you create in your regular email program and then send that message to as many recipients as you want.

You learned how to attach files to email messages back in Chapter 28, "Sending and Receiving Email." Because a digital photo is just another type of computer file, the process is the same when you want to send a photo. Create a new message in your email program or web mail service, click the attachments button, and then select those photos you want to attach. Click the Send button, and your message is sent on its way, complete with the photos you selected.

As easy as this process is, you need to be aware of one issue before you start emailing your photos far and wide—the size of the photo files you email.

If you're emailing photos pretty much as they were shot with your camera, you're probably emailing some large files. This can be a problem if you or your recipients are using a slow dial-up Internet connection; the larger the attached files, the longer it takes to send or receive an email message. In addition, some ISPs have trouble handling messages that are too large; you want to avoid messages more than 1 or 2MB in size.

note

You can use any photo-editing program, including Windows Live Photo Gallery, to resize your pictures. For more detailed instructions, turn to Chapter 32.

For this reason, you probably want to resize your photos before you email them. If your recipients will be viewing your photos only on their computer screens, you should make your photos no larger than the typical screen—no more than 1024 pixels wide or 768 pixels tall. Anything larger won't fit on a typical computer screen.

In Windows 7, resizing can be automatic. As you learned in Chapter 32, both the Pictures Explorer and Windows Live Photo Gallery include an E-mail button. When you click this button, Windows displays an Attach Files dialog box. You use this dialog box to select a size for the picture you want to send; you can choose to send the photo as small as 640×480 pixels or as large as its original size. A copy of the selected picture is then resized appropriately and attached to an email message. The original photo remains at its original size on your hard disk.

On the other hand, if your recipients will be printing the photos, you probably don't want to resize them. A photo resized to 1024×768 pixels doesn't have enough picture resolution to create a detailed print. You'll want to keep your photos at their original size if they're going to be printed; any resizing will result in fuzzy prints.

Sharing Photos at an Online Photo Site

If you're sharing your photos with many people, an even better solution is to post your pictures on an online photo website. These sites let you store your photos in online photo albums, which can then be viewed by any number of visitors via their web browsers—for free. These sites also offer photo printing services, and some sell photo-related items, such as picture tee shirts, calendars, mugs, and so on. Most of these sites are free to use; they make their money by selling prints and other merchandise.

To use a photo-sharing site, you start by signing up for a free account. After your account is created, choose which photos on your PC you want to share. After the photos are selected, the site automatically uploads them from your PC to the website. You then organize the photos into photo albums, each of which has its own unique URL. You can then email the URL to your friends and family; when they access the photo site, they view your photos on their computer screens. If they like what they see, they can order their own photo prints (which they pay for, not you).

The most popular of these photo-sharing sites include

- **dotPhoto** (www.dotphoto.com)
- **DropShots** (www.dropshots.com)
- **Flickr** (www.flickr.com)
- **Fotki** (www.fotki.com)
- **FotoTime** (www.fototime.com)
- **Kodak EasyShare Gallery** (www.kodakgallery.com)
- **PhotoWorks** (www.photoworks.com)
- **Picturetrail** (www.picturetrail.com)
- **Shutterfly** (www.shutterfly.com)
- **Snapfish** (www.snapfish.com)
- **Webshots** (www.webshots.com)

For example, Shutterfly, shown in Figure 33.1, lets you create any number of photo albums. You create a new album and upload photos by clicking the My Pictures tab and then clicking the Upload button. You can then choose to create a new photo album or upload new photos to an existing album. When the Choose Pictures window appears, select the photos to upload and then click the Add Selected Pictures button.

FIGURE 33.1

The Shutterfly photo-sharing website.

After the pictures are uploaded, you can view your photo albums by clicking the My Pictures tab. As you can see in Figure 33.2, each album is displayed separately; click an album to view the photos in that album.

FIGURE 33.2

Online photo albums at the Shutterfly site.

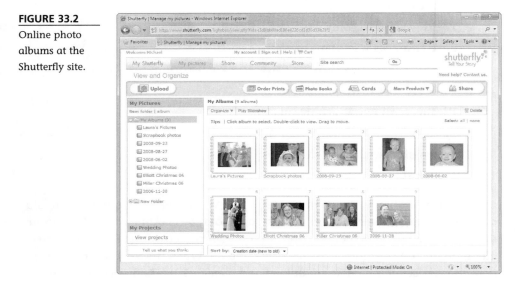

To share your photos with others, click the Share tab. This lets you create share sites—personal web pages that host the photos you want to share. You can choose your own customized page layout and then mail the URL for the new site to friends and family.

Printing Photos Online

Most of these photo-sharing websites also offer photo-printing services. After you've uploaded your photos, all you have to do is select the photos you want to print and then click the appropriate button. (On Shutterfly, this is accomplished by clicking the Order Prints button on the My Pictures tab.)

You'll probably have the option of choosing different sizes of prints. For example, Shutterfly offers 4×6-, 5×7-, 8× 10-, 11×14-, 16×20, and 20×30-inch prints and also wallet-sized prints, in either matte or glossy finish. Choose the size and quantity you want for each print and then enter your payment and shipping information.

Most sites ship within a day or two of receiving your order; add shipping time, and you should receive your prints in less than a week. Shipping is typically via the U.S. Postal Service or some similar shipping service.

THE ABSOLUTE MINIMUM

Here are the key points to remember from this chapter:

- The easiest way to share photos with friends and family is to send your photos as email attachments.
- Before you attach a photo file to an email message, resize it to a maximum of 800 pixels wide.
- Multiple people can view your photos when you create an online photo album at a photo-sharing website.
- Most photo-sharing sites also let you order photo prints, which are delivered via postal mail.

34

PLAYING, RIPPING, AND BURNING CDs

Your personal computer is a full-featured digital music machine. Not only can you download music from the Internet (which we talk about in Chapter 35, "Downloading and Playing Digital Music"), but you can use your PC to play music on CDs. Just insert a CD into your PC's CD drive, and the music starts.

In addition, assuming that you have a recordable CD drive (called a CD *burner*) in your system unit, you can make your own audio mix CDs. You can take any combination of songs on your hard disk and "burn" them onto a blank CD—and then play that CD in your home, car, or portable CD player. You can also use your PC to make copies of any CD you own and to "rip" songs from a CD to your PC's hard drive.

And the good thing is, all of this is quite easy to do. You don't have to be a geek to create your own computerized music library!

Choosing a Music Player Program

In most cases, playing a CD is as simple as inserting a disc into your computer's CD or DVD drive. This should automatically launch a music player program, which should start playing your music or movie.

Which music player program you use depends on what's installed on your PC. Assuming that you're using Microsoft Windows, you have the Windows Media Player (WMP) program preinstalled and ready to go. Music player programs also come with most portable music players; for example, the popular Apple iPod comes with the iTunes music player.

Usually, it doesn't matter which music player software you use; they all perform pretty much the same functions, in pretty much the same fashion. That said, I recommend that you use iTunes if you have an iPod, or Windows Media Player if you have any other type of portable music player. Windows Media Player is also good if you don't have a portable music player; it's my favorite program for playing, ripping, and burning CDs.

This chapter looks at the two most popular player programs—Windows Media Player and iTunes— and how to use them to play, rip, and burn CDs.

note

The latest and greatest version of WMP is Windows Media Player 12, which is included with Microsoft Windows 7. You can also download WMP from the Windows Media website (www.microsoft.com/windows/windowsmedia/).

Using Windows Media Player

For most users, the music player of choice is the one that comes free with Microsoft Windows. Windows Media Player is a great little program you can use for many purposes—playing CDs and DVDs, ripping and burning CDs, listening to Internet radio broadcasts, and watching web videos. It works similarly to most other music players, so if you know how to use WMP, you should be able to figure out any other media player program.

You launch Windows Media Player from within Windows by clicking the Start button and selecting All Programs, Windows Media Player.

Whether you're playing a CD, DVD, or digital audio file, you use the controls located at the bottom of the WMP window, shown in Figure 34.1. These are the normal transport buttons you find on a DVD player or VCR, including Play/Pause, Stop, Previous, and Next. WMP also includes buttons to turn on/off the shuffle and repeat functions, along with a volume control slider and mute button.

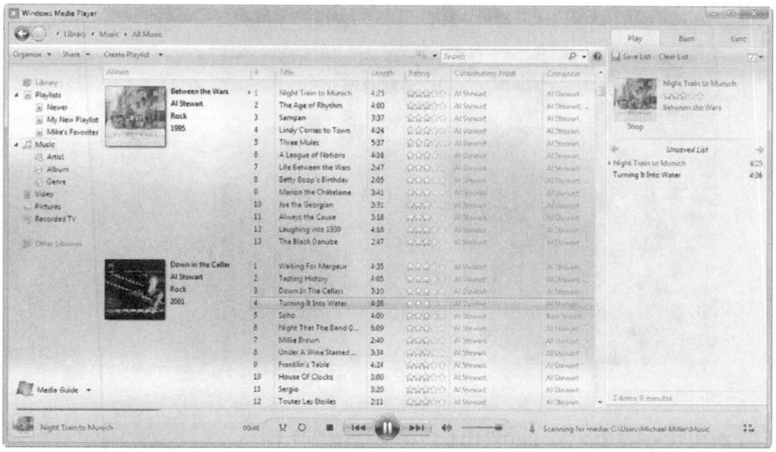

FIGURE 34.1

Playing CDs and other audio files with Windows Media Player.

To the left of the playback controls is a playback status area. This area displays the title of the currently playing track; the track's artist, album, and other metadata; the amount of time elapsed; and a small spectrum analyzer, which is kind of interesting if not totally useful.

What you see in the main part of the WMP window depends on which tab you select from the row of tabs at the top of the window. Windows Media Player assigns different functions to different tabs, and the contents of the main window vary from tab to tab. For example, to view all the contents of your media library, select the Play tab; to burn music to a CD, select the Rip tab; and so forth.

Playing a CD

If you're using WMP as your main music player, CD playback should start automatically when you insert a CD into your computer's CD drive. New to WMP 12 is the Now Playing window that you see when playing CDs. As you can see in Figure 34.2, the Now Playing window is a smaller and simpler playback window that takes up a lot less desktop space than the normal WMP window.

> **tip**
>
> The Previous and Next buttons serve dual duty as Rewind and Fast Forward buttons. Just click and hold down the button to access the Rewind and Fast Forward functions.

> **tip**
>
> To view more options associated with a given function, click the down arrow beneath that particular tab.

FIGURE 34.2

Playing a CD in WMP's Now Playing window.

To pause playback, click the Pause button (in the same location as the Play button—it switches back and forth depending on whether you're playing or pausing the CD); click Play again to resume playback. To skip to the next track, click the Next button. To replay the last track, click the Previous button. You stop playback completely by clicking the Stop button.

By the way, if WMP doesn't start automatically when you insert a CD, you can launch the program manually from the Windows Start menu and then click WMP's Library tab; the CD should be listed in the Navigation pane. Highlight the CD title, and you'll see the list of CD tracks in the Contents pane; click the Play button to begin playback.

Ripping Songs from CD to Your PC

When you want to store your music digitally or transfer music to a portable music player, you need to copy that music from a compact disc to your computer's hard drive. This process is called *ripping*. If you have a large enough hard disk, you can rip an entire library of CDs or individual songs to your computer. Naturally, you can use Windows Media Player for the entire ripping procedure. It's easy to do.

tip

To switch from the Now Playing window to the larger Windows Media Player window, click the Switch to Library button in the upper-right corner.

tip

To play the songs on a CD in a random order, click the Shuffle button on the far left of the transport panel. WMP also offers a repeat function, which repeats the selected song(s) over and over. You activate this function by clicking the Repeat button, which is next to the Shuffle button in the transport panel.

Before you begin ripping, however, you have to tell WMP what format you want to use for your ripped files. You also have to choose the bit rate for recording.

Let's start with the file format. Windows Media Player lets you rip audio files in a number of different formats: MP3, WMA, or WAV. For most users, the regular WMA format is good, although you might want to go with Windows Media Audio Lossless for the highest sound quality, or the MP3 format for almost-universal compatibility with all portable music players.

To select a file format, click Rip Settings, then Format. You can select either the Windows Media Audio or MP3 format. Next, click Rip Settings, Audio Quality, and then select the desired bit rate; the available options vary by the type of file you select.

After you've set the format and bit rate, it's time to start ripping. All you have to do is insert the CD you want to copy into your PC's CD drive and, when the Now Playing window appears, click Rip CD.

Alternatively, you can rip a CD from the main WMP window by selecting the Play tab, shown in Figure 34.3. Check all the tracks you want to copy, and then click the Rip CD button on the toolbar.

note

Learn more about digital music file formats in Chapter 35.

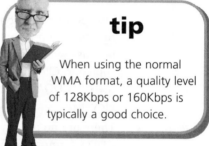

tip

When using the normal WMA format, a quality level of 128Kbps or 160Kbps is typically a good choice.

FIGURE 34.3

Ripping tracks from a CD to your PC's hard drive.

Whichever method you use, Windows Media Player extracts the selected tracks from the CD and converts them from their original CD Audio format to the file format you selected, sampled at the bit rate you selected. The converted files are written to your PC's hard disk and added to the Windows Media Player Library.

Burning Your Own CDs

If you can copy tracks from a CD to your hard disk, what's to stop you from going in the other direction—copying files from your hard disk to a recordable/rewritable CD?

tip

Make sure you're connected to the Internet before you start ripping so that WMP can download album and track details. (If you don't connect, you won't be able to encode track names or CD cover art.)

This process of recording your own custom CDs is called *burning* a CD. Unlike CD ripping, CD burning doesn't require you to set a lot of format options. That's because whatever format the original file is in (WMA, MP3, or WAV), when it gets copied to CD it is encoded into the CDDA (CD Digital Audio) format. All music CDs use the CDDA format, so if you're burning an MP3 or WMA file, Windows Media Player translates it to CDDA before the copy is made.

There are no quality levels to set, either. All CDDA-format files are encoded at the same bit rate. So you really don't have configuration to do—other than deciding which songs you want to copy.

Here's all you have to do to burn a CD:

1. Insert a blank CR-R disc into your PC's CD drive.

2. From within WMP, click the Burn tab, shown in Figure 34.4.

3. Drag the desired tracks, albums, or playlists from the Content pane to the Burn List in the List pane.

4. Click and drag items within the Burn List to place them in the desired playback order.

5. When you're ready to burn the CD, click the Start Burn button.

tip

If you want to make a copy of a CD to another CD, you use a combination of ripping and burning. That is, you rip the files from the original CD to your hard disk (in WAV format) and then burn those files to a second blank CD. Alternatively, you can use a program specifically designed for CD copying, such as Easy Media Creator (www.roxio.com); this program makes copying pretty much a one-button operation.

FIGURE 34.4

Creating a Burn List on the Burn tab.

WMP now inspects the files you want to copy, converts them to CD-DA format, and copies them to your CD. When the entire burning process is done, WMP displays a message to that effect and ejects the newly burned CD from the disc drive.

Using Apple iTunes

Windows Media Player isn't the only music player software you can use to play, rip, and burn CDs. If you're the proud owner of an Apple iPod or iPhone, you're probably already familiar with the iTunes program, which functions as a music manager/player program for the iPod.

The iTunes player functions much like Windows Media Player. The difference is that it's optimized for use with the iPod; it automatically rips music in Apple's somewhat-proprietary AAC file format.

The main iTunes window looks a lot like the main WMP window. The left-hand pane includes sections for your music and media library, a link to the online iTunes Store, and a list of all your playlists. The obligatory transport controls (Play/Pause, Rewind, Forward, and Volume) are located at the top of the window. Next to the transport controls is a panel that displays the currently playing song and artist, as well as total and elapsed time for the track.

What you see in the main part of the iTunes window depends on which view you select. (The View buttons are to the right of the track display panel.) The first button displays a text list of available songs, which can be sorted by song, artist, album, genre, and so forth. The second button displays songs grouped by album, along with a thumbnail of the CD art. The third View displays iTune's unique Cover Flow view, shown in Figure 34.5, which presents an interactive display of all the albums you have stored on your PC.

FIGURE 34.5

iTunes in Cover
Flow view.

Playing a CD

When you insert a CD into your PC's CD drive,
that CD automatically appears in the iTunes
window. To start playback, all you have to do is
click the Play button. You can then use the
transport controls to pause the CD or go backward and forward through the tracks.
Naturally, the volume control adjusts the playback level.

Ripping Songs from CD to Your PC

iTunes makes copying songs from CD to your
PC's hard drive relatively easy. As with WMP,
you first have to configure iTunes to use the
desired file format and bit rate for the songs it rips.

tip

To play the songs on a CD
in a random order, click the
Shuffle button at the bottom
left of the iTunes window.
iTunes also offers a repeat
function, which repeats the
selected song(s) over and
over. You activate this function by
clicking the Repeat button, which
is next to the Shuffle button.

Unlike WMP, iTunes doesn't rip songs in Microsoft's WMA format. Instead, it can rip
in Apple's AAC format, as well as the MP3 and WAV formats. To choose a rip format, select Edit, Preferences to display the iTunes dialog box. Then, select the
General tab and click the Import Settings button. This displays the Import Setting
window, shown in Figure 34.6. Pull down the Import Using list and select the file format you want. Then pull down the Setting list and select the bit rate you want to
use.

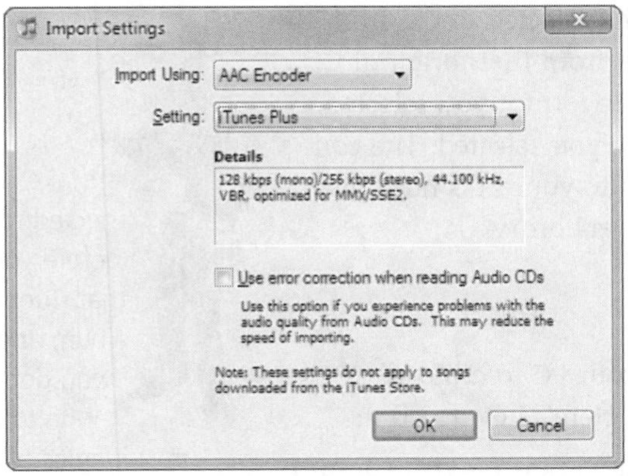

FIGURE 34.6

Configuring iTunes for ripping music.

After you've set the format and bit rate, it's time to start ripping. Follow these steps:

1. Insert the CD you want to copy into your PC's CD drive.

2. As you can see in Figure 34.7, all the tracks from the CD are now listed in the iTunes window. Check those tracks you want to copy.

3. Click the Import CD button at the bottom of the iTunes window.

> **tip**
>
> By default, iTunes uses the AAC Encoder at a bit rate of 128Kbps; this is a good setting for most users.

FIGURE 34.7

Getting ready to rip a CD using iTunes.

iTunes now extracts the selected tracks from the CD and converts them from their original CD Audio format to the file format you selected, sampled at the bit rate you selected. The converted files are written to your PC's hard disk and added to the iTunes library.

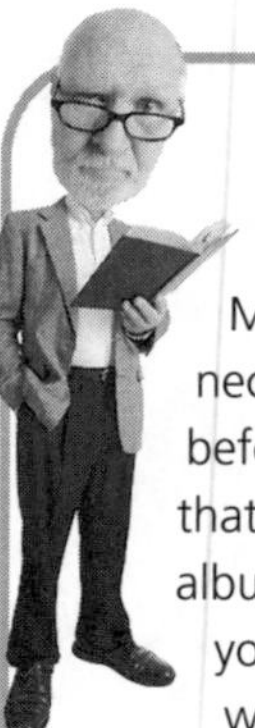

tip

Make sure you're connected to the Internet before you start ripping so that iTunes can download album and track details. (If you don't connect, you won't be able to encode track names or CD cover art.)

Burning Your Own CDs

Burning music from your PC to a blank CD is also easy with iTunes. Here's how to do it:

1. In iTunes, create a new playlist containing all the songs you want to burn to CD. Make sure that your playlist is less than 74 minutes (for a normal CD) or 80 minutes (for an extended CD) long.

2. Insert a blank CD-R disc into your PC's CD drive.

3. Select the playlist that contains the songs you want to burn, as shown in Figure 34.8, and make sure that all the songs in the playlist are checked.

4. Click the Burn Disc button at the bottom of the iTunes window.

FIGURE 34.8
Burning a playlist of songs to CD.

iTunes converts the selected files to CDDA format and copies them to your CD. When the entire burning process is done, iTunes displays a message to that effect and ejects the newly burned CD from the disc drive.

note

Learn how to create iTunes playlists in Chapter 35.

THE ABSOLUTE MINIMUM

Here are the key points to remember from this chapter:

- The process of copying songs from a CD to your hard disk is called *ripping*.

- The process of copying digital audio files from your hard disk to a blank CD is called *burning*.

- You can use either Windows Media Player (included with Windows) or iTunes (included with the Apple iPod) to play, rip, and burn CDs.

- For best audio quality, rip files using the WMA or AAC formats; for best compatibility with music player programs and portable music players, use the MP3 format.

35

DOWNLOADING AND PLAYING DIGITAL MUSIC

In Chapter 34, "Playing, Ripping, and Burning CDs," you learned how to play music from CDs and how to rip your CDs to digital files stored on your PC's hard drive. But CDs aren't the only route to PC-based digital music; a lot of music also is available on the Internet, ready for you to purchase and download.

The music you download from the Internet can be played back on your PC or transferred to your iPod or other portable music player. It's a great way to beef up your music collection—with no physical CDs to buy!

Understanding Digital Audio Formats

Before we get into the mechanics of creating your own digital music library, you need to understand the various audio file formats available for your use. There are many ways to make a digital recording, and different online music stores (and portable music players) use different file formats.

Digital audio files are of two types. *Uncompressed* files reproduce the exact file contained on a compact disc; these files are large but have excellent sound quality. *Compressed* files remove bits and pieces of the original music to create a smaller file (easier to store and download from the Internet) but with reduced audio fidelity. The most common uncompressed file format is the WAV format; the most popular compressed file formats are AAC, MP3, and WMA.

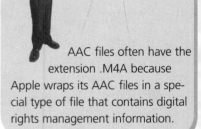

note

AAC files often have the extension .M4A because Apple wraps its AAC files in a special type of file that contains digital rights management information.

Which file format should you use for your digital music? There's no easy answer to that question; each format has its plusses and minuses. That said, Table 35.1 details the pros and cons of the most popular digital music file formats.

TABLE 35.1   Digital Audio File Formats

Format	Pros	Cons
AAC	Compresses songs into small files Used by Apple's iPod portable music player and iTunes Store Can play in Windows Media Player 12	Not CD quality Not compatible with non-Apple portable music players and online music stores Digital rights management can restrict playback to a set number of PCs and players
MP3	Compresses songs into small files The most universal of all audio file formats; compatible with virtually all music player programs and portable music players No digital rights management, so files can be played on any number of PCs and music players	Not CD quality
WAV	CD quality	Large file size
WMA	Compresses songs into small files Used by most online music stores Compatible with most music player programs and portable music players	Not CD quality Not compatible with Apple's iPod Digital rights management can restrict playback to a set number of PCs and players

Of the compressed formats, the MP3 format is the oldest and most universal; almost every music player program and portable music player is MP3-compatible. The WMA format was developed by Microsoft and is used by most commercial online music stores; it's compatible with all music player programs except Apple's iTunes, and with all portable music players except Apple's iPod. The AAC format is used by Apple in both iTunes and iPod; it's not compatible with many other music player programs and portable music players—although AAC files can be played in Windows Media Player 12.

If you're downloading music, you probably don't have a choice of formats; you have to take the music in the format that it's in. Practically, that means if you have an iPod and use the iTunes store, you'll get your music in AAC format. If you have any other type of player (such as the Microsoft Zune or Creative Zen) and get your music from any other online music store (such as Napster or the Zune Marketplace), you'll get your music in either WMA or MP3 format.

When you're copying files from your CD to your PC, however, you have your choice of format. For compatibility with all portable music players (including the iPod), use the MP3 format. If you have an iPod and only want to play your files on other iPods, you can use the better-sounding AAC format. Or if you have a non-Apple player and never want to play your music on an iPod, you can use the equally good sounding WMA format.

Here's another consideration: What if you want to play your digital music not on a PC or portable audio player, but rather on your home audio system? Neither the AAC, MP3, or WMA formats have good-enough audio quality to sound good when played through a quality home system. In this instance, you can save your files in WAV format, although that will take a lot of disc space—about 650MB per CD. A better alternative is to use a format that incorporates *lossless compression*, such as WMA Lossless (for Windows PCs) or AAC Lossless (for compatibility with the iPod). These formats reproduce the exact sound of the original, with no deterioration in audio quality, but at a smaller file size than the noncompressed WAV format. (Lossless files are larger than compressed AAC, MP3, or WMA files, however.)

Dealing with DRM

Until quite recently, most music you downloaded from online music stores was encoded with *digital rights management* (DRM) technology. DRM was designed to prevent the unlawful distribution, copying, and sharing of copyrighted music. If a track you downloaded is protected with DRM, you're limited as to how you can copy and listen to that song.

DRM works by encoding the audio file in a type of wrapper file format. This wrapper file includes a user key, which is used to decode and play the track—under specified conditions. For example, a DRM license might dictate how many different PCs or portable music players the track can be copied to, whether it can be burned to CD, and so on. If you try to use the song in a way not permitted by the license, the DRM protection keeps it from playing.

It's important to know that while DRM technology can be applied to audio files in the AAC and WMA formats, it cannot be applied to MP3 files. This is why most online music stores encoded their music as either AAC or WMA formats, to facilitate DRM.

Recently, however, the trend has been away from DRM to selling DRM-free tracks, most often in the MP3 format. (Apple iTunes is an exception to this, selling its DRM-free tracks in its own AAC format.) The benefit to DRM-free music is that once you purchase it, you can use it however you wish; you can play it on any number of PCs or portable music players and burn it onto an unlimited number of custom CDs. It's a much more listener-friendly solution, which is why many online music stores are now offering DRM-free music.

tip

Check with the individual online music store to see if it encodes its tracks with DRM—and if so, what the terms of its DRM license are.

Downloading from Online Music Stores

One of the great things about digital music is that you can listen to just the songs you want. You're not forced to listen to an entire album; you can download that one song you really like and ignore the rest. Even better, you can take songs you like from different artists and create your own playlists. It's like being your own DJ or record producer!

Where do you go to download your favorite songs? You have a lot of choices, but the easiest is to shop at an online music store. These are websites that offer hundreds of thousands of songs from your favorite artists, all completely legal. You pay about a buck a song and download the music files directly to your computer's hard disk.

caution

When you're downloading music, it's best to have a high-speed broadband Internet connection. Although nothing's stopping you from downloading via a dial-up connection, the process can get a tad tedious. These are big files to download!

iTunes Store

The most popular online music store today is Apple's iTunes Store. The iTunes Store (www.apple.com/itunes/store/) offers more than four million songs at prices ranging from 69 cents to $1.29 each.

All songs offered for sale in the iTunes Store are in Apple's somewhat-proprietary AAC file format, which means that they won't play in many third-party music player programs or on most non-Apple portable music players. But you can use Apple's iTunes software to play the files, and (of course) play all downloaded songs on your Apple iPod.

To use the iTunes Store, you first have to download the iTunes software. We'll examine this software later in this chapter, but don't worry—it's a fairly easy program to use. To download the software, all you have to do is click the Download Now button on the iTunes Store home page and then follow the onscreen instructions.

note

As of early 2009, most tracks in the iTunes Store were being offered without DRM encoding. Prior to this, all iTunes tracks had DRM encoding.

After the iTunes software is up and running on your computer, you access the iTunes Store by clicking the iTunes Store icon in the Source pane; click the Music link to view music tracks to purchase. As you can see in Figure 35.1, there are several ways to find music in the iTunes Store. You can browse by genre, view new releases, or use the Power Search feature to search for specific songs or artists.

FIGURE 35.1
Shopping for digital music at the iTunes Store.

When you see the results of your searching or browsing, such as the page in Figure 35.2, click the Buy Song button to purchase a particular song, the Buy Album button to purchase an entire album, or the Buy Video button to purchase a video. After you confirm your purchase, the track(s) will be downloaded automatically to your PC and added to your iTunes Library. You can listen to your downloaded music in the iTunes music player or transfer the music to your iPod.

FIGURE 35.2

Downloading
songs from the
iTunes Store.

Other Online Music Stores

If you don't have an Apple iPod, you'll want to
check out some of the non-Apple online music
stores. These stores offer tunes in either the
MP3 or WMA file formats; both of these formats can be played in most music player programs (including Windows Media Player) and
portable music players—Apple's iPod being the
notable exception.

When you're shopping for songs to download,
here are some of the other big online music
stores to check out:

> ■ **Amazon MP3 Downloads** (www.
> amazonmp3.com)
>
> ■ **Dada** (www.dada.net)
>
> ■ **eMusic** (www.emusic.com)
>
> ■ **iMesh** (imesh.com)
>
> ■ **MP3.com** (www.mp3.com)
>
> ■ **Napster** (www.napster.com)
>
> ■ **Puretracks** (www.puretracks.com)
>
> ■ **Rhapsody** (www.rhapsody.com)
>
> ■ **Wal-Mart Music** Downloads (mp3.
> walmart.com)

note

The first time you make a
purchase from the iTunes Store,
you'll be prompted to create a new
account and enter your credit card
information.

note

If you have a Microsoft Zune
music player, you use the Zune
Marketplace (www.zune.net) to purchase your music. It's only for Zune users.

All of these offer similar pricing, although the selection tends to differ from site to site.

Playing Digital Music on Your PC

After you download a bunch of digital music, what do you do with it? You can, of course, transfer the songs to a portable music player, like the iPod, but you can also play your music right there on your personal computer. Just make sure you have a good set of speakers or headphones connected and a music player program installed. The two most popular such programs are Windows Media Player (provided with Windows) and the iTunes player (used with the Apple iPod). We'll look at both in brief.

Using Windows Media Player

No matter which version of Windows you're using, you have the Windows Media Player (WMP) program preinstalled. You can use WMP to play back all your downloaded digital music—and to keep it organized on your system.

Playing Digital Audio Files

In Windows 7, all the music files you download should be stored in the Music folder, typically under subfolders for artist and album. All music stored in these folders is automatically sensed by Windows Media Player and added to WMP's Library.

To play a digital audio file in WMP12, you first have to load that file into the player. You do this by clicking the Library tab (shown in Figure 35.3), navigating to the song you want to play, and then either double-clicking the song title or selecting the song and clicking the Play button.

caution

You can download music from noncommercial websites and unofficial file-trading networks—although I don't recommend it. Not only is downloading from these sources legally questionable, these sites are breeding grounds for computer viruses and spyware. If you're going to download from an unofficial site, run both antivirus and anti-spyware software.

note

Learn more about transferring digital music to a portable music player in Chapter 36, "Using Your PC with an iPod or iPhone."

note

You can also download WMP from the Windows Media website (www.microsoft.com/windows/windowsmedia/).

FIGURE 35.3

Playing music from WMP's Library.

You can also play back an entire album by selecting Album from the Navigation pane, navigating to the album, and then clicking the Play button. Same thing with playing back all the songs by a particular artist or in a particular genre: Select either Artist or Genre in the Navigation pane, navigate to the artist or genre you want, and then click the Play button.

Creating a Playlist of Your Favorite Songs

By default, the music stored in the WMP Library is organized by album and artist. Although it's fine to listen to music a complete album at a time, Windows Media Player lets you organize your music however you want by creating custom *playlists*.

A playlist is simply a list of individual songs, assembled from any album or artist in your music library. A playlist can be as short as two songs or can include every song on your PC.

tip

You can choose to display the contents of WMP's Content pane in various ways. The default view is what Microsoft calls Expanded Tile; also available are Icon and Details views. You change the Content pane view by clicking the View Options button next to the Instant Search box at the top of the Library tab. Click the button itself to cycle through the different views, or click the down arrow next to the button to select a specific view from the drop-down menu.

To create a playlist in Windows Media Player 12, follow these steps:

1. From the Play tab, go to the Navigation pane and select Create Playlist.
2. This creates an item called Untitled Playlist. Select this item and enter a new name for the playlist.

3. To add a track to your playlist, select it in the Library's Content pane and drag it onto the playlist name in the Navigation pane.

4. Repeat step 3 as many times as you want to add more songs to your playlist.

To play a playlist, go to the Navigation pane in the Library tab and click the Playlist item. This displays all your playlists in the Content pane. Double-click a playlist to select it, and then click the Play button to begin playback. All the tracks in your playlist will play, one at a time, in the order listed.

tip

To skip a track within a playlist, click the Next button in the WMP transport. To repeat a track you really like, select the track and then click the Turn Repeat On button. You can also play the tracks in a playlist in random order by clicking the Turn Shuffle On button.

Using the iTunes Player

If you have an Apple iPod, you have the iTunes music player program installed on your PC. You can use the iTunes player for all your music playback needs, as you'll soon see.

Playing Digital Audio Files

Playing songs with iTunes is as easy as it is with any music player program. Make sure you have Music selected in the Library section of the Source pane, and then iTunes displays all the songs you have stored on your computer. You can click the View buttons to display your music in different ways; most people like the cool-looking Cover Flow view, which lets you "flip" through all the album covers for your digital music.

As you can see in Figure 35.4, a text list of music is displayed beneath the cover display. Click a cover to view all the songs contained in that particular album. To play an individual song, double-click the title in the song list—or select the song and click the Play button in the transport controls. To play an entire album, just double-click the album cover.

note

When you create a playlist, you don't actually make copies of the individual songs. Instead, the playlist points to the songs where they continue to reside on your hard disk. When you play a playlist, Windows Media Player accesses each song file in turn on the hard drive. However, if you change the location of your music files or their filenames, your existing playlists might not be able to locate your music.

FIGURE 35.4

Playing music in the iTunes player.

Creating a Playlist of Your Favorite Songs

Just as WMP lets you create playlists for filtered playback, so does the iTunes player. The playlists you create are displayed in the Playlists section of the Source pane; double-click a playlist to play it.

To create a new playlist, follow these steps:

1. Select File, New Playlist (or click the + button in the bottom-left corner of the iTunes window).

2. A new "untitled playlist" item appears in the Playlists section of the Source pane. Double-click this item and enter a title for the playlist.

3. Click the Music item in the Library section of the Source pane.

4. Select a song you want to add to the playlist; then use your mouse to drag that item onto the name of the playlist in the Source pane.

5. Repeat step 4 as many times as you want to add more songs to your playlist.

tip

You can sort the songs displayed in the music list by name, time, artist, album, and so forth. Just click the header at the top of the column by which you want to sort; some columns sort differently if you click them a second or third time.

Listening to Internet Radio

Downloadable music isn't the only music available on the Internet. Many real-world radio stations—as well as web-only stations—broadcast over the Internet using a technology called *streaming audio*. Streaming audio is different from downloading an audio file. When you download a file, you can't start playing that file until it is completely downloaded to your PC. With streaming audio, however, playback can start before an entire file is downloaded. This also enables live broadcasts—both of traditional radio stations and made-for-the-Web stations—to be sent from the broadcast site to your PC.

tip

Although you can listen to Internet radio over a traditional dial-up connection, you'll hear better quality sound over a broadband connection.

You can listen to Internet radio within many music player programs. For example, the iTunes music player has a Radio function (shown in Figure 35.5) that facilitates finding and listening to a variety of Internet radio stations. In addition, many Internet radio sites feature built-in streaming software or direct you to sites where you can download the appropriate music player software.

FIGURE 35.5

Listening to Internet radio with iTunes.

When you're looking for Internet radio broadcasts (of which there are thousands, daily), you need a good directory of available programming. Here's a list of sites that offer links to either traditional radio simulcasts or original Internet programming:

- **AOL Radio** (music.aol.com/radioguide/bb/)
- **Jango** (www.jango.com)

- **LAUNCHcast** (music.yahoo.com/launchcast/)
- **Live365** (www.live365.com)
- **Mike's Radio World** (www.mikesradioworld.com)
- **Pandora** (www.pandora.com)
- **RadioTower.com** (www.radiotower.com)
- **SHOUTcast** (yp.shoutcast.com)
- **XM Radio Online** (xmro.xmradio.com)

note

Some of these sites offer original programming for a subscription fee.

THE ABSOLUTE MINIMUM

Here are the key points to remember from this chapter:

- Digital music is typically stored in one of three compressed file formats— MP3, AAC, or WMA.

- Of these formats, MP3 is the most universal; the AAC format is proprietary to Apple's iPod and iTunes; and the WMA format is used by Windows-compatible sites and players.

- You can download songs from online music stores such as the iTunes Store; songs cost 69 cents or more.

- You can use any audio player program—such as Windows Media Player or the iTunes player—to play back digital audio files.

- If you prefer to listen to a stream of digital music, Internet radio is the way to go; hundreds of real-world and web-only radio stations are broadcasting on the Internet.

36

USING YOUR PC WITH AN iPOD OR iPHONE

One of the hottest consumer electronics gadgets today is the portable music player, sometimes called an *MP3 player*. These players are small enough to fit in the palm of your hand and, depending on the storage medium used (either micro hard drive or flash memory), can store from 512MB to more than 100GB of files. That's big enough to hold tens of thousands of songs, as well as photos and (depending on the player) videos.

The most popular portable audio player today is the Apple iPod—or, in its smartphone incarnation, the iPhone. You get the music for your iPod either by downloading from the Internet or ripping from your own CDs. The music you download or rip is stored on your computer and then transferred to your iPod when you connect it to your PC.

Getting to Know the Apple iPod

The iPod is the market's best-selling portable audio player for a reason—it's easy to use and does what you need it to do. Apple sells several versions of the iPod, including the large-capacity iPod Classic, the touchscreen-operated iPod touch, the compact iPod nano, and the ultra-small (and screenless) iPod shuffle, all shown in Figure 36.1.

FIGURE 36.1

Apple's iPod family of portable music players. (Photo courtesy of Apple.)

Then there's the iPhone, which has taken the mobile phone market by storm. The iPhone blends an iPod music player with a touchscreen-operated smartphone—and throws in WiFi portability, to boot. The iPhone lets you play music, talk on the phone, surf the Internet, send and receive email, and use all sorts of applications that you can download from the iPhone Apps Store, accessible directly from the iPhone. It's a nifty device and worth considering if you need either a new music player or cell phone.

Unlike every other product that Apple sells, the iPod is the one device that works equally well with Macintosh or Windows computers. To use the iPod with your PC, however, you first have to install Apple's iTunes software.

As we discussed in Chapter 35, "Downloading and Playing Digital Music," iTunes is a music player program that is fine-tuned to work with both the

note

As popular as the iPod is—and it's far and away the most popular portable audio player today—it has one drawback: It plays digital audio files only in the AAC and MP3 formats. (AAC, the format used for music downloaded from the iTunes Store, is somewhat proprietary to Apple.) It does *not* play files in Microsoft's WMA format. So you won't be able to play WMA files on your iPod device.

iPod and Apple's iTunes Store. You use the iTunes software to transfer music files to your iPod, as well as to purchase and download digital music from the iTunes Store.

Connecting the iPod to your PC is as simple as connecting the cable that comes with your iPod to a USB port on your computer. When the iPod is connected, your PC automatically launches the iTunes software and downloads any new songs and playlists you've added since the last time you connected.

note

Your iPod's battery is also recharged when the cable is connected to your PC.

Managing Your Music with iTunes

The key to managing the music on your iPod is mastering Apple's iTunes software. As you learned in Chapter 35, iTunes looks like most other music player programs. You have a set of transport controls (for playing music on your PC) in the upper-left corner, a list of music files in the main window, and a list of playlists in the Source pane on the left. Select a source or playlist in the Source pane, and its contents are displayed in the main window.

Your master collection of songs is stored in the Music section of the Library, which is the first source in the Source pane. (iTunes creates separate libraries for Movies, TV Shows, Podcasts, and Radio.) When you first install the iTunes software, it imports all AAC, AIFF, MP3, and WAV format files in your Music or My Music folder and lists them in the Library. If you have WMA-format files that you've ripped from CDs in these folders, it asks whether you want to convert them to import into the Library. (iTunes won't convert WMA files you've purchased from an online music store, due to the files' included copyright protection.)

To transfer songs to your iPod, all you have to do is check them in the Library list. When you connect your iPod, your device automatically appears in the Source pane. Click the entry for your iPod or iPhone, and you see the summary screen shown in Figure 36.2. All the checked songs in your Library are downloaded to your iPod; your device's capacity and used space are shown at the bottom of this screen.

tip

You can specify which items are synced to your iPod by clicking the various tabs on your iPod screen in iTunes. For example, if you have a large-capacity iPod, you can choose to download videos, photos, and even your personal contacts to the iPod device.

FIGURE 36.2

Downloading tunes to an iPhone.

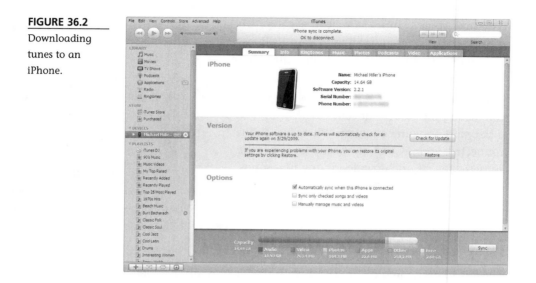

Downloading Music from the iTunes Store

In Chapter 35 you learned how to download music from various online music sites. As discussed in that chapter, one of the most popular online music stores is Apple's iTunes Store. The entire iTunes Store is designed for users of the iPod and iTunes software.

Connecting to the iTunes Store is as easy as clicking the iTunes Store icon in the iTunes Source pane. After you're online, you purchase songs as described in Chapter 35; all the songs you purchase are automatically added to your iTunes Library. Then, the next time you connect your iPod, the songs are automatically transferred to your portable device.

THE ABSOLUTE MINIMUM

Here are the key points to remember from this chapter:

- Copying digital music files from your PC to a portable music player is typically as easy as connecting the player to your PC—the transfer occurs automatically.

- You manage the files you want to copy on your PC beforehand using the appropriate music player program.

- The most popular portable music player today is the Apple iPod, which uses the iTunes software to manage all of its song transfers.

37

PLAYING DVDs AND VIDEOS ON YOUR PC

Your personal computer can play back more than just music. You can also use your PC to play back full-length movies on DVD!

Video playback is especially useful if you have a laptop computer. Watching a movie on your laptop is a great way to pass time during a long plane flight or car ride (if you're a passenger, of course—you should never watch movies while driving!). Just charge up your laptop's battery, load up on the latest movies, and settle back to be entertained.

Using Windows Media Center to Play DVDs

Playing a DVD on your computer is easy—assuming that your PC has a DVD drive, of course. You can use most media player programs, such as Windows Media Player, to play back your DVDs; some DVD-specific playback programs are also available.

That said, if you're running Microsoft Windows, there's a better way to play full-screen movies on your computer. Windows Media Center is a full-screen interface for all manner of digital media playback, but it's particularly suited for watching DVDs and other videos. That's why I recommend it over Windows Media Player for watching movies on your PC.

To watch a movie DVD with Windows Media Center, all you have to do is insert the DVD into your PC's DVD drive. Windows will prompt you to choose a playback device, as shown in Figure 37.1; select Play DVD Movie Using Windows Media Center.

note

Windows Media Center can also be used to listen to digital music, view digital photos, and (if your PC has a built-in TV tuner) watch and record television programs. It's particularly useful for driving a home theater PC in your living room.

FIGURE 37.1

Choose Windows Media Center to watch movies full-screen.

Windows Media Center should now open, and the movie should start playing automatically, as shown in Figure 37.2. To pause the movie, click the Pause button; then click Play to resume playback.

note

You can also opt to watch the DVD using Windows Media Player, which can be run full-screen if you like.

Other transport controls let you move to the next or previous DVD chapter, or fast forward or rewind through the disc.

FIGURE 37.2

Watching a DVD movie with Windows Media Center.

Playing Other Video Files

If you download video files from the Internet or transfer home movies from a digital camcorder, you can view those files on your PC using either Windows Media Player or Windows Media Center. Whichever software you choose, playing a video file you've stored on your PC's hard drive is similar to playing back a DVD.

To view video files in Windows Media Center, go to the main menu and select Pictures + Video, Video Library, as shown in Figure 37.3. All your video files should be there; click a thumbnail to start playback.

FIGURE 37.3

Navigating to Windows Media Center's Video Library.

Extras
TOSHIBA Games
Pictures + Videos

play favorites

video library

4:39 PM

To view video files in Windows Media Player, click the down arrow beneath the Library tab and then select Video. This changes the Library list in the Navigation pane to display only video files. Make your selection in the Navigation pane, and thumbnails of the available videos appear in the Content pane, as shown in Figure 37.4. To begin playback, double-click a video clip, or select the clip and click the Play button.

FIGURE 37.4

Selecting a video file for playback in Windows Media Player.

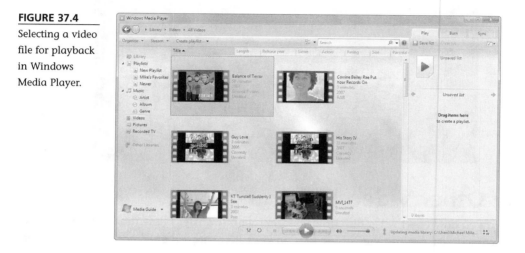

THE ABSOLUTE MINIMUM

Here are the key points to remember from this chapter:

- To play DVDs on your PC, use a media player program—such as Windows Media Player or Windows Media Center.

- Windows Media Center offers full-screen playback of DVDs and digital video files, as well as playback of digital music and digital photos.

38

MAKING YOUR OWN DIGITAL HOME MOVIES

If you have a camcorder and make your own home movies, you can use your computer system to make those movies a lot more appealing. With the right hardware and software, you can turn your PC into a video-editing console—and make your home movies look a *lot* more professional. All you have to do is hook up a few cables and start editing!

Connecting Your Camcorder

Preparing your PC for video editing is fairly simple. All you have to do is connect your camcorder to your PC system unit.

Most new camcorders today record either to a built-in hard disk or memory card. You can connect the camcorder directly to your PC using the supplied USB or FireWire connection. Or, if the camcorder records to memory card, insert the camcorder's memory card into your computer's memory card reader. In the case of a direct connection, use the software that came with the camcorder to transfer the digital movie files from the camcorder to your computer's hard drive; if you're using a memory card, you can copy files from the card to your computer using Windows Explorer.

tip

If you have an older VHS, VHS-C, SVHS, 8mm, or Hi8 camcorder, you need to convert the camcorder's analog video signal to digital format. You do this by using an outboard video capture device that connects to your PC via USB or FireWire. You'll plug your camcorder into the jacks on the video capture card or device (typically using standard RCA connectors), and it will convert the analog signals from your camcorder into the digital audio and video your computer understands.

Choosing a Video-Editing Program

Once you've transferred your digital movie files to your personal computer, you can then edit your movies. You might, for example, want to cut out some boring footage, combine two or more clips, insert transitions between clips, and even add titles and credits to your movie.

You can do all of these things—and more—with a PC-based video-editing program. These programs perform many of the same functions as the professional editing consoles you might find at your local television station. Today's video-editing programs are surprisingly easy to use—and the results are amazing!

The most popular Windows-compatible video-editing programs cost around $100 and include

- **Adobe Premiere Elements** (www.adobe.com/products/premiereel/)
- **Pinnacle Studio** (www.pinnaclesys.com)
- **Sony Vegas Movie Studio** (www.sonycreativesoftware.com)
- **Ulead VideoStudio Pro** (www.ulead.com)
- **Windows Live Movie Maker** (download.live.com)

This last program—Windows Live Movie Maker—is part of the Windows Live Essentials suite that you can download for free from Microsoft. It's probably the easiest to use of all these programs, and the price (free) is certainly right!

Most video-editing programs work in much the same fashion. You select the video files you want to include in your movie and then drag and drop the clips onto a timeline of some sort. You can then rearrange and trim the clips and add transitions from clip to clip. Titles can be created and inserted at the front of the video; likewise, credits can be inserted at the end. Depending on the program, additional special effects and editing functions might be available. (Figure 38.1 shows the editing window for Sony Vegas Movie Studio.)

> **note**
>
> Windows Live Movie Maker is a new version of the Windows Movie Maker program that was built into Windows XP and Windows Vista. The program is no longer included as part of Windows 7, but is instead offered as an optional free download.

FIGURE 38.1

Editing movies with Sony Vegas Movie Studio.

Burning Your Movie to DVD

Whether you want to use the raw video from your camcorder or edit it with a video-editing program, you'll want to save your results so that you can share your movies with friends and family. There are a number of ways to do this.

First, you can email the movie file as an attachment to an email message. The problem with this method is that movie files are large, which makes them difficult to send and download. You might not want to go this route.

Second, you can upload your video to YouTube, for all the world to share. Of course, all the world might not be as interested in your home movies as your family is, which might mean YouTube is a bit of overkill.

Third, you can burn your movie to a DVD, which can then be played in any DVD player. All you need is a DVD burner drive in your PC and a DVD creation software program.

Fortunately, Windows 7 comes with its own DVD creation program built in. Windows DVD Maker lets you quickly and easily create DVDs from your digital home movies. Burning a DVD, complete with custom menus, is as easy as working your way through a wizard.

When you launch Windows DVD Maker, click the Add Items button. When the next screen appears, as shown in Figure 38.2, select the items you want to include on your DVD and then click Select.

You're then returned to the first screen, with the videos you added listed in order. To change the order of the videos, use your mouse to drag them up or down the list.

note

Learn more about uploading movies to YouTube in Chapter 24, "Watching Videos on the Web."

tip

To include a slideshow of still photos on your DVD, select JPG-format files from the Add Items to DVD dialog box. You can then click the new Slideshow item to change the order of photos in the slideshow.

FIGURE 38.2

Adding videos to your DVD list.

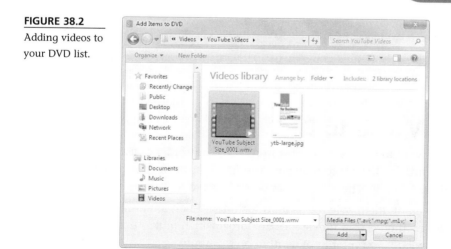

When you click the Next button, you can choose which types of menus you want for your DVD. As you can see in Figure 38.3, available menu styles are listed in the right pane; scroll through the list and click the style you want. You can also, if you want, click the Menu Text button to select different fonts and font sizes.

FIGURE 38.3
Choosing a menu style for your DVD.

With these choices made, it's now time to burn the DVD. Insert a blank DVD into your PC's DVD drive; then click the Burn button. Your selected videos and menus are now burned to DVD. Know, however, that the burning process can be lengthy; go get a pizza or something while you wait!

THE ABSOLUTE MINIMUM

Here are the key points to remember from this chapter:

- For the best results, stay all-digital throughout the entire video-editing process; this lets you transfer your digital movie files directly from your camcorder to your computer for editing.

- You use a video-editing program, such as Windows Live Movie Maker, to combine multiple video clips, add transitions, and create titles and credits for your movies.

- To burn your home movies to DVD, use a DVD creation program such as Windows DVD Maker.

Index

How can we make this index more useful? Email us at indexes@quepublishing.com

W

How can we make this index more useful? Email us at indexes@quepublishing.com

How can we make this index more useful? Email us at indexes@quepublishing.com

FREE Online Edition

Your purchase of **Absolute Beginner's Guide to Computer Basics** includes access to a free online edition for 45 days through the Safari Books Online subscription service. Nearly every Que book is available online through Safari Books Online, along with more than 5,000 other technical books and videos from publishers such as Cisco Press, Exam Cram, IBM Press, O'Reilly, Prentice Hall, Addison-Wesley Professional, and Sams.

SAFARI BOOKS ONLINE allows you to search for a specific answer, cut and paste code, download chapters, and stay current with emerging technologies.

Activate your FREE Online Edition at
www.informit.com/safarifree

> **STEP 1:** Enter the coupon code: XQWPFDB.

> **STEP 2:** New Safari users, complete the brief registration form.
> Safari subscribers, just log in.

If you have difficulty registering on Safari or accessing the online edition, please e-mail customer-service@safaribooksonline.com